SÁNDOR BALOGH

AUTONOMY AND THE NEW WORLD ORDER

A SOLUTION TO THE NATIONALITY PROBLEM

1999

MATTHIAS CORVINUS PUBLISHING

Toronto - Buffalo

Special thanks to our long-time major supporter

Gyula Palinay

for his substantial donations to our endeavors.

ISBN

1-882785-11-8

Library of Congress Catalog Card Number:

98-74725

Jacket by Nicholas Ybl, Jr.
Maps by Lajos Desy-Nagy

Printed in the
United States of America

HISTORIA EST MAGISTRA VITAE....

MAJOR HOT AND COLD SPOTS IN EUROPE

COLD SPOTS: With Autonomy
1. Catalonia,
3. Basques in Spain,
5. Scotland,
7. Walles,
9. Aaland Islands,
11. South-Tyrol,
13. Gagaus in Moldavia

HOT SPOTS: without autonomy
2. Basques in France
4. Corsica,
6. Albanians in Kosovo,
8. Hungarians in Voivodina,
10. Hungarians in Romania
12. Hungarians in Slovakia
14. Hungarians in Ukraine

TABLE OF CONTENTS

V. SOVEREIGNTY, FEDERALISM, AND THE THEORY OF AUTONOMY

VI. AUTONOMY IN PRACTICE

VII. AUTONOMY PROPOSALS IN THE CARPATHIAN BASIN

CONCLUSION

APPENDICES

INTRODUCTION

There are two reasons for writing this book. The first is practical and political, the other is theoretical and political. The practical reason is the attempt to promote peace that is punctuated with violent local skirmishes in various trouble spots in the world in an effort to realize the noble goal of national self-determination. The theoretical is to clarify the concept of and the reasons for "self-determination," Finally, the political reasons are (a) to take the discussion outside the legal profession and introduce practical and theoretical considerations, and (b) to argue that it is time for the governments comprising the United Nations to step in, define self-determination, and establish a new mechanism for the 21st Century that can facilitate peacefully the right to self-determination.

Of the several dozen trouble spots three of the most critical at this writing in the late 1990's are Bosnia and Kosovo, two provinces of the former Yugoslavia, Israel in the Middle East, and the Congo, the former Dutch colony.

Bosnia is a small country that few people outside Central Europe heard of until the assassination of Austrian Crown Prince Ferdinand in Sarajevo, Bosnia's capital, in 1914. It has received attention again since ethnic violence erupted there just a few years ago.

Medieval Bosnia was nominally a banat (client state) of Hungary, but by the 13th century it enjoyed autonomy under its rulers, the bans. The Ottoman Turks conquered the area in 1463. As Turkish power waned in the 19th century Bosnia's Muslim nobility repeatedly rebelled against the sultan; a general revolt in 1875-76 was supported by Serbia, which claimed Bosnia and Herzegovina as part of its territory. After the revolt had been quelled, the Congress of Berlin (1878) allowed Austria-Hungary to occupy the two provinces, which remained nominally part of the Ottoman Empire. Austria-Hungary's outright annexation of Bosnia-Herzegovina in 1908 further increased tensions with Serbia, and the Bosnian Serbs agitated against Austrian rule. In June 1914, Gavrilo Princip, a Bosnian Serb, assassinated the Austrian archduke FRANZ FERDINAND in Sarajevo. The resulting conflict between Serbia and Austria-Hungary quickly escalated into World War I. Thus, while Bosnia is a distinct region and Bosnians are a distinct ethnic group, Bosnia had never enjoyed independence with her own sovereign government until the recent break-up of the artificial state of Yugoslavia.

Kosovo is also a province of the former Yugoslavia and now Serbia. Kosovo, having some 90 per cent Albanian population, once was an autonomous province, but its autonomy was withdrawn several years ago by the Serbian dominated government of Yugoslavia. Kosovo remained in the romp-Yugoslavia, and legally is part of Serbia.

Israel, now incorporating the former Palestine, is also a major trouble spot, due to the conflicting claims of the Arab and Jewish population of the area.

Finally, the multi-ethnic Congo is a former colony of France, and later that of Belgium. It has been independent since 1960, but had been involved in almost constant turmoil, including secession of Katanga in 1961, which had been condemned by the UN, and several bloody inter-ethnic conflicts. The Congo question is still far from being settled at the time of this writing.

The conflicts in both Israel and Bosnia are frustrating, because all of the traditional means of diplomacy, including threat of force, or when diplomacy fails, even actual use of force fails to achieve peaceful coexistence of the different ethnic and religious groups within one community or even one state. Much has been said and written about Israel, while Bosnia is interesting only to specialists in foreign affairs, or to those who hail from that part of the world, and to the families of those soldiers who are there, exposed to daily danger, to maintain the fragile peace.

The tragedy behind the Bosnian conflict is that, just like in Israel, on the one hand there are conflicting ethnic and/or cultural/religious communities involved, and on the other hand one side uses a territorial argument, the other has human rights grievances, so there is little common ground for a solution and neither side is able and willing to compromise. I believe that as far as the diagnosis is concerned, the Middle East situation and the Balkan conflict have important similarities. As for the prescription, there might be different factors that make the recommendation for one dispute unworkable in the other, yet, the principles of a possible solution must be the same not only in these two, but in most of them where ethnicity plays a role.

Unfortunately, Bosnia is not alone in that part of the world that include peoples with conflicting religious and cultural traditions. Except for Hungary and Albania, the other countries of Central Europe all contain sizable minorities who belong to different ethnic groups and/or religions. It is only a matter of time before the conflict in some of these countries also erupt into violence, if no precaution is taken. Even without violence, however, the conflict absorbs and diverts precious national resources from economic and cultural development that would improve the lot of both the majority and the minorities.

There is a growing concern, arguing from the humanitarian side, for urgent official action to end the violence and bloodshed. An essay of two scholars, associated with the Brooking Institute, was published in the recent issue of FOREIGN AFFAIRS on the world refugee problem and claim a total of over twenty million people are refugees within their own country, due to "armed conflict, internal strife, and systematic violations of human rights, ... constituting the newest global crisis."[1] Their conclusion is that

> (U)nless accompanied by steps to address the causes of crisis, military solutions are only temporary. Humanitarian assistance alone can prolong conflicts. Conflict and internal displacement can be resolved only through a broader commitment to the peaceful management and mediation of disputes....

> Conflicts that are allowed to fester can produce mass displacement and leave political and economic scars that damage the economic well-being and political security of neighboring states, regions, and the international system as a whole. The world community cannot let this newest challenge go unchecked.[2]

This situation that Cohen and Deng call a "global crisis" is caused by ethnic, religious or cultural divisions and conflicts within countries, and the lack of effective means and international rules to allow diverse groups a sufficient degree of independence and self-determination in their linguistic, cultural, or religious matters.

We might point out here that modern political science is discovering that political culture is often more important than economic factors. It becomes more and more obvious that for many people ideas are more important than economic or material factors, or even a full stomach. The terrorists forego a quiet job and peaceful home-life for the dangerous mission to advance the cause and the perceived interest of their nation or religion.

Therefore the thesis of this book is that peace and order suffers, and even world peace might be endangered when political, territorial, economic and perhaps other considerations are given preference over and at the expense of ethnic, linguistic and cultural, especially religious factors. History shows that both creating countries with culturally diverse population like the ones

---

1 Roberta Cohen and Francis M. Deng, "Exodus within Borders," FOREIGN AFFAIRS, July-August, 1998, p.12.

2 Ibid., p. 1

already mentioned, and dividing ethnic groups, like Germans, Koreans, Vietnamese, to mention only a few examples, into separate states under different political and ideological systems, lead to conflict and even wars. The folly of these methods has been proven repeatedly by modern history.

This global crisis does not even include the sufferings of tens of millions of people who are either too weak or too meek to start armed rebellion and quietly suffer the most insidious economic discrimination, attacks on their culture and their values, and often even on their physical person and may even be threatened with biological elimination.

The second reason is that while all this domestic violence has been taking place, the concept of self-determination has ripened for consideration by the United Nations. Although Hurst Hannum, in his monumental and ground breaking work on autonomy complained in 1990 that "(S)overeignty, self-determination, and human rights .... are terms of international law, although to date international lawyers have expressed little interest in analyzing them ..."[3] the situation was not that bleak even then. But, probably due to the volume of violence caused by internal strife since the break up of the Soviet Union, there seems to have been an explosion of essays written on the subject. On 1997 Ved P. Nanda, one of the foremost experts in the world on international law, was able to list some twenty four major works in the footnote to substantiate the claim that "(t)he literature of self-determination is vast."[4] But even this list is just the tip of the iceberg. The literature on self-determination is so vast that it is practically impossible to utilize it fully for a project like this one. But the general tone of the books and articles is that the time has come for an official and authoritative definition of the concept and the standards, and for the creation of an effective machinery for the peaceful implementation of this right.

While humanitarian groups are busy helping the millions of victims of internal violence, and international lawyers and other experts have been honing the concept of self-determination, the United Nations miserably fails in her responsibility to outlaw and effectively prevent "future Kosovas, " whole sale human rights violations by governments that should provide protection to its minorities. The UN seems to focus on using military threat to prevent violence, instead of taking bold and decisive action to nip ethnic violence in the bud by setting up an effective mechanism to provide for minority rights.

---

3 Hans Hannum, AUTONOMY, SOVEREIGNTY, AND SELF-DETERMINATION, The Accommodation of Conflicting Rights (Philadelphia, University of Pennsylvania Press, 1990). p. 5.
4 Ved P. Nanda, "Revisiting Self-Determination as an International Law Concept: a Major Challenge in the Post-Cold War Era, "ILSA JOURNAL OF INT'L & COMPARATIVE LAW, vol. 3, # 2; p. 443,

Therefore the conclusion of this book will be an urgent appeal to the leaders of governments to bring the matter of self-determination, both internal and external, before the UN General Assembly and pass a resolution that will effectively solve the problem and establishes a peaceful mechanism to provide for the implementation of the by now internationally recognized right to self-determination. It will be suggested that the key to world peace is in the hands of the United Nations in not only permitting or even mandating autonomy and/or secession when warranted, but also guaranteeing that granting autonomy would not lead to secession, if the autonomy is granted and protected in good faith and leads to democracy. This would satisfy the minorities on the one hand, and should allay the fears of the majority population by providing higher requirements for secession than for autonomy.

The author believes that the best way to proceed in our study is by borrowing the methodology from medicine. For the best treatment the doctor needs a family history to establish the role of possible genetic and environmental or cultural factors, then proceeds with the examination and diagnosis, followed by the prescription, and finally, a treatment plan, choosing the best one from several alternatives, taking into consideration possible harmful side-effects. The prognosis depends on so many factors that it will not even be attempted at this point.

To follow this plan, it is felt by the author that of the several approaches, political science is the most appropriate. Hannum explains that international lawyers "have been content to leave the technical definitions (of self-determination) to the pens of academics and their political implications to politicians."[5] Thus, the present work is an attempt, using the political science approach, to create a bridge tying the work of these three groups together and facilitate finding a solution within a legal framework that follows the definitions of academicians, motivates the politicians, and satisfies the human rights advocates.

First I shall discuss the symptoms in some multi-disciplinary detail, using some concepts and conclusions from sociology, anthropology, and state of the art political science to show where we are coming from and where are we heading.

It should be noted that scientific disciples, like almost everything in life, undergo certain evolution, and what may have been modern concept or theory some fifty years ago, is outdated at the turn of the new millennium. Some of the most important such changes include the development of the concept of human rights from the rights of the individual to collective rights

---

5 Hannum, AUTONOMY, p. 5

and the right of self-determination, and of national sovereignty, the basis of international politics. The modern concept of human rights is accepted more and more even by politicians--or at least the legislative branch of the U.S.

Hurst Hannum wrote that "human rights norms are widely accepted and give legitimacy to U.S. and UN actions.... U.S. law requires them to be a primary concern of U.S. foreign policy." The establishment of the famous MFN, the Most Favored Nation category, for example, explicitly discriminates among countries based mainly on their human rights record. [6] This was not the case a few decades ago! [7] But MFN in itself is not sufficient, because many governments would rather forego the advantages of being an MFN country than improve its human rights policy. The former Rumanian dictator Ceausescu openly refused even to apply for MFN status when it was made clear that in order to receive it his government would have to improve its human rights policies and practices.

This is one reason while international lawyers might feel uncomfortable to get into the debate, because when boundaries and territory were the dominant factors, it was easy to pass laws and protect territories. Also, when the emphasis was on economic factors, experts could easily assess damages. But when it comes to religious freedom or cultural rights, it is not easy to draw legal boundaries. Ideally the conflict should be solved with social means. But it seems that social means are inadequate for ethnic conflicts, as we are finding it out even here in the United States. So international lawyers are more and more willing to jump into unknown waters and chart a course for the peaceful resolution of ethnic conflicts through legal means, including coercion. The direction of evolution is clearly in this direction.

In the following there will be much discussion of ethnic groups and nationalism. [8] Therefore, we should be aware of an important distinction made by His Holiness Pope Pius XI, between two kinds of nationalism. After explaining that "nations were made by God," he stated that "there is ... room for fair and moderate nationalism, which is the breeding ground of many virtues, but beware of exaggerated nationalism as of a veritable curse." [9] It would be unfair to characterize the minorities as always standing for fair and moderate nationalism and the majorities as always representing exaggerated nationalism, but there would be much less conflict and violence in the world today, if both the majorities and in some cases even the minorities have shown more moderation. The majority regimes' and populations' policy of

---

6 see Section 402 (Jackson Vanik Amendment) of the Trade Reform Act of 1974.

7 Hannum, "The Specter...", p. 15

8 Although the popular meaning of these and other terms used is obvious, more technical explanations and definitions will be provided in the text as necessary.

9 *Address Le Missioni il Nazionalismo*, August 21, 1938.

"ethnic cleansing" and "forced assimilation" along with the radical demands of small groups of ultra-nationalists like the French-Canadian terrorists, are examples of exaggerated nationalism endangering or even destroying moderate nationalism.

The focus of the argument will be on the minority issues in non-colonial countries, especially in East Central Europe and the Carpathian Basin where many countries also have sizable ethnic, cultural or religious minorities.

Nothing ... is more likely to disturb
the peace of the world than the
treatment which might in certain
circumstances be meted out to
minorities...

Woodrow Wilson

I.

FROM THE MELTING POT TO THE CULTURAL FAULT-LINE

Politicians were enamored with the seeming success of the American Melting Pot theory without realizing that the American experiment has taken place in a much more open, liberal context, and even then, in reality it has worked much less successfully than some believe.

Assimilation, Accommodation, and the Balkan Model??

According to sociologist Rodney Stark,

> (F)or a long time, people believed that intergroup conflicts in North America would be resolved through assimilation. As time passed, a given ethnic group would surrender its distinctive cultural features and disappear into the dominant American or Canadian culture. At that point, people would no longer think of themselves as ethnic, nor would others continue to do so.
>
> Today many once formidable intergroup conflicts have been resolved in North America.... The important point is that conflict vanished without the disappearance of noticeable differences; conflict ended because the differences became unimportant. Such conflict resolutions are called accommodation, not assimilation. The growth of mutual interest between conflicting groups enables them to emphasize similarities and de-emphasize differences.
>
> When intergroup conflict ends through accommodation, the result is ethnic or cultural pluralism--the existence of diverse cultures within the same society....
>
> Obviously, accommodation and assimilation are not the inevitable outcomes of intergroup conflict. Conflict has sometimes been extermination of the weaker group, as has happened with the Jews in Nazi Germany, (or) Catholics in Elizabethan England, ... Intergroup conflicts have also led to expulsion of the weaker group.[10]

In the American Experience ethnic groups have learned a new form of relationship: accommodation, a peaceful midway solution between conflict and assimilation. Accommodation requires a degree of detachment from your

---

10 Rodney Stark SOCIOLOGY , 3rd ed. (Belmont, CA: Wadsworth Publishing Company, 1989) p. 294. Emphasis in original.

own culture, a great degree of tolerance, and opportunity to progress economically and the free choice to either maintain your own culture or assimilate into your neighborhood. Sociologists have replaced decades ago the melting pot concept with the mosaic image of ethnic relations: many small ethnic communities live side by side with other ethnic communities and with larger, homogeneous and assimilated areas creating beautiful, colorful tapestry. Within the dominant American culture one finds the various ethnic subcultures, like the Irish, Italian, Jewish, Hungarian, Polish, etc. Scores of cities in America and Canada have yearly Festivals with the various ethnic groups, dressed in their traditional folk-costumes, present their folk dances and songs and serve delicious ethnic food.

On the other hand, as will be shown, such accommodation is impossible in some multi-cultural countries and ethnic relations are in a constant state of conflict. Czechoslovakia, Rumania and Yugoslavia, in their seventy years of history following World War One failed to provide the conditions for peaceful accommodation and the free development of ethnic subcultures. Minorities had to fight off efforts to either forcefully assimilate them or expel them. In extreme cases, not only in Serbia and Bosnia and in other Central European countries but in other ethnically and/or culturally heterogeneous areas like the Middle East or some African countries the conflict often deteriorated into ethnic cleansing which is a combination of extermination and expulsion, or cases of intolerance, aggression and even acts of terror against members or installations of the other group. Even the United States has experienced conflict between ethnically different communities and discrimination against or even persecution of minorities.

At the time the foundations of modern foreign policy were developed, most Americans still believed in the melting pot approach, assuming that you can just throw people with different cultures together, and when enough heat is generated, they will melt into a great, amorphous society.

It is on this basis that the question of autonomy was perceived by many Americans, including the Chairman of The Subcommittee on Territorial Problems of the Advisory Committee on Post-War Foreign Policy within the State Department. According to the secret minutes of the Subcommittee's February 12, 1943 meeting the topic under discussion was granting autonomy to minorities as opposed to changing the borders. During the discussion

> (T)he chairman considered that the subcommittee should examine very closely the word autonomy. It raised the question of invasion of national sovereignty and the whole minority problem. He pointed out that such autonomy would be comparable to an international guarantees (sic) for the minority rights of French Canadians in New

England. Any such international political action would be highly resented in the American melting-pot. [11]

Thus, Mr. Isaiah Bowman, presiding officer of the Subcommittee, equates the situation of French Canadians in the United States with that of Hungarians or Germans in Rumania, Czechoslovakia or Yugoslavia, and seems to assume that the fate of all minorities, including the French Canadians, should be the same: disappear in a melting pot. The chairman was answered by one of the subcommittee members, Mr. Philip Mosley, who

> pointed out that the French Canadians had their own church schools, and could elect local officials from their number, as in some towns in New England. The Szekelys of Transylvania would be content with comparable advantages and with the absence of discrimination against them in the national fiscal policy. The Szekelys had actually had autonomy for a very long period...

> Mr. Pasvolsky noted that this suggestion raised the question of the part to be played by the state in the maintenance of the schools.... Mr. Mosley explained that in Transylvania much support for the schools came through the church. Mr. Cannon pointed out that education in Europe was not a mere matter of teaching people to be literate but also a question of political activity. He knew of many cases where a dozen or so families have been planted in certain localities in order that they might claim after a few years that a school for them should be established in that town. In Transylvania the church has been used to promote nationalism....

> ...Mr. (Melvin M.)Knight declared that he would like to support Mr. Mosley's suggestion. He did not think that there was a complete parallel between the situation in Massachusetts and in Transylvania. In Massachusetts the French Canadians had come of their own will to a country whose laws they could learn before they arrived. In Transylvania, on the other hand, the Szekelys had been there before the formation of the Rumanian state and the latter had been imposed over their heads. This seemed to him to justify some degree of autonomy for the Szekely. [12]

The subcommittee chairman did what chairmen do in trouble: formed a sub-sub committee on Transylvania and appointed the three complaining

11 Ignac Romsich, ed., WARTIME AMERICAN PLANS FOR A NEW HUNGARY; Documents from the U.S. Department of State (Published by Social Sciences Monographs, Boulder CO and the Atlantic Research and Publications, Highland Lakes, NJ; Distributed by New York: Columbia University Press, 1992), p. 131.
12 Ibid., pp. 131-2.

members, Messrs. Mosely, Cannon and Knight to the sub-sub committee. It should be noted that while these gentlemen did react to the chairman's suggestion to extend the melting pot concept, none of them had objected to the melting pot concept on the basis that there is a conflict between human rights and the government creating a melting pot. Nor did they point out that the French Canadians do not need international guarantees because the U.S. constitution effectively protects their human and minority rights. If the Rumanian or Slovak constitutions gave similar, effective protection, there would be no need to worry about autonomy or border changes.

Unfortunately, in the final treaties between Hungary and her neighbors neither border changes nor effective constitutional protection with or without minority autonomy was included, and the government sponsored melting pot concept had prevailed.

One reason why the minority issue is making such a slow progress is that the melting pot concept still seems to be alive and well in some important circles. In January 1990, after the ousting of the Ceausescu regime, representatives of the National Federation of American Hungarians (NFAH) had visited the U.S. Commission on Security and Cooperation in Europe and had an opportunity to talk to Judy Ingram, a staff member of the Commission. She seemed very friendly until some of the visitors had suggested the need for positive rehabilitation of the Hungarian community by restoring the ethnic composition of certain areas and returning some Hungarians who had been forcefully moved to Rumanian regions. This suggestion was made to correct a situation that the Commission's own report had cited, namely, that Hungarians had been replaced, as the result of official Rumanian policy (among others, the offering of 15,000 lei and guaranteed housing to Rumanians moving to Hungarian dominated communities), with Rumanians to break up Hungarian communities, and at the same time Hungarians were assigned, or even forced to move into purely Rumanian communities where they were harassed and discriminated against.[13]

Ms. Ingram's attitude suddenly turned hostile, claiming that the proposal to restore homogeneous ethnic communities was contrary to the policy and practice in the United States and should not be pursued in Rumania. She claimed that the goal of US affirmative action policies was to create "heterogeneous communities."[14] This sounds as a desperate effort to keep the idea of melting pot alive into the 1990's. In response to the written

---

13 see CSCE Report 101-1-10, pp. 20-22.
14 It should be noted that Ms. Ingram also seems to have misunderstood the concept of "affirmative action." Its legitimate goal was not to produce "heterogeneous communities" (which would be unconstitutional if the national government wants to do it) but to end discrimination and guarantee equal treatment of minorities.

complaint by the Chairman of the National Federation of American Hungarians, about Ms. Ingram's insensitivity to the plight of ethnic Hungarians and seeming support of a melting pot type solution, Senator DeConcini attempted to minimize Ms. Ingram's efforts by suggesting that "I believe that Ms. Ingram tried to point up some of the difficulties inherent in the 'positive rehabilitation' plan you are developing."[15] But in reality she had completely rejected the proposal for positive rehabilitation, without ever considering how the admitted difficulties could be overcome.

This shows that even those whose job is to protect the rights of minorities in the spirit of the Helsinki process, at least subconsciously, still believe in the melting pot theory and apply it to situations where it is completely inappropriate. Also, while the American CSCE group criticized the forced relocation of Hungarians, it did not effectively oppose the de facto melting pot effect of these re-locations. This produces split results: while our rhetoric is pro-minority right, our efforts seem to be pro-melting pot.

This belief in the melting pot approach applies not only to the Americans. European and Soviet policy makers made the same mistake. Ethnicity is one of the strongest bonds in any society. Even in spite of the famous Marxist slogan, Proletarians of the world, unite! the proletarians of the world failed to unite because ethnicity has proved stronger that class affiliation or pure materialistic or economic considerations.

The French and the British had their multi-cultural empires that were governed with guns and bayonets, gun-ships and the famous Foreign Legion. Yet, none of them could produce a homogeneous society under the French or British rule. The colonial empires collapsed as soon as the colonial force was removed. In Russia, following in the footsteps of absolutist Tsarist Russian imperialism, the Communists continued to maintain with force and terror this great multi-cultural empire under the name of Soviet Union, in the name of Proletarian Internationalism until it broke up as soon as the Communist terror was over and was not replaced by Tsarist terror to hold it together. The same applies to Yugoslavia, which broke up as soon as Tito's iron hand was removed by death. The makers of foreign policy did not show any sensitivity or appreciation for ethnic and cultural traditions of peoples. Thus, the melting pot had failed not only in the United States but world-wide, and it is time to publicly renounce it!

To classify relationship between culturally diverse population I propose seven categories or models of ethnic and cultural relations:

---

15 Letter to Dr. Sandor Balogh, Chair, Human Rights Committee, NFAH; January 26, 1990.

1. The melting pot model is an ideal that has seldom if ever worked with larger groups and minorities that had their own communities. According to this model ethnic and cultural differences will freely and naturally disappear and the result will be a homogeneous society. It may have worked in the distant past, before ethnic consciousness became as strong, and even then it might have taken centuries. It may also work with individuals who are completely outside or on the fringes of their ethnic group and are easier to assimilate, but will fail with others who have stronger affiliation with their ethnic group, or when people's culture is under attack. A siege mentality seems to strengthen the cohesion of any out-group.

2. The more realistic American model is a pluralistic, mosaic like society where the different ethnic groups accommodate each other, and the diverse cultures are allowed to coexist (e.g. U.S.), or multi-culturalism is even promoted (e.g. Canada).

3. Regional autonomy also known as the Swiss model where the different cultures are geographically separated and exercise regional autonomy, and the regions coexist as equals in a federal relationship.

4. Shared autonomy where major ethnic groups within a region share political power according to a set constitutional schedule.

5. Personal autonomy where minority individuals are constitutionally guaranteed a degree of cultural autonomy.

6. The apartheid model, where races are kept apart by law and social policy, producing segregation and discrimination.

7. The Balkan model, where minorities are forcefully assimilated, expelled, or even annihilated, like in Bosnia. Unfortunately, this is not restricted to the Balkan. There are several countries and regions of the world where this is the dominant form of relationship.

A New Switzerland ... or the Old Balkan in Slovakia?

It seems that after World War I the Allied and Associated Powers expected that the new, artificially created or enlarged countries will become so many small melting pots, and the nationality problem that they had used as an excuse to break up the multi-national Austro-Hungarian empire will resolve itself. Or, at least they had hoped that these countries will develop into peaceful pluralistic societies like the United States or Switzerland. They were wrong, however. They did not even developed according to the Swiss model that Dr. Benes presented in Paris on May 20th, 1919, in the name of the yet to be created Czechoslovak Government:

> The Czechoslovak Government intends to organise its State by taking as the bases of the rights of the nationalities the principles applied in the constitution of the Swiss Republic, that is to say, the Government designs to make the Czechoslovak Republic a sort of Switzerland....[16]

Needless to say, that Czechoslovakia never became a second Switzerland, and Slovakia's current leadership is working hard to become a new successor or Ceausescu's fascist Rumania. Benes had changed his tune as soon as the Peace Conference closed. In less then three decades after his pledge to create a new Switzerland in Central Europe he has traveled from the Switzerland plan to the expulsion of all minorities.

> When the Second World War ended, the ancient city of Kassa became the temporary seat of the Czechoslovak government. President Benes soon issued a declaration that Czechoslovakia was to be exclusively the native land of the Czechs and Slovaks. This statement was followed up by systematic expulsion of the Hungarians and the Sudeten Germans. At that time there were living in Southern Slovakia, in a broad border zone that formerly had been part of Hungary, some 650,000 Hungarians The government in Kassa now decided to Slovakize some 200,000 of them. About 100,000 of them were to be exchanged for Slovaks who had hitherto lived in central Hungary, and the remaining 400,000 were to be scattered throughout all of Czechoslovakia in order to promote their assimilation.

> First, the Hungarians were stripped of their citizenship. There followed the dismissal of all Hungarians from central and all municipal civil service jobs. Their salaries were cut off, their businesses expropriated without any compensation. Henceforth they were not allowed to work in industry and commerce. They had to turn their houses and other properties over to Slovak Partisans. All Hungarian elementary and intermediate schools were closed. A decree prohibited the giving of religious instruction in Hungarian language.... No Hungarian newspapers and books could be printed.

---

16 PROTOCOL PRESENTED BY DR. BENES ON BEHALF OF CZECHOSLOVAKIA TO THE COMMISSION FOR THE NEW STATES AT THE PEACE CONFERENCE. Memorandum No. III (emphasis in original); reproduced in David Hunter Miller, MY DIARY AT THE CONFERENCE OF PARIS (New York: Appeal Printing Company, 1924), XIII, pp. 69-70, reprinted in Charles Wojatsek, FROM TRIANON TO THE FIRST VIENNA ARBITRAL AWARD (Montreal: Institute of Comparative Civilizations, 1980) p. 191.

Many Hungarian priests were expelled...Only those who were prepared to deny or renounce their Hungarian background and accepted "Slovakization" could count on forbearance.

In the summer of 1945 the Czechoslovak government requested the great powers at Potsdam to approve the plans for resettlement. The conference approved the resettlement of the Sudeten Germans but not that of the Hungarians. Nevertheless, shortly afterward some 20,000 of them were expelled.[17]

Cardinal Mindszenty as the Primate of Hungary had issued a pastoral letter on April 27, 1947, to ask Hungarian Catholics to aid the 20,000 refugees who were expelled from zechoslovakia into Hungary consequent to the signing and ratification of the population transfer between Hungary and Czechoslovakia, and has asked prayers for the almost 100,000 Germans expatriated from Czechoslovakia into Sudeten Germany.[18]

After the expulsion of these Germans and Hungarians, those that remained were exposed to constant harassment, discrimination, forced assimilation and even persecution. After Czechoslovakia broke up, the situation became even worse under the Slovak regime.

US Senator Alfonse D'Amato, in his official capacity as Chairman of the US Helsinki Commission (Commission on Security and Cooperation in Europe, CSCE), delivered on April 22, 1997 a detailed statement on the floor of the US Senate about the human rights situation in Slovakia, long after the conclusion of the bi-lateral treaty with Hungary on minorities that was supposed to protect the Hungarian minority. Senator D'Amato contrasts the treatment of Hungarians and the Roma (Gypsies) in Slovakia:

> While Hungarians suffer from a more direct form of government intolerance, other ethnic groups suffer more indirectly. Put it another way, it is not so much government action that threatens Romani communities in Slovakia, it is government inaction.[19]

In the case of Hungarians, however, according to Senator D'Amato,

> (T)he Slovak Government continues to pursue a minorities policy that would be laughable if it were not so wrong and harmful. This policy has included everything from banning the playing of non-

---

17 Jozsef Cardinal Mindszenty MEMOIRS (New York: McMillan Publishing Co., Inc., 1974) p. 59.
18 cf. Pastoral Letter of Cardinal Mindszenty, Circ. Strig., V., Archg. Primate. Proc. V-700-22.287.
19 Alfonse D'Amato "Slovakian Human Rights Issues," CONGRESSIONAL RECORD--SENATE, April 22, 1997, p. S3465.

Slovak national anthems last year to the more recent decision to bar the issuance of report cards in Hungarian language, reversing long standing practices. Such petty gestures are beneath the dignity of the Slovak people, whose heritage has survived more than a thousand years of foreign--and often markedly repressive--rule. The Slovak language and culture, now protected in an independent Slovakia, are not so weak that it can flourish only at the expense of others.[20]

Looking at it superficially, the Senator is correct. Such behavior is childish and does not seem to advance Slovakian interests at all! But in the context of the oppressive policies of Slovakia, this symbolic gesture is a stage in their policy of ethnic cleansing to create a Slovakia for the Slovaks only! They want to make life for Hungarians so miserable, that eventually they will want to escape from the land their ancestors lived on for centuries. According to the chauvinistic leaders of Slovakia, there is nor room for Hungarians in a land that was part of Hungary for over a thousand years, and where the Hungarians were the first to create sovereign government. By the way, Senator D'Amato adds a touch of irony pointing out that Hungarians permitted the Slovak language to survive and flourish for a thousand years under Hungarian rule and now the Slovaks want to eliminate Hungarian in one generation. If the Hungarians were as repressive as the Slovaks claim, or as the Slovaks himself are, there would be no Slovak language and Slovak ethnicity today!

Observing the trends concerning the treatment of minorities in Rumania and in Kosovo, Serbia, the Senator is not too optimistic about Slovakia's minority policies: "(A)ccordingly, these seemingly small restrictions on the Hungarian minority in Slovakia may very well be the harbinger of more repressive tactics ahead" the treaty with the Hungarian government notwithstanding. But this is not all! The Senator continues:

> With this in mind, the failure of the Slovak parliament to adopt a comprehensive language law, and the recommendation of the Ministry of Culture that such a law is not even necessary, defy common sense. Current laws on minority-language use in Slovakia do not provide adequate or satisfactory guidance regarding the use of Hungarian for official purposes, as the recent report-card flap shows. Much harm can be done until a minority language law is passed based on a genuine accommodation between the majority and minority communities.

---

20 Idem.

Finally, recent reductions in government-provided subsidies have had a disproportional negative effect on the Hungarian community. The Slovak Government's defense, that all ethnic groups have been equally disadvantages by these cutbacks in unpersuasive in light of the Culture Minister Hudec's stated intent to "revive" Slovak culture in ethnically mixed areas and to make cultural subsidies reflect that goal.[21]

Considering these and other human rights violations, D'Amato issues a stern warning to Prime Minister Meciar:

It is time and past time for Prime Minister Meciar to use his moral authority and political leadership to set Slovakia on the right course. He must make clear, once and for all, that Jan Slota--who also called the Hungarian minority "barbarian Asiatic hordes"-- is not his spokesman, and that the Slovak National Party's unreconstructed fascists do not represent the majority of the people of Slovakia.[22]

Unfortunately, in this last point the Senator is wrong. It does seem that Meciar's National Party is an unreconstructed fascist party, but unfortunately, it does represent the mentality of the Slovak majority, because the majority has been brainwashed into a fascist state of mind, so much so, that if the West will not stop making an issue of human rights and if Slovakia is refused an invitation to join NATO, they might turn to their Slav brothers in Russia, (as detailed elsewhere in this essay) knowing that the Russians will receive them with open arms, since they could not care less how the Slovaks would treat their non-Slavic minorities.

After explaining how the Slovak government responds to criticism by blaming somebody else, the Senator ends his statement on a negative tone:

the leadership of the Helsinki Commission [which was chaired by Senator D'Amato; S.B.] ... have raised our concern about developments in Slovakia with Slovak officials on a number of occasion. Unfortunately, all we hear from the Slovak leadership is one excuse after another, and all we see is a search for one scapegoat after another: it is the Hungarians, it is the Czechs, it's the Ukrainian Mafia, it's the hostile international community seeking to destroy Slovakia's good name, it's the public relations problem abroad, not real problems back home--in short, there is always somebody to blame besides those who are, in fact, running the country

---

21 Idem.
22 Idem.

... I make this statement today in the hope that the leadership in Bratislava will start to make real reforms, like their colleagues in Romania, and begin to restore the promising future that the people of Slovakia deserve. Their present policies are leading down a path of international isolation, increasing criticism, and economic deprivation for their people.[23]

But again, the Senator is wrong! The Slovaks are not interested in economic well-being as long as there are unassimilated Hungarians in their country! No carrot or stick policy works where bigotry is so deep in the people's heart as it is in the three Central European countries, Slovakia, Rumania and Serbia.

As expected, Slovakia's Foreign Ministry, through the Slovak Ambassador to the United States has responded to Senator D'Amato's April speech given on the Senate floor. But the response did not satisfy the Senator, who officially acknowledged the response in the Commission's June 20, 1997 letter to the Slovak ambassador. The letter points out that although the Ministry's

> statement rightly draws attention to a number of positive aspects of the Slovak record, including your government's legislation on the restitution of Jewish communal property and efforts to prosecute effectively the murderers of Mario Goral. On many other points, however, we remain unpersuaded by the Ministry's efforts to reassure us that democratic reform is on track in Slovakia. In fact, we remain profoundly troubled by the situation in Slovakia.[24]

Then the Senator cites three examples where the Slovak record falls short of the expected. First is the troubled relationship between the ruling majority party and the "loyal opposition," preventing true democratic methods to take hold in Slovakia, second, the high level of "political violence" in Slovakia, and third, the minority relations. Concerning the latter, the Senator wrote:

> On the matter of minority-majority relations in Slovakia, we found the Ministry's statement regarding the playing of the national anthems particularly revealing. On this point, the Ministry justified its restrictions by asserting that the playing of foreign (not Slovak) national anthems is a political, not a cultural act--even equating it with treason. We believe the expression of one's political beliefs--even in a musical form--should not be equated with treason but should be protected free speech. Accordingly, the Ministry's statement has only fostered rather than lessened our concern that

---

23 Ibid., pp. S3465-6.
24 Letter to H.E. Ambassador Branislav Lichardus, June 10, 1997, by Senator Alphonse D'Amato, Chairman, and Christopher H. Smith, M.C., Co-Chairman of CSCE.

the current government's policies are designed to restrict the rights of the Hungarian community in Slovakia

The Slovak situation was also on the agenda of OSCE High Commissioner on National Minorities (HCNM), whose office is in the Hague, Netherlands. High Commissioner van der Stoel paid a three day visit to Slovakia in October, 1997, and talked with government officials, including the Ministers of Culture and of Education, and with political leaders, both from Slovak and Hungarian parties.

> The talks concentrated mainly on issues directly related to minorities, such as the use of minority languages in official communications, the issuing of bi-lingual school certificates, and the principles that govern the allocation of cultural subsidies. Another important subject covered in the HCNM's discussions was the situation of the Slovak minority in Hungary.[25]

If the Czechs, who were hailed between the two world wars, and even after the Second World War as the great bastions of democracy in Central Europe, and the Slovaks, who belong to the Western Christian tradition, could not live with ethnic minorities, how could one expect the Balkan peoples, like the Byzantine Rumanians and Serbs, or the peoples in the third world countries to create conditions that are the hallmark of democracy, and what we enjoy in the United States, the world's oldest democracy?

World Peace and World Government?

After World War II and the Holocaust the world leaders started to show more interest at least in Human Rights, if not political culture in general.

Arthur M. Schlesinger, in describing the foreign policy direction of the United States, developed by "the wiser men of an older generation,"[26] explained that these wise men envisioned a peaceful world united under one government. The vital center, that gave the title of Schlesinger's book, is the center where the US and the Soviet should meet: we progress toward socialism, and they progress by giving their people more human rights.

---

25 Report from the HCNM, OSCE Newsletter, Oct. 1997, vol. 4, #10, p. 12.
26 Arthur M. Schlesinger THE VITAL CENTER; The Politics of Freedom (Boston: Houghton Mifflin Company, 1949) p. vii.

"When Russia loosens the totalitarian grip, then the noble dream of world government will begin to make some contact with reality."[27]

Had Schlesinger studied the Russian Mind[28], however, he would have recognized that the differences between the American and Russian culture are much deeper than the mere existence of a totalitarian government. Totalitarianism in Russia is not like a piece of clothing that one can put on and take off at will but has deep roots in the Russo-Orthodox belief system and religio-political culture.

An interesting debate about world government is presented by Robert Goldwin in READINGS IN WORLD POLITICS[29] by including two papers.

The argument for World Government had been based on the existence of the nuclear bomb. According to this view, espoused here by Robert M. Hutchins, President of Fund for the Republic, to avoid total annihilation we need world government.

> Here it will not do to say that common principles cannot be found. They must be found. And they can be found in the common humanity of all mankind. By patience, tolerance, and good will we can come to understand other human beings, because they are human beings like ourselves.[30]

But tell the Serbs in Bosnia, or the Rumanians in Rumania, that the Bosnians, Croatians or Hungarians are fellow human beings and they should show patience, tolerance, and good will toward their minorities! They will laugh in one's face! In fact, Hutchins' argument that common principles must be found is similar to the argument behind ethnic cleansing and terror: the country, be it Bosnia, Slovakia, Rumania, Palestine or Israel, it must be of the same race or ethnicity. When something must happen, it is easy to invoke force as the only means of carrying out the goal. We obviously need more, a great deal more in common than being the children of Adam and Eve. Even following the same God is not enough!

---

27 Ibid., p. 240.

28 For a detailed analysis see Sandor Balogh, CULTURAL AND POLITICAL PATTERNS OF COMMUNISM IN CENTRAL EUROPE: A Case Study of the Soviet-Hungarian Relationship, 1948-56, a doctoral dissertation by the present author (Ann Arbor, MI: UMI Publisher, 1987), Ch. One, "The Russian Mind" pp. 88-120.

29 Robert Goldwin et al., editors, READINGS IN WORLD POLITICS (New York: Oxford University Press, 1959).

30 Hutchins, "World Government Now," in Robert Goldwin, p. 416. First published as "The Constitutional Foundations for World Order," in FOUNDATIONS FOR WORLD ORDER (Social Science Foundation, Denver, CO: University of Denver, 1947).

On the other hand, Walter F. Berns of Yale opposes Hutchinsons's position and suggests that to assume that the US and the USSR could agree on a world government is naive. Burns argues that the cultural differences between the superpowers are so great that, at least in the foreseeable future, it is unreasonable to expect them to submit to one government.

> Their argument is too simple; it is abstract; it is based on abstractions from all the relevant elements in the political situation....
>
> One does not appeal to the sense in these men. One does not attend cultural congresses with them with any justifiable hope of finding a common principle needed to form the basis of a non-Communist world state. "How many divisions does the Pope have?" Stalin asked. Well, will his successors not also ask, how many divisions do the World Federalists have?
>
> These are the "simple and irrefutable" facts controlling the answer to the political question. We cannot persuade the Soviets to join a world government; we cannot force them to join by any method short of atomic war; there can be no world government without them.[31]

Mutatis mutandis, the principle still applies: we cannot force the Serbs to join the Bosnians and Croats in a unified Bosnia short of foreign troops enforcing a hopeless agreement, drawn up under tremendous pressure at Dayton, and agreed to by the Serbs with the clear expectation that it will not be implemented. Both parties want an ethnically pure country, under their rule, of course, and it can be achieved only through violent means.

Still, at this late date (end of September, 1997) the only alternative seen is extending the stay of NATO troops. Daniel N. Nelson, editor of the journal INTERNATIONAL POLITICS, a professor of international politics at Old Dominion University and former foreign policy advisor to presidential candidate Rep. Richard Gephardt, summarizes the Bosnian situation in a column:

> Two years and billions of dollars after the Dayton Peace Accord, NATO's intervention in Bosnia-Herzegovina has lead to peace with no future. Although the fighting ended, the war did not end.
>
> NATO's military power, the combined international bureaucracies, including the United Nations, and legions of private humanitarian and other non governmental organizations that now occupy

---

31 Walter F. Berns "The Case Against World Government," in Goldwin, pp. 428-9.

Sarajevo as the Serbs could not--all have enforced no principle and guaranteed no lasting peace.[32]

A few days later a "senior NATO commander" was quoted in the same paper that "the question no longer is if the Muslims will attack the Bosnian Serbs, but when. The only way to prevent such an attack, at this point, is for the peacekeeping mission to extend its mandate."[33] This is a false alternative, of course, since between renewed fighting and extending the stay of NATO troops is the third alternative of re-drawing of boundaries creating at least new autonomous regions if not new sovereign countries, possibly combined with a fair population transfer. Not an easy solution, but at least if offers hope for peace and allows normal relationship and development within the larger communities.

The Hungarian musician and social philosopher Ervin Laszlo, one of the leaders of the Club of Rome that has been doing some futuristic studies, including what has been called "doomsday models" of the future, is much more realistic than Schlesinger or Hutchinson. At the 1992 III. World Congress of the Hungarian World Federation in Budapest, they distributed a brief booklet prepared especially for the Congress, with excerpts from one of Laszlo's recently published book. In Chapters IX and X he emphasizes the creative nature of culture, and the value inherent in cultural pluralism. "True creativity cannot co-exist with uniformism.... The many different views and ideas, that characterize the peoples with different cultures, make our world rich and resilient." [34] Chapter XI talks about the creation of a new world order. According to Laszlo the international order

does not require a world government, but rather effective and successful ordering systems in the different areas of the new world order. Of the utmost importance is the creation of balance between colorful pluralism and unity.[35]

In another book Laszlo takes the idea a step further and suggests that

(T)hough long overtaken by globalizing processes in the economy, the sovereign nation-state is still the de jure apex of social, political, and even economic organization on Earth. Blind adherence to it

32 Daniel H. Nelson "Bosnian peace cannot survive without resolute intervention", ALBANY TIMES UNION, September 28, 1997.
33 Report by Chris Hedges (NYT) "Muslims reported rearming in Bosnia" ALBANY TIMES UNION, October 3, 1997.
34 Ervin Laszlo, A VILAG TULELESE, 2000+ (SURVIVAL OF THE WORLD 2000+) (Budapest: Akademia Kiado, 1992) p. 9.
35 Ibid., p. 10.

could become a major roadblock to evolutionary convergence in the human community.[36]

Thus, there is a great deal of stress in world affairs between these defenders of the strong, fully sovereign nation-state and the promoters of this evolutionary process. According to Laszlo

> interdependence has grown too fast for contemporary societies... They were pushed into one another's arms without being ready for a close embrace. In consequence, the international system lapsed into disorder, its level of integration insufficient to coordinate its economic, political, and ethnic differentiation.[37]

So, Laszlo seems to suggest, the current culturally or ethnically heterogeneous societies must evolve into more homogeneous societies but not by forced assimilation but by creating smaller homogeneous subsystems which can then be integrated into larger systems to produce a more peaceful world.

> The evolutionary trend ... also catalyzes growing differentiation among grass-roots subsystems.... This also involves articulation, the process whereby the regional and ethnic components of societies become more distinct and autonomous.
>
> Integration is not uniformization, the domination of one element and the subordination of others. It is the coordination of all elements in a shared and mutually beneficial order. Thus integration does not flatten cultural diversity, it only orchestrates it.[38]

Accordingly, forced assimilation has no place in the new world order, and the New World Order will not have to be run by a World Government, but by a governing principle that will effectively organize systems to safeguard plurality in unity, including autonomy of culturally diverse ethnic groups.

Applying this principle to the problem discussed, one of the urgent needs of the international system in the new millennium is to find a way that would do just that. Since the current, multi-cultural unitary states tend to stifle plurality and the majority often aims to exterminate, or at least to force the assimilation of groups of different ethnic subcultures, languages, and/or religions, for countries with populations of different cultures, ethnicity or religion, at the end of this paper some form of autonomy, whether regional,

---

36 Ervin Laszlo, THE CHOICE: EVOLUTION OR EXTINCTION? A Thinking Person's Guide to Global Issues (New York: G. P. Putnam's Sons, 1994) p. 164.
37 Ibid., p. 165.
38 Ibid., p. 164.

personal, or districts where larger ethnic groups share power for will be proposed.

The thesis of this essay does not argue whether world government is good or bad, desirable or undesirable, nor whether it is possible or not.[39] The only point that is argued here is that cultural differences do not have to be disregarded if one's aim is a better ordered, more peaceful world; in fact, disregarding cultural differences mankind will suffer a great deal, without ever succeeding in establishing   world government. On the other hand, allowing cultural differences to flourish and safeguarding it by granting autonomy to such groups will alleviate much conflict and suffering, whether the world will ultimately evolve into world government or not, is not only a worthy goal in itself, but, according to Laszlo, would hasten the evolution into a new, more peaceful world order. Therefore the foreign policy of the next millennium should start with developing the concepts of political culture and autonomy into foreign policy objectives and goals.

Bob Hand, a staff member of the US CSCE office, in an analysis of the Bosnia situation reminds us that we have been talking about national self-determination for decades, yet no clear cut definition and method to achieve it has yet been articulated.[40] He argues that it is urgent to create ways to assure a sufficient degree of self-determination to bring peace to Bosnia. It is suggested that based on Laszlo's approach and Bob Hand's urging, the international community place on its agenda the matter of self-determination and autonomy.

The Kissinger Approach

When one talks about the two great foreign policy failures of the Post World War II era, the Vietnam war and the Middle East conflict, the name of Dr. Henry Kissinger comes to mind. Dr. K, as he was fondly referred to by the media, even received the Nobel Peace Prize for his efforts to make the Israelis and Arabs live peacefully in one country. We know, of course, that his efforts failed (yet, he is allowed to keep the Nobel Prize, and in fact, based on his reputation, I understand, he operates a successful foreign policy consulting firm).

Dr. Kissinger has also been famous for his repeated suggestions that the East Central European countries should become organic parts of the Soviet

---

39 See the debate between Robert M. Hutchins and by Walter F. Burns above at #'s 29-31.
40 CSCE DIGEST, July 1997.

Union. It seems he had failed to realize that organic means "a system of interrelated parts" according to Webster, and the relationship between the Soviet and the countries involved was more of a deadly conflict than interrelatedness. President Reagan was right when he rejected the Kissinger plan out of hand.

When Dr. Kissinger proposed his plan again after the 1988 election to the new Bush administration, this writer had written a critique for Dr. Janos Nadas, the President of the World Federation of Free Hungarians, in opposition of the Kissinger proposal. After the Kissinger proposal was rejected, the Dr. Nadas and this author, who was Secretary General of the Federation, had received a letter from James W. Swihart, Director, Office of Eastern European and Yugoslav Affairs in the State Department, informing us of the outcome, and he concluded the letter with this sentence:

> Finally, I would like to point out at least one benefit Dr. Kissinger's proposal brought us--your thoughtful letter which, in itself, was a welcome addition to our thinking on Eastern Europe.[41]

The rejection of the Kissinger proposal was significant for Central Europe and world peace, because when President Bush left for Poland, Hungary and Western Europe in July 1989, instead of carrying the Kissinger proposal with him, his message was that the U.S. will not turn over those countries to the Soviet. At every public opportunity he had, the President emphasized the great importance the U.S. attaches to the changes taking place in Central Europe[42], and there is every reason to assume that in private talks he had also encouraged the leaders of Hungary and Poland to continue the democratization and the opening toward the West.

After leaving Hungary, at a press conference held aboard Air Force One en route to Paris, the President was asked if he thought that his trip made any difference. The answer was a definite "Yes, I do," and Mr. Bush added: "I could tell them what I thought we would be able to do, how much we shared their desire for change, I think it was fruitful for them.... And I think that makes a difference to the leaders..."[43]

It was after the Bush trip and encouragement that Hungary opened its borders to the East Germans, and the Iron Curtain started to crack in the fall of 1989. It is doubtful that all this would have happened if the Kissinger line

41 Letter to Drs. Janos Nadas President, and Sandor Balogh Secretary General, WORLD FEDERATION OF FREE HUNGARIANS; May 1, 1989.
42 See US Govt. Printing Office, Weekly Compilation of PRESIDENTIAL DOCUMENTS, Volume 25, # 29, July 24, 1989, pp. 1065-96.
43 Ibid., July 13, p. 1093.

had won the debate over US foreign policy. The hero of the collapse of communism in Hungary was Mr. Bush and the Hungarian community in the United States that had opposed the Kissinger proposals, and not Gyula Horn or Miklos Nemeth, who actually opened the border. It seems that Messrs. Reagan and Bush had greater appreciation for political culture[44] and national self-determination than many of his predecessors or his successor, or Dr. Kissinger, for that matter.

The Political Culture Approach And the Cultural Fault Line

One important factor behind the tragedy of Bosnia, that also makes finding a workable solution to other similar conflicts near impossible, has been that politicians and statesmen, along with historians and political scientists disregarded the findings of anthropologists and sociologists. As the result, they continue to neglect to consider the political culture of peoples, and even if they had considered it within the context of American domestic politics, they had failed to understand the political culture of other countries. So they had either applied American standards to other countries, or in their foreign policies they had only focused on boundaries and political institutions. The seriousness of the problem is indicated by the problems faced in Bosnia, and the near impossible task of maintaining peace between the different factions.

It is beyond the scope of this introductory essay to analyze the study of political cultures, but a brief review is in order.[45] Political scientists started only in the mid 1960's to understand, analyze and compare political systems on the basis of political culture as opposed to political institutions, constitutions, and boundaries. It was a decade later that the political culture concept was used to compare communist regimes. But in this fledgling area of study there was not even an agreement about the definition of political culture. Mary McAuley suggests that the political culture approach should go back as far as necessary to explain the contemporary political institutions and belief system:

> (I)f today's political culture has its origins in yesterday's political culture, we would expect our authors to seek the source of the traditional political culture--not in the yesterday's politics and

---

44 See his comments about *Mittel Europa* below.
45 This review is based on "The Political Culture Approach," Balogh, pp. 7-15.

society--but in the belief system of an even earlier stage of that society.[46]

For example, if one were to trace the British political culture to its earliest beginning, one should go beyond even the Magna Carta of 1215, to the mythical pre-history of the British people. Investigating the origin of basic concepts of the Rights of the Englishman, which was only demonstrated by the Magna Carta but is of much earlier origin, one would end up at the famous Stone of Scone of Jacob, the Biblical patriarch. It is believed that the Stone, which was built into the coronation chair until just recently, was returned to Scone in Scotland, served as Jacob's famous pillow when he had his dream as recorded in the Bible.[47] Jacob's dream seems to prophesy that Jacob's descendants will rule over a great empire, a fitting description of the role England had played in world history.

According to the Biblical story Jacob received Isaac's blessing that should have been given to Esau, the first born son. But Jacob purchased the rights of the first born from Esau for a bowlful of porridge. These rights included not so much the right to salvation or to spiritual goods but the political right not to be ruled but to rule and to dominate. The British still seem to cherish them, not as the rights of the first born but the rights of the Englishman[48] individually, as if they were a special, privileged race, and to national prosperity and the right to rule over nations collectively. The Stone served in the coronation of Scottish kings from 839 till 1292, when Edward I., the British king took it to Westminster Abbey in 1296, and every British monarch since has been crowned while sitting over the Stone since then.[49] To understand the British mind today one should go back as far as one can, in this case to the blessing Isaac gave to Jacob.

On the other hand, to understand the American mind and their concept of democracy, one should go back to the rebellious ideas of Thomas Paine and the famous words of the Declaration of Independence: All men are created

---

46 Quoted in Ibid., p. 9, from Mary McAuley, "Political Culture and Communist Politics: One Step Forward, Two Steps Back," in Archie Brown and Jack Gray, editors., POLITICAL CULTURE AND COMMUNIST STUDIES (Armonk, NY: Sharpe Inc., 1984) pp. 13-39.
47 Gen., 28;10-18.
48 Americans are familiar with this mentality from the study of the American Revolution and the claim that *taxation without representation* was a violation of their rights as *Englishmen*.
49 cf. Bill Gladder (Baltimore Sun, Perth, Scotland by-line), "Scottish Sites Vie To Be Resting Place For Historic Stone of Scone" (Albany TIMES UNION, Sep. 29, 1996) According to popular belief the stone has some magic properties. "It was said that the stone groaned if a true royal sat upon it to be crowned. If the sitter were a pretender, the stone remained silent... The stone is also known as Stone of Destiny" (Idem). The occasion for the article was the decision to return the stone to Scotland, after being 700 years in British possession. According to the announcement the stone will remain the property of the Crown, and will be returned to England for future coronations.

equal! There is no privileged nation or people, not at least in the political arena.

Similarly, to understand the Bosnian, Hungarian, Rumanian, Serbian or Slovak minds one must go back to both the true and the perceived earliest history of each of these national groups, until one finds the roots of today's political culture.

The deep roots of today's political cultures of the conflicting parties in Bosnia shall be analyzed to some extent in the next chapter. For the purposes of this paper it is sufficient to call attention to the importance of political culture and to show that the cultures of the dominant groups and the minorities in each of the listed countries are quite different, and it seems to be an impossible task to reconcile them in a peaceful pluralistic society. Instead, we shall consider the possible results when people with so different cultures are thrown into one political entity.

Donald Devine in a Washington TIMES column critiques the Clinton Administration's Bosnian policy, and quotes Professor Samuel Huntington, a former National Security Council adviser, to support his views.[50] According to Huntington, the President projects the American approach of "multiculturalism," the peaceful coexistence of different races and cultures in one country, to the rest of the world, including Bosnia. The Catholic Croats, the Orthodox Serbs and the Muslim Bosnians must live together in a multicultural country even if it kills them.

It is interesting to note that while the American ideal of the melting pot had been used to justify non-interference in ethnic minority issues, the new American ideal, promoting multiculturalism, is being used to justify intervention, and neither approaches leads to lasting peace in ethnically heterogeneous countries.

In line with the Clinton approach, Warren Christopher, President Clinton's former secretary of state proclaimed that "the US would not recognize any fundamental divide among Catholic, Orthodox and Islamic parts of Europe." The three fundamentally different religious and political cultures cannot be separated by a boundary line, because our ostrich like politicians and statesmen dig their heads in the sand and fail to realize that in other countries ethnic, religious, or cultural differences count!

This writer has made this point over a decade ago in his dissertation:

---

50 Donald Devine, "Imminent mission creep?" in WASHINGTON TIMES, September 12, 1997; p. A21.

The significance of understanding the people and culture of a country, especially as important as the Soviet Union and the Central European nations ... should be obvious. During World War II, US marines and other troops were provided detailed information on the native cultures in the South Pacific. This material, collected from the Human Relations Area File, "is said to have prevented many costly mistakes and saved many lives."[51] Yet, influential policy makers and opinion molders seem not to take into consideration the basic cultural features of ... people in Central Europe .... Their failure to realize this has led to many costly mistakes... The average GI participating in W.W.II knew more about the culture of a small tribe in the South Pacific than ... US Presidents know about ... Poland or Hungary.[52]

Unfortunately, the facts of life do not care what we know and recognize and what we do not know or recognize. The fundamental divide is there, whether Mr. Christopher and other liberal universalists recognize it or not. According to Devine,

Mr. Huntington calls the universalist dilution of the importance of religion "secular myopia," while he makes religion "possibly the most profound difference that can exist between people," that will lead in the post-Cold War world to fault line conflicts between these different world views. He argues that conceptions of a benign, universal, democratic-capitalist world can only be imagined by ignoring history...

To Mr. Huntington, liberal universalism not only is an inaccurate description of world reality, it is a threat to world peace. The United States does not have the power to keep demanding that other civilizations act in accord with western values and rights as if these were accepted by all, when they are not....

As Mr. Huntington says, those who ignore civilizational divides are "doomed to be frustrated by them."[53]

Messrs. Huntington and Devine are right, of course, except that they put the emphasis on religion alone and overlook ethnicity. Religious differences tend to become much more important when they are combined with ethnic differences, as is the case in Bosnia. Over the centuries religious views and

---

51   Pauline V. Young, SCIENTIFIC SOCIAL SURVEYS AND RESEARCH 3rd ed., (Englewood Cliffs, NJ: Prentice Hall, 1956), pp. 132-3.
52 Balogh, pp. 4-5.
53 Ibid.

attitudes tend to permeate the entire culture, and peculiar national political cultures develop that go way beyond dogma and worship.

Devine also draws the wrong conclusion. The problem is not that the US and the West had intervened militarily. The tragedy is that the intervention was made necessary by Western (including US) insistence that the traditional boundaries of Bosnia must be maintained, and these incompatible religious groups must stay together. The Serbs wanted their region attached to Greater Serbia, the Croatians wanted to be attached to Croatia, and the Muslims wanted peace and their own country, and all this was denied by the international community, led by the country whose president, Woodrow Wilson, once had made the notion of national self determination a major factor in world politics! Let the boundaries reflect the cultural divide, and there will be no need for foreign troops!

According to Devine,

> Bosnia may well be the best test case of liberal universalism's theme that liberal democracy and regulated capitalism are the only meaningful futures of world society. Mr. Huntington specifically rejects this "expectation of harmony" and convergence, and sets his opposing theme that "modernization is distinct from Westernization," ... and that the world is increasingly "multi-civilizational...,"[54]

as Ervin Laszlo had pointed out. In other words, if one aims to world peace, instead of forcing every country and people on the Procrustes bed of Western civilization, as a first step, we must take the fault lines seriously and draw the political boundaries along the ethnic and cultural fault lines as much as possible. This would at least assure peaceful and civilized relations within a country, on the neighbor to neighbor level.

The unfortunate thing is that Bosnia is not an isolated situation. After World War One Yugoslavia was created and Muslim Bosnia was forced into a shot gun union, along with the Catholic Croatia and Slavonia, dominated by the Orthodox Serbs, as the Serbs' reward for the assassination of Arch Duke Ferdinand in Sarajevo, thus igniting the spark that led to the first World War. Rumania, where the Byzantine Orthodox Church dominates, was given a huge minority population of Catholic and Protestant Hungarians and Germans in Transylvania, and the Protestant Czechs and the Catholic Slovaks were united with a half million mostly Catholic Hungarians thrown in, without any regard to religion, language and political culture. Thus, all three countries created after World War One were built on major fault lines,

---

54 Ibid.

and when the earthquake came after the dissolution of the Soviet Empire, the buildings started to shake.

The fault line is clearly illustrated by Stjepan Buc, a former member of the Yugoslavian Parliament. After escaping from communist Yugoslavia, he became a political science professor in Argentina. According to Professor Buc,

> (B)ecause of her origin, development, culture, and entire nature, Croatia belongs to the Central European area. Conversely, Croatia does not belong to the East, nor to the Balkans. Separated from the Western world by treachery and violence, and thanks to the fabricated "Slavic Union" that never really existed, Croatia was handed over to a traditionally aggressive Eastern foreign rule. May we, at the same time, refer to the Hungarian example, because our situation is best illustrated by it. The Croatians and the Hungarians are peoples of Western culture..."[55]

Professor Buc attributes this tragic mistake to a

> surprising ignorance of sociology in Eastern European history (that) has had harmful results regarding the interpretation of Croatian history. Even worse, however, are the quite false political conclusions generated by this ignorance. The catastrophic consequences can be best illustrated if one realizes that the present unsound political structure of Central Europe represents one focus of the current world crisis, and that, this results from the above mentioned ignorance concerning the nature of the peoples of the Indo-Germanic-Slavic linguistic group. Old Byzantine fairy tales about fictitious ethnic "Slavic Unity" (continuously accepted and carried on also by the romanticism of the 18th and 19th centuries) resulted in the fabrication of those artificial states in the first half of the present century. Not only different peoples and hostile races strangers to each other were forced into such states, but actually two worlds--the East and the West--were supposed to unify. Such was the case of the Croatian people who became one of the victims of the false doctrine of so-called "Slavic unity." They were forced into an artificial state--i.e., Yugoslavia--which they never considered their home but rather a prison. The fundamental error made was that a European, Western people were (sic) isolated from their organic, natural connection with Europe--let us say, from Central Europe,--and were forced to be part of an Asiatic-Byzantine power,

---

55 Stjepan Buc, "Croatia and Central Europe," in Francis S. Wagner, ed., TOWARD A NEW CENTRAL EUROPE (Astor Park, FL: Danubian Press, 1970), p 65.

such as Yugoslavia, as far as the ethnic and cultural aspects are concerned.[56]

From this it is obvious that the cultural fault line Professor Huntington mentions is not his invention but a very real one, that western policy makers better take into consideration. But is should be made clear that Buc is not racist and does not consider the Eastern culture as inferior:

> It would not be correct, however, to classify the Eastern man and his world as something generally inferior. That world is simply different from ours. Because of these essential differences we simply do not wish to be under the rule of that world. We just cannot endure its domination. We prefer to enjoy our right of self-determination and we wish to live freely in our own state.[57]

The same applies to Hungarians forced to live under Slovak, Rumanian or Serbian rule. In fact, this very same logic led the Hungarian people to rebel against the Soviet rule in 1956, as the Doctoral dissertation of this author[58] argues. As for Croatia, events over the past few years have demonstrated that Professor Buc was stating the feeling of the overwhelming majority of Croats when they have rebelled against Serbian rule and became independent. Writing in the 1960's, Buc was not a prophet in the usual sense but a perceptive political scientists who understood the role and importance of political culture in the lives of peoples. The tragedy is that the Croats, when their turn came, opposed giving the Serbs and Hungarians living in Eastern Croatia the same right to secede and join their compatriots across the Croatian border, and also failed to apply the same standard in Bosnia.

Rumania is the only country among those that were given a substantial number of Hungarians by the Trianon Treaty, that has survived--with Western protection and complicity, and due to the fact that Transylvanian Hungarians so far have attempted to solve their problem diplomatically, using civilized means. But it should not surprise one if they lose their patience and resort to more effective means that the West seems to need to pay attention to a crisis.

But just what are the religio-cultural differences on the two sides of the fault line? In a 1982 study of cultural differences in Central Europe[59] they found that the human rights record of the several communist states is quite diverse:

---

56 Ibid., pp. 60-1.
57 Ibid., p. 63.
58 Sandor Balogh, CULTURAL ...
59 cf Stephen White, John Gardner and George Schopflin, COMMUNIST POLITICAL SYSTEMS, An Introduction (New York: St. Martin Press, 1982) Chapter 6: "Democracy and Human Rights," pp. 221-264; discussed in Balogh, pp. 13-16.

some do better than others.[60] Political scientist Stephen White at al. finds that there is a line up of East Germany, Poland, Czechoslovakia and Hungary on one side, Rumania, Yugoslavia, Albania and Bulgaria on the other side on issues as "extension of human rights,[61] the independence of the courts in the political system,"[62] press censorship[63] and samizdat activity,[64] free association and assembly, including the attitude toward the traditional Communist May Day demonstrations,[65] and religious freedom, where the authors of the study note that "in Eastern Orthodox societies such as Bulgaria the churches have never claimed the same degree of autonomy and by and large they have been integrated into the framework of the state."[66]

Interestingly, George Bush, as vice president, made the same point in his famous Mitteleurope speech in 1983. Upon returning from a visit to Rumania and Hungary, as he stood on the Western side of the Iron Curtain, he stated: "As I look out to the East, I had the momentary impression that I was standing in a lonely outpost on the edge of Western civilization... Historically, of course, it could not have been more false."[67]

Then the Vice President went on to talk about "Mitteleurope--Central Europe,"[68] quoting Ceszlav Milosz, a dissident Polish intellectual. Milosz wrote about his fellow intellectuals in Central Europe and their "extinguishment" seeing their countries, which "are rightfully part of an ancient civilization, one that is derived from Rome rather than from Byzantium 'surrender to a hegemony of nations',"[69] which has such a different, a Byzantine civilization.

"It has been often remarked, continued the Vice President, that the three great events--the Renaissance, the Reformation, the Enlightenment-- Russia took part in none. But Mitteleurope ... took part in all."[70]

Thus, in addition to the ancient Byzantine heritage, the Orthodox world was left behind in the evolution of its culture, since due to its isolation, the three

---

60 see White, pp. 221-2; Balogh p. 13.
61 Ibid., p. 236.
62 Ibid., p. 238. On the issue of independent courts Rumania is on the pro-democracy side, but it is only because the Hungarian and German minorities demanded it, not the ethnic Rumanians.
63 Ibid., pp. 241 and 239-40.
64 Ibid., p. 243.
65 Ibid., pp. 243-8.
66 Ibid., pp. 248-50.
67 "Address by George Bush, Vice President of the United States: Vienna, September 21, 1983;" The Vice President's Office; p. 1.
68 Idem.
69 Ibid., p. 2; Cf. Czeszlav Milosz, THE CAPTIVE MIND (New York: Vintage Books, 1951) No page reference given by Bush.
70 Bush, p. 2, quoted in Balogh, p. 16.

major reform movements that help define Western civilization and political culture, the Renaissance, the Enlightenment and Reformation, for better or worse, did not have an effect in the East. This applies, of course, not only to Russia but to Rumania and Serbia as well.

One of the best descriptions of the difference between the Western Christian and Orthodox world views is Vladimir Sergeyevich Solovyev's RUSSIA AND THE UNIVERSAL CHURCH, written in 1889 by this mystic poet and philosopher. Solovyev was raised in the Orthodox faith but became disillusioned and became Catholic. In his book he describes the result of the thousand year old schism combined with slavofile ambitions, resulting in a messianic complex intent to re-make the world in their image.

Another, more contemporary study of the problem is a book[71] written by Imre Zsolnay, a Hungarian historian in 1963-4, but the author could not have it published until 1993, after the communist regime had collapsed and the Russian troops were withdrawn from Hungary.

While Solovyev concentrates on the Byzantine influence on Czarist Russia, Zsolnay does the same regarding the Soviet Union. Interestingly, if one relates the two works, one will conclude that as far as political culture is concerned, there is not much difference between the politico-cultural ideologies of nationalist and pan-Slav Russia and the internationalist proletarian Soviet Union. Both had been separated from the Western Christian culture by a deep cultural fault line.

If one wants to include Bosnia in the picture, we must add another political culture, that separates the Muslim Bosnians from the Catholic Croats and the Byzantine Serbs. Thus in the Bosnian conflict the fault line is compounded. Without taking these differences into account, there can be no effective solution for the Bosnian, or the other ethnic conflicts in East Central Europe, or in any other area of the world, for that matter.

Among the books of more recent vintage Colin S. Gray's book, NUCLEAR STRATEGY AND NATIONAL STYLE[72] is the most outstanding example of taking political culture seriously, although its topic seems to be dated. But it contains excellent analyses of certain aspects of both the Soviet/Russian and the American political cultures. Another book, somewhat older but one of the best available on the problems of East Central Europe considering the cultural background of the region is one written by John Flournoy Montgomery, a former US Ambassador to Budapest. But because it

---

71 Imre Zsolnay, BIZANCTOL A BOLSEVIZMUSIG (From Byzantine to Bolshevism) Budapest, 1993. ISBN # 963 450 067 6.
72 Colin S. Gray, NUCLEAR STRATEGY AND NATIONAL STYLE(Lanham, MD: Hamilton Press, 1986)

considers culture, an approach the liberal universalist movers and shakers of international politics disdain, it is quite unpopular among the liberal universalist policy making Establishment, although if they had studied it carefully, they could have avoided the Bosnian crisis, for example. Montgomery's book should be required reading by all statesman and diplomats who have anything to do with Central European or Bosnian policy.

Finally it might be presumptuous to recommend this writer's above quoted dissertation, but it should also be useful to understand the problems resulting from the political fault line and different political cultures in the region.

To disregard such a deep and obvious fault line in dealing with conflicts in Central Europe is not only a sin and a crime against humanity and Western values of freedom and democracy but a political blunder. In order to create a more peaceful world, under one government or many, it is imperative that where geographically feasible, homogeneity must be made the corner stone of state-hood. Where historic reasons justify, such homogeneity must be secured by autonomous regions to reduce intra-community conflict and to protect minorities.

To summarize, the old approach to international politics, based on treating countries and regions as just plain real-estate and attempting to introduce solutions that might or might not have worked in other cultures and societies, without any regard to the ethnic and cultural features of the people involved, has led the world to the brink of disaster.

Therefore it is proposed that a new policy, emphasizing cultural differences, be introduced to shape the world into the 21st century. Central Europe, which has been notorious for its ethnic problems, could be used as a laboratory to see if the new approach would work. It might not be easy, but a major mistake like Trianon that further messed up the already complex nationality picture there, could be fixed only by a major surgery.

II.

HISTORICAL BACKGROUND

This essay focuses on how to remedy, if it is humanly possible, the tragic consequences of the Peace Treaties of Trianon. These treaties disregarded cultural differences and created new, multi-cultural countries under the rule of peoples who were not ready and able to handle the resulting conflicts. A dominant radical element makes these countries as a whole culturally, and as individuals, psychologically unable--it is more than unwillingness--to switch from ethnic conflict to accommodation. While in Rumania there were long periods of violent ethnic cleansing alternating with periods of cultural assaults on the minority, and still there are groups who advocate the most radical form of ethnic cleansing and even extermination. In Slovakia ethnic cleansing takes the more moderate form of forced assimilation and making conditions such that the minority would want to emigrate. After World War II entire Hungarian villages in Serbia were treated the same way by Serbs as we have seen in Bosnia, but after the War there were no CNN TV crews reporting it and the world has paid no or little interest. Bosnia is just a repetition of earlier terror acts by the Serbs, with the only exception that this time the world has paid attention to the extermination of entire villages of people of another culture or ethnic background.

Trianon could be regarded as a giant--and cruel-- experiment in creating artificial multi-cultural political units. It is suggested that this experiment should be officially declared a failure, and it is proposed that the Great Powers and Schlesinger's wiser men start a new experiment in Central Europe by drawing boundaries that follow ethnic and cultural dividing lines.

The Creation Of The Nation State

The nation state idea has been a major development in history that laid the foundation for the modern era. In the middle ages Society, Church and the State were competing for supremacy. Eventually, after Machiavelli popularized the idea of the absolute power of the Prince, i.e. the ruler, who most often was a hereditary monarch, the State has emerged victorious. The classical form of fully sovereign nation-state first officially appeared in the Peace Treaty of Westphalia in 1648.

One role of the monarch was to unite the forces of nationalism and serve as a symbol of the nation, leading to the development of the nation state. This concept included three elements: population, well defined territory with boundaries, and sovereignty, i.e. a government with supreme authority over its territory.

Initially the nation state included one dominant national group and the state's boundaries were drawn to reflect the nationality of the inhabitants. The existence of large minority ethnic groups was the exception. The treatment of the minorities was subject to the principles of Christian brotherhood. Before the early 19th century, nationalism was a cohesive force, holding the majority together to form the state and defend it against other states, rather than a dividing force, separating groups within the state. The basic division within society was the feudal class system, and after the Reformation, religion also became such a separating feature, often creating conflict between various religions, while at the same time acting as a cohesive force within. Even in multi-ethnic countries that may have developed as the result of wars and conquests, ethnicity was a latent feature. Most disputes, conflicts and persecutions were along religious lines. If the ethnic majorities of those countries had followed the chauvinistic policies of some of today's multi-ethnic states, by the 19th century there would have been no minorities, or at least no minority languages and consciousness to demand equal rights and self determination.

The minority's position in Hungary was quite similar to that of the rest of Europe, except that partly due to the devastation by the Tartars and Turks, and thanks to Saint Stephen's written and well publicized advice to his son to make foreigners welcome in his country, Hungary had larger minority populations than most other countries. Under the Crown Doctrine that has governed Hungary and stated that all residents of Hungary, including minorities, are members of the Crown, and all should be treated equal, her minorities had flourished.[73]

But it is a mistake to identify the Crown Doctrine as a unique Hungarian development. From the very beginning of Hungary's history, the Hungarian royalty had strong cultural and family ties to the West,[74] so Hungary's constitutional development was close to that in the West. It is possible that at times constitutional developments in Hungary had influenced Western

---

73 Kocsis István, A SZENT KORONA TANA, Multja, jelene, jövöje [THE DOCTRINE OF THE HOLY CROWN; Its Past, Present, Future] (Budapest: Pesky, 1996) pp. 125-127.

74 For example, St. Margaret of Scotland was a relative, possibly a grand daughter of Saint Stephen, and Saint Stephen's wife, Saint Gisella, was the sister of Henry, the Emperor of Germany. Similar dynastic relations existed throughout the middle ages between the House of Arpad, later the Anjou's and Hapsburgs and other royal houses.

developments. Thus, the Western and the Hungarian concepts of the king and the crown were, and remained very similar until the abolition of Hungary's monarchy in this century.

Initially the person of the king as ruler was the focus of all power, and gradually,

> on a more basic level, sacred objects imparted a splendor to the royal or imperial personage. The crown, scepter, and throne were seen as far more than the mere symbols of an exalted position, which they suggest to the modern mind. Instead, they radiated the authority of a divinely chosen ruler from something within them.... With the growth of the territorial conception of the monarchy--of kings as ruling countries with the people in them, as opposed to the earlier conception of kings ruling peoples in whatever land they happened to be--the splendor of the sacred objects began to cover the territorial integrity of a kingdom.[75]

Although this has been written about Western developments, it also fully applies to the Hungarian concept of the Holy Crown Doctrine and is still followed in the West, as England's defense of some useless islands as Crown Territory in the Falkland War demonstrates.

Thus, on the one hand, following Saint Stephen's admonition to welcome foreigners in the land, Hungary had an open-door policy toward refugees or people seeking opportunity to live in peace in a country that was famous for her hospitality. On the other hand, all new-comers to the territory governed under the Crown were protected under the Crown as equals, in respect to their nationality. For centuries the number of minorities had grown and the Hungarian majority never forced the assimilation of minority groups. Therefore there was no nationality problem in Hungary until the 19th century.

Nationalities in Central Europe and the Boundary Issue

The rise of national consciousness was created by the ideas of Rousseau, followed by the French Revolution "when French philosophers like Diderot and A'Alambert began to differentiate between nation, state and language, declaring that if the state were to flourish, language must adjust to the

---

75 Henry A. Myers, MEDIEVAL KINGSHIP, The Origins and Development of Western Monarchy in all Stages from the Fall of Rome to the Fifteenth Century (Chicago: Nelson-Hall, 1982) p. 168.

requirements of the state."[76] But, ironically, at first this effected only the dominant groups that in the past had been independent nations of Europe, but at the moment did not have a nation state of their own, like the Poles, the Germans and the Italians, and even this effect was reversed: instead of forcing members of a state to use the same language, it instigated people of the same language to form a state of their own! Instead of the "language must adjust to the requirements of the state," for the Poles, Germans and Italians it meant that the state (in this case the new state to be created) must adjust to the language area!

The nationality problem assumed a new dimension when the Hapsburg Court in Vienna used the several nationalities residing in Hungary against the Hungarian nationalists themselves who wanted to separate the Hungarian state from Austria with which it was united under the common monarch in the Austro-Hungarian Empire since the 16th century. The irony is that the Hapsburg emperor, who was also the crowned King of Hungary and sworn to uphold the Hungarian laws and interests, as Austrian emperor, serving the interest of the Austrian side of his Empire, instigated the ambitious leaders of the various nationalities against his own Hungarian Kingdom. In modern days they would call this a conflict of interest or even treason! These efforts during the 19th century had a major role in the beginnings of hostile nationalism in Central Europe.

A contemporary Transylvanian poet has captured the essence of the situation when he compared the minorities who were accepted and shielded by Hungarians for centuries in historic Hungary to the parasitic cuckoo bird who lays her eggs in the nests of other, smaller birds. As the baby cuckoo bird gets larger, it throws out its step-brothers and step-sisters from the warm nest that their parents built, and of whose naive hospitality he is taking advantage, becomes the only survivor from among a nestful of birds.[77] Similarly, Hungarians, ever since Saint Stephen founded the Hungarian Kingdom, welcomed refugees from other lands, and even invited foreigners to populate areas that were left de-populated due to Tartar invasion and the Turkish wars. Some of these nationalities have re-paid their welcome with kicking the families of their hosts out of their ancestral homes.

In one of the great ironies of history, not only one but two successive heirs to the Hapsburg throne, first Crown Prince Rudolph[78] and next Crown

---

76 Istvan Sisa, THE SPIRIT OF HUNGARY, 3rd ed. (Morristown, NJ: Vista Books, 1995) p. 126.

77 Bencze Mihály, "Garcsin-költö," in LÉLEKVÁNDORLÁS (Brasso: Fulgur Kiadó, 1996) p. 34

78 Crown Prince Rudolf of Austria, b. Aug. 21, 1858, was the only son of Emperor FRANCIS JOSEPH. Rudolf's death (Jan. 30, 1889) in a hunting lodge at Mayerling, near Vienna, was

Prince Ferdinand,[79] fell victims of the monarchy's orchestration of the nationality problems within the empire. Once the genie of nationalism was unleashed by the Court, it could not be returned into the bottle. The pro-Hungarian Rudolf, was murdered (officially committed suicide) for his sympathy with Hungarians. Ferdinand, who worked out with his Czech, Serb, and Rumanian supporters the plan for breaking up Hungary in a design[80] very similar to the final outcome of the Trianon Peace Treaties that mutilated Hungary after World War I, was assassinated himself in Sarajevo, in 1914.

Hungarian historian Tibor Baráth[81] places the tragedy of Rudolph in the context of a power struggle between Crown Prince Rudolph, who was soon to be crowned King of Hungary with the Emperor's blessing and thus carry out the Emperor's and Empress Elizabeth's plan to gradually place the center of the Empire to Hungary.[82] Ferdinand, next in line to the throne after Rudolph, was thinking more in terms of extending Austria's influence in Europe, and wanted to appease not only the Slavs in the empire by partitioning Hungary between the minorities residing in or around Hungary, but Rumania itself by promising them Transylvania if Rumania joins the Empire.[83] He failed to recognize that neither Russia, who also had designs on the South Slavs and wanted to strengthen her position there to get exit to the Adriatic Sea through the Balkan, nor France, who was jealous of the growing Germanic influence in Southern and Central Europe, would tolerate such a plan. Thus, Ferdinand's miscalculation led to his own assassination in Sarajevo in 1914. According to Baráth's sources, Ferdinand himself

---

officially ruled the result of a suicide pact with his mistress. According to some rumors, however, he was murdered because of his sympathies with Hungarian nationalism. ("Rudolf," The 1996 Groliers Multimedia Encyclopedia)
79 Franz Ferdinand, b. Dec. 18, 1863, was the Austrian archduke whose assassination by a Serbian nationalist at Sarajevo on June 28, 1914, sparked WORLD WAR I. After the alleged suicide (1889) of Archduke Rudolf, Ferdinand, a nephew of Emperor Francis Joseph became heir apparent. The Emperor, however, disapproved of his marriage (1900) to a Czech commoner, Sophie Chotek, and their children were barred from the succession. Although reactionary, Franz Ferdinand for a time favored the reorganization of AUSTRIA-HUNGARY to create a third kingdom of Croatia. This was one reason for his assassination by the Serbian nationalist Gavrilo Princip. (Cf. "Franz Ferdinand, Austrian Archduke," in Grolier).
80 According to Sisa,...the re-organization was much more comprehensive than just an independent Croatia. Cf. Sisa, SPIRIT..., pp. 185-6.
81 See Tibor Baráth, "A mayerlingi tragedia uj megvilágitásban" (The Tragedy of Mayerling in New Light"), in Tibor Baráth, A KÜLFÖLDI MAGYARSÁG IDEOLÓGIÁJA (Montreal: Sovereign Press, 1975). Baráth's source is Ugek, LA TRAGEDIA DE MAYERLING (Brussels, 1953) p. 223.
82 See Sisa, Ch. 28 "Queen Elizabeth: The 'Guardian Angel' of Hungary," pp. 171-174.
83 Istvan Sisa, NEMZET HATAROK NELKUL (A NATION WITHOUT BOUNDARIES) (Cleveland, OH: Arpad Publishing Co. 1993) p. 16.

participated, along with his "Mafia" of Czech officers in the assassination of his cousin, the 31 year old Rudolph.

Ferdinand's hatred of Hungary is demonstrated by not only his many openly hateful remarks about Hungary, but by his plan not to crown himself king of Hungary after the death of his uncle, Franz Joseph, but first dismember Hungary, that would be impossible if he were the crowned king, and then accept the Crown of Saint Stephen and be the king of a truncated country, while being the Emperor of a re-organized and enlarged federation.[84]

Consequently, Hungary's dismemberment at the Trianon Peace Conference only ratified the plans that Ferdinand and his advisors, leaders of the nationalities residing in historic Hungary, had developed but without Ferdinand, of course, and not as autonomous territories within the Empire, but as independent countries.

Adding to the irony was the fact that Ferdinand was assassinated by a radical Serb, supported by Serbian officials, including the secret police, who were not satisfied with a greater Serbia as an autonomous part of the Austrian Empire as Ferdinand had envisioned, but wanted an independent Serbia yet subservient to Russia. The Serbian government was instigated and supported by the Russian government and other pan-Slavists who wanted to unite all Slavic peoples and in the process provide Russia with direct access to the Adriatic Sea. Also, studies[85] and recently released documents in France seem to implicate the French government who, on the one hand, wanted a war to stop the German influence in the Balkan and the Middle East that would have resulted from completion of the proposed Baghdad Railway, and on the other, opposed Ferdinand's plan of extending Austrian influence in Western Europe. Therefore, France seems to have channeled money through Russia to the Serbian ultra-nationalists.

Yet, at the end of the war that followed the assassination, Hungary was treated as the main party responsible for the outbreak of the war by the true aggressors, including the French Clemenceau, rather than the innocent victim of the great-power struggle between the four players, Austria, Germany, Russia and France, that she really was. Even Austria, one of the instigators of the conflict, was given a portion of Hungarian territory.

It is beyond the scope of this essay to describe and analyze in detail the circumstances and the injustices committed against Hungary by the Treaty of Trianon. But to consider appropriate solutions to the problem one must go

---

84 cf. Ibid., pp. 15-16.
85 See L. W. Cramer, THE DIPLOMATIC BACKGROUND OF THE WORLD WAR (New York: Columbia University, 1928).

back and analyze the Treaty of Trianon both in its local and its global context as well as its political and legal aspects.

The local aspects involve the creation of minority problems, [86] and the economic consequences for the region, causing long term damage created by the Treaty of Trianon, at least in terms of Hungary. To understand the root of the current minority problems involving millions of Hungarians, and the reason why the minority issue still festers, with occasional flare ups, and also to consider effective solutions, one must find an answer to the question: why were millions of Hungarian nationals whose ancestors have lived in the area for centuries, if not for a thousand years, assigned to minority role by a treaty that was supposed to uphold the national self-determination principle? Why wasn't the same principle applied to Hungarians?

Even before and during the Great War, as W.W.I. was called before WW II had devastated the world for a second time in one lifetime, certain secret promises and agreements were made by the Allied and Associated Powers that were contrary to international law as then understood and to the "open diplomacy" principle. President Wilson in a speech to a joint session of Congress on January 8, 1918, announced his famous 14 points and had strongly endorsed open diplomacy. The very first of the fourteen points states that "Open covenants of peace, openly arrived at, after which there shall be no private international understandings of any kind but diplomacy shall proceed frankly and in the public view." Unfortunately, Wilson did not insist on its realization and the treaties, especially the one with Hungary, were based on promises concerning the partitioning of Hungary, made during, and even perhaps before the war.

According to Quigley's monumental work on "the history of the world in our time,"

> The peoples of the victorious nations had taken to heart their wartime propaganda about the rights of small nations, making the world safe for democracy, and putting an end to both power politics and secret diplomacy. These ideals had been given concrete form in Wilson's Fourteen Points. Whether the defeated Powers felt the same enthusiasm for these high ideals is subject to dispute, but they have been promised, on November 5, 1918, that the peace settlements would be negotiated and would be based on the Fourteen Points. When it became clear that the settlements were to be imposed rather than negotiated, that the Fourteen Points were lost in the confusion, and the terms of the settlements had been

---

86 Two chapters (23 and 30) in Stephen Sisa's monumental work, THE SPIRIT OF HUNGARY, details the development of nationalism in the Austro-Hungarian Empire.

reached by a process of secret negotiations from which the small nations had been excluded and in which power politics played a much larger role than the safety of democracy, there was a revulsion of feeling against the treaties.[87]

As the result, "the treaty of Trianon [with Hungary] signed in 1920 was the most severe of the peace treaties and the most rigidly enforced."[88]

The secret agreements made with the so called Little Entente countries included partitioning Hungary to benefit Rumania[89] and to create the countries of Czechoslovakia and Yugoslavia at Hungary's expense. Although the exact boundaries, it seems, were determined at the Peace Conference, the Hungarian delegation was excluded from the discussions, and the United States Senate refused to ratify it.

If one looks at the ethnic map of the Carpathian basin, one will find huge chunks of territory populated by Hungarians, but attached to the newly created or enlarged countries. When the Hungarian government demanded plebiscites in these territories, the Four Powers that prepared the treaty allowed plebiscite only in Sopron, a city that was to be given to Austria. The rest of the Hungarian populated cities or regions that fell outside the proposed boundaries were denied the right to determine their own future.

This would seem puzzling, unless one looks at another map, one showing the railroad lines of Hungary. Most of the railroad lines radiated from Budapest, but then, just before the Carpathian Mountains begin, the radiating lines are connected, creating a grand circle at the perimeter of the Great Plains. The designers of the Treaty were determined to give this vital railroad line, encircling the Plains, to the successor states.[90] The Subcommittee on Territorial Problems of the Advisory Committee on Post-War Foreign Policy within the State Department in a 1941 document on "Transylvania: Alternative Territorial Solutions" admits that

> (A)t the peace Conference in 1919, the railway connecting these cities was considered to be so great and strategic importance to

---

87 Carroll Quigley, TRAGEDY AND HOPE, A History of the World in Our Time (New York: Macmillan Company, 1966) p. 268.
88 Ibid., p. 274.
89 In the English language there are three acceptable versions to spell the name of the country and people: *Romania* is more suggestive of the connection with the Roman legions stationed in Dacia; Rumania, suggesting no such connection, and Roumanian, which seems to be more neutral and is used in diplomatic circles and documents. In this essay in direct quotations I shall use the original spelling, and in the text I shall follow the practice of most American scholars and historians, using *Rumania* or *Rumanian*.
90 See Zoltan Palotas Dr., A TRIANONI HATAROK (The Trianon Boundaries), (Budapest: Interedition, 1990).

Rumania that boundary was drawn to the west of it. The American territorial experts had recommended a line which cut across the railway in several places but was intended to secure a more just ethnic division.[91]

Of course, the American delegation was overruled, and millions of ethnic Hungarians were detached from the main body of the nation and made a minority in their own ancestral homeland, just because they happened to live on the wrong side of the tracks, as the saying goes. This is why no plebiscite was allowed, because it would have meant that major portions of the railroad would have had to be returned to Hungary if the people on the other side voted to stay united with Hungary. In the case of Sopron along the Western border of Hungary there was no such danger, so the plebiscite was allowed. The residents of Sopron overwhelmingly voted to remain with Hungary rather than being attached to Austria as the peoples of Nagyvárad and the other cities given to Rumania would have.

Thus, almost the entire border with Rumania, and more than half with the then Czechoslovakia, was determined by where the railroad tracks were (see map in Appendix #1), without a plebiscite that international law and Wilson's points required. The rest of the Czech border was drawn at the Danube, to create a natural boundary. As the result only about 40 per cent of the Trianon border around Hungary follows ethnic lines (much of it along the Drava river, separating Hungary and Croatia), while 60 per cent cuts into Hungarian ethnic territory.[92] This explains why Hungary lost seventy two per cent of her territory and 64 per cent of its population.[93] Of the total population transfer of 13.3 million people only 7.5 million (that includes the Croatians, who were Slavs, and thus were placed under Serbian rule in Yugoslavia) had belonged to the main ethnic category of the new country, which means that 5.8 million, that is 44% of the people detached from Hungary, was not Slovak, Rumanian, Serb, Croatian or Austrian. About 4 million of the 5.8 million were ethnic Hungarians who were transferred to become subjects of governments that have shown the deepest hatred of Hungary and Hungarians. All this was done in the name of self-determination.

To add insult to injury, even the 1.7 million Croats and the 1.9 million Slovaks were not given independence but were thrown under Serbian and

---

91 Romsics, "Transylvania: Alternative Territorial Solutions" p. 216.
92 Ibid., p. 93.
93 The figures in this paragraph are taken from Zoltan Bodolai, Ph.D., and Endre Csapo THE UNMAKING OF PEACE; The Fragmentation and Subsequent Destruction of Central Europe after World War One by the Peace Treaty of Trianon (Cleveland: Arpad Publishing, 1984), pp. 25-6.

Czech domination, respectively. Only the 2.5 million Rumanians, the 1.0 million Serbs and the .2 million Germans who were attached to Austria, a total of 3.7 million, out of 13.3, less than thirty per cent, and, incidentally, less than the number of Hungarians thrown into minority role, were truly "liberated" from under foreign domination while a total of 9.6 million people, including the Slovaks and Croats were placed under new oppressors who were proven to be much worse than the allegedly oppressive Hungarian rule. In addition, probably a large number of Rumanians, especially the intelligentsia, might have preferred to remain with Hungary. The newly created racist regimes were (and are) second in cruelty only to South Africa, formerly infamous for her apartheid policies.

The end result of Trianon was a series of ethnically heterogeneous countries, and it bears repeating, in the name of national self-determination. Based on data compiled between 1960-65, of 135 nations examined Hungary ranks 35th, with 90% homogeneity rate, Rumania ranks 59th, with 75%, Czechoslovakia was 80th, with 51%, and Yugoslavia ranked 118th of the 135 countries, with only 25% of population belonging to the dominant ethnic group![94]

In retrospect, especially in light of the recent events in Bosnia, it is easy to see that entrusting the Serb ultra-nationalist with the right to govern all Southern Slavs and create a mini-empire in Yugoslavia was a grave error. Careful study of the minority situation in Rumania and Czechoslovakia, and since the break up of the Czechoslovakian state, in Slovakia, would lead one to similar conclusion.

From a different perspective the Treaty of Trianon had another important consequence in the region: by following the railroad tracks, on the one hand, Hungary was deprived of a natural defense line, since the entire boundary line of Hungary with Rumania, is on the Great Plain, while on the other side there are mountains. To understand the situation one should compare this with the Golan Heights in the Middle East, and the importance Israel places on that strategic territory. On the other hand, while the railroads at the peripheries of Rumania and Czechoslovakia added little to their economic well-being, it deprived Hungary of a vital link to connect major economic centers directly, thus seriously disrupting the economic life at a time when the most cruel reparation burden was meted out to the country.

---

94 George Thomas Kurian, THE BOOK OF WORLD RANKINGS, (New York: Facts on File, Inc., 1984) pp. 48-49; from Theodore A. Couloumbis & James H. Wolfe, INTRODUCTION TO INTERNATIONAL RELATIONS: POWER AND JUSTICE (Englewood Cliffs, NJ.: Prentice Hall, 1986) pp. 66-7. The index was designed by the USSR Academy of Sciences, Moscow, and originally published in ATLAS NARADOV MIRA.

The Global Aspect

The global aspects of the situation in Central Europe involve two aspects: geo-politics and political culture. The geopolitical aspect was recognized by Halford J. Mackinder, a Scottish geopolitical expert and presented in a paper, "The Geographical Pivot of History," before the Royal Geographical Society in 1904.[95]

According to Mackinder, the Carpathian Basin is part of the strategically most important region on Earth. It connects the West through the Balkan with the oil rich Middle East and the Orient, and along with Poland, the region separates East and West, expansionist Russia and Germany. Mckinder called this region the Heartland, and believed that whoever controls the Heartland, could control the World Island, that is, Europe and Asia, and whoever controls the World Island controls the world.

After Mckinder made up this rule he warned the western democracies during and after WW I that to preserve world peace they should not allow Russia and Germany to be united, and should take control of this region to create a "tier of neutral countries," from the North Sea to the Adriatic. He feared that if one superpower, either Germany or Russia, would control the Heartland, it would be able to gain power over the Eurasian land mass, with its navy having access to both oceans and uniting German technological know-how and organizing ability with Russia's natural resources and man power. Such a combination would become such a powerful force that the democracies could not defend themselves.

The makers of the Treaty of Trianon, instead of heeding McKinder's advice, broke up the Austro-Hungarian empire and fragmented the region into artificial countries with sizable ethnic minorities and without much experience in self government. Under the disguise of self-determination, the main political goal of these countries, and the unifying force between the successor states in their foreign policies, was blind nationalism and a dream of an ethnically pure country to be achieved by expulsion, genocide, or forced assimilation of the millions of Hungarians and other ethnic groups, including Germans, Jews and Gypsies living in their ancestral lands.

The democracies failed to heed Mackinder's warning after WW I and, in spite of the international relations expert Spykeman's caution, repeated the same mistake after WW II, and finally, even after Colin Grey's warning about Russian imperialism during and after the Cold War, the democracies still have no policy to effectively deal with the problem of Central Europe and the

---

95 Reprinted in Halford J. Mackinder, DEMOCRATIC IDEALS AND REALITY (New York: W.W. Norton and Co, 1962), pp. 241-264.

Heartland, or the long-term relationship between Russia and Western Europe. Russia seems to be the only power interested in having a buffer zone for her protection and in preventing Poland and Hungary from joining NATO.

Nicholas John Spykman of Yale University in the conclusion of his monumental work on the world following W. W. II gives a searing criticism of Trianon and suggests how to correct the errors of Versailles and Trianon, albeit thirty years late, after the horrors of World War II, and the loss of millions of lives, not counting the economic destruction that could have been avoided by listening to Mackinder. According to Spykman, after the war ends,

> (T)he temptation will be almost irresistible to repeat the fatal blunders of 1919 and to believe that, the war having been won, we can return to our insular domain...[96]

> The greatest difficulty will be that of balancing Germany and Russia..... The easiest solution would be to give them common frontier. But if this should prove impossible, then the political unit between them should be a great eastern European federation from the Baltic to the Mediterranean, not a series of small buffer states... The Versailles settlement sacrificed economic and power considerations to the exclusive demands of the principle of self-determination.... The new peace will not only have to correct the balkanization of Europe, which was introduced after the First World War, but it also will have to achieve the integration of the other states into a few large units.[97]

Colin S. Gray[98] reinforces both Mackinder's and Spykman's views, although he is worried primarily in terms of a Soviet take-over of the Heartland, but he

---

96 Nicholas John Spykman, AMERICA'S STRATEGY IN WORLD POLITICS, The United States and the Balance of Power (New York: Harcourt, Brace and Company, 1942, p. 464. It should be noted that while Spykman writes as an American, and represents the American perspective, a strong case can be made that his views also represent a global interest, since peace and balance of power *is* global issue. His views are presented here not to glide over the minority issue, but as an added argument that the U.S. and the world democracies should be concerned about Central Europe and solve the problem that can lead to global conflict as the Bosnian situation has demonstrated.

97 Ibid., pp. 466-7.

98 See Colin S. Gray, THE GEOPOLITICS OF THE NUCLEAR ERA, Heartland, Rimlands, and the Technological Revolution (New York: Crane, Russak & Company, Inc., 1977), Colin S. Gray, NUCLEAR STRATEGY AND NATIONAL STYLE (Lanham, MD., Hamilton Press, 1986), and Colin S. Gray, WAR, PEACE, AND VICTORY, Strategy and Statecraft for the Next Century (New York: Simon & Schuster, 1990).

is just as adamant concerning the pivotal role of the region. According to Gray, the nuclear era does not diminish the significance of the region. Neither does the post-nuclear era. If we may hope to put the fears of a nuclear annihilation behind us, we are only returning to the times and concerns of Mackinder and Spykman. So there is every reason to continue to be interested in what is going on and who is likely to control East Central Europe should a crisis over the minority issue erupt again.

But even this geopolitical context does not tell the whole story. East Central Europe lies not only between East and West, but along the fault line between the two major cultural worlds: Western Christianity and Russified Byzantine Orthodoxy. The conflicting political cultures of some of the peoples around Hungary make the region a veritable time bomb waiting to explode, unless strong preventive action is taken. This division does not follow ethnic lines either. The Rumanians, for example, belong to the Byzantine sphere, except the Germans and Hungarians in Transylvania while Croatia and Slavonia, along with Hungary, belong to the Western Christian sphere. These are not just different religions but different world views and relationship to authority and other human beings. One of the causes of the troubles following the World War I treaties was the throwing together of various religious groups, like the Protestant Czechs and the Catholic Slovaks, the Catholic or Protestant (including Unitarian, a religion that originated in Transylvania) Hungarians and the Orthodox Rumanians, the Orthodox Serbs, the Catholic Croatians and the Muslim Bosnians.

It seems as if the major powers dictating the terms of the peace and setting up a new Europe had been mesmerized by the representatives of the Czechs, Serbs and Rumanians, and defying reason, gave in with very little resistance, to their propaganda and their demands.

Without wishing to submerge in the details of the Peace Treaty of Trianon, at least three more aspects should be mentioned, as part of the background

The Political and the Legal Aspects

The Treaty was forced on Hungary by blackmail. After the signing of the Armistice the Hungarian army was disbanded by the Hungarian government. If Hungary had refused to sign the Treaty, the Allied representatives had threatened Hungary to unleash the Rumanian army on the by then defenseless country. The nation was forced not only to ratify the Treaty but to make it law. It is known as the 1921:XXXIII Law. The First Paragraph begins: "Tekintettel a kényszerhelyzetre..." ("Considering the forced situation..."). That is, the treaty was forced on Hungary, and by the most basic rules of justice, only freely entered contracts are valid.

The second point may be raised after reading Quigley's analysis. He points out that the Hungarian leadership

> was persuaded to sign the Treaty of Trianon by a trick and ever afterward repudiated it. Maurice Paléologue, secretary-general of the French Ministry of Foreign Affairs (but acting on behalf of France's greatest industrialist, Eugene Schneider), made a deal with the Hungarians that if they would sign the Treaty of Trianon as it stood and give Schneider control of the Hungarian state railways, the port of Budapest, and the Hungarian General Creditbank of France would eventually make Hungary one of the mainstay of its anti-German block in Eastern Europe, would sign a military convention with Hungary, and would, at the proper time, obtain a drastic revision of the Treaty of Trianon. The Hungarian side of this complex deal was largely carried out, but British and Italian objections to the extension of French economic control into Central Europe disrupted the negotiations and prevented Hungary from obtaining its reward.[99]

It is hard to imagine that the secretary-general of the ministry could enter (and be taken seriously) in such a significant and complex deal without the approval of his boss, French Premier Georges Clemenceau (known as the Tiger), or at least of the Foreign Minister. But if Clemenceau was involved with this deal, is it possible that he had endeavored on purpose to make the terms of the Treaty especially harsh on Hungary, to give reason to agree to the deal in the hope of getting it modified in due time (that had never materialized), and at the same time blackmail Hungary and get a foothold for French industrial interests in there? Thus, the Treaty of Trianon not only violated Wilson's promise of open diplomacy, but also violated his promise of no more power politics in the region.

It is indeed a triple irony that France, seemingly the instigator of the events that had led to the outbreak of the war to prevent the spreading of German influence in the Middle East, was not only sitting in judgment over Hungary, a victim of the Hapsburg aspirations and the only opponent of the war at the Imperial Crown Council (while the representatives of the minorities were all enthusiastic supporters of the line that eventually led to the war), and French businessmen not only benefited at the expense of Hungary but France made Rumania, Hungary's deadly enemy, the main stay of her Central European policy!

It seems that after the discovery of secret documents in Paris President Mitterand made some comments in Budapest in the late 1980's (for which

---

99 Quigley, pp. 274-5.

he was severely criticized by the Rumanians) that some might consider an apology and admission of an error. There are also some signs, albeit weak and somewhat ambiguous, that now France is ready to at least accept steps that would help to remedy the human rights situation in the successor states, and at times obvious friction has developed between the Rumanian and French governments.

One example of such friction occurred at the 1989 UN Human Rights Commission Hearings in Geneva. M. Michel Rocard, the Prime Minister of France and a member of the Commission, stated in his remarks on February 6 that

> The Commission should not hesitate to investigate situations similar to the one experienced by the unfortunate people of Romania, whose leaders had cut themselves off from the great current that had just been enshrined in Europe with the adaptation, in Vienna, of procedures to safeguard human rights.[100]

The Rumanian response as reported next day in a Press Release never denied the charge. Instead, managed to insult France and compare the situation in France to that of Rumania:

> The observer for Rumania said the guest of honour yesterday had made insinuations concerning his country--insinuations he rejected. If the Prime Minister of France had looked clearly at the question of human rights, including in his own country, he might have seen millions of human beings dying of disease, and deprivation, millions of unemployed and hundreds of thousands homeless. Would it not have been wiser for the representative of France to start by "sweeping in his own backyard"? he asked.[101]

This exchange took place, of course, in the waning months of the Ceausescu regime. Also, the Rumanian response compares apples with oranges. It is one thing if in spite of positive government policies unemployment and poverty exists, and government sponsored discrimination, terror and genocide is another thing. But even after the fall of the hated dictator, the situation for Rumania's minorities had not changed much until the recent elections in 1996. In statements even after the fall of Ceausescu, French officials seem to have indicated their interest in keeping the issue alive and putting pressure on Rumania to mend her ways.

But in these days of reparations and apologies the least that France owes Hungary and the Hungarian nation is, if not a strong and direct apology, at

---

100 UN Information Service, February 7, 1989.
101 Ibid., February 8, 1989.

least a belated but sincere effort to right the wrongs committed at Trianon over 75 years ago!

Concerning the threat of force and use of trickery to make Hungary accept the harsh terms of the Treaty of Trianon one may attempt to argue, of course, that the consent of Hungary was not required, since the decision of the Allied and Associated Powers was based on international law.

But international law is a nebulous concept. There is no international law in the sense of positive, legislated law that we are familiar with and that can be enforced, and violators punished. Usually four sources of International Law are mentioned by textbooks: the principles laid down by the Dutch Hugo Grotius, the "Father of International Law,"[102] agreements in bi- or multilateral treaties, tradition, and international court decisions (precedents).

But there are problems with these "laws" based on any of these sources. First, there is a basic conflict between the concept of binding law and the concept of sovereignty. Sovereignty, being the supreme authority over a certain territory and the population thereof, would be compromised if outside, international organizations would interfere in the internal matters of a country. Therefore traditional international law does not provide enforcement machinery in domestic matters. Second, even if a court is available to decide disputes, international courts have jurisdiction only if both parties agree, just like in domestic arbitration cases and even then, complying with a court decision is up to the "boy scout honor" of each of the parties. Third, treaties are signed and ratified voluntarily and there are provisions to abrogate a treaty if it does not serve the interest of a party anymore. Fourth, the principles proposed by Grotius are general, and lastly, one can find cases in tradition to justify just about anything. Yet, it should be noted that the kind of boundary changes and application of self-determination introduced at Trianon were not based on any of the above sources, and has never become a tradition! In addition, general legal concepts that have been used, although not explicitly invoked at Trianon, like ex post facto laws, or use of threats to obtain compliance and other similar morally objectionable behavior, even if used sporadically, are generally shunned in international relations also. Although both Trianon and the Nuremberg Trials seem to prove that might makes right, might is not considered a source of international law!

---

102 Hugo Grotius wrote THE LAW OF WAR AND PEACE, first published in 1625, following the Thirty Years' War.

III.

THE DIAGNOSIS

Medicine distinguishes genetic or inherited and acquired diseases. There are no comparable genetic causes of problems in international relations. Human nature is not inherently violent and no conflict is inevitable. Every conflict and problem is acquired in the sense that it is caused by some human mistake in the course of history. So it is with the minority problem in Central Europe. International law, as designed by Grotius, was a set of common sense rules intended to reduce conflict and maintain international peace and order. Violating or circumventing such law can only cause conflicts and violence. And the more one waits in correcting the situation, just like with human illnesses, the more radical operation is needed.

Neither of the two main pretenses used to mutilate Hungary at the Trianon Peace Conference has been known and accepted in international law, and even if it was accepted, the first pretense is patently false, invented only to justify a preconceived conclusion.

The Question Of Responsibility

The first pretense was articulated by M. Millerand in his cover letter of transmittal: "The Allied and Associated Powers ... cannot forget how great is Hungary's responsibility for the outbreak of the world war, and in general, for the imperialist policies of the Dual Monarchy."[103]

In other words, Hungary had to be punished for her responsibility for the outbreak of the war. First, even if true, at best adequate (or even punitive) material compensation is the proper method of punishment. Although the amount of compensation required in Part VIII of the Treaty is unjustified and exorbitant, based on Hungary's responsibility as stated in Art. 161, in the case of compensation only the amount is disputed and not the principle. But mutilating a country as punishment for aggression, or deciding that Hungary could not handle her minority problem and detaching even minority inhabited territories, let alone areas with pure or majority Hungarian population from Hungary as the solution, is nowhere allowed in international law, except in the principle of might makes right.

---

103 Cover letter, The Allied and Associated Powers to the President of the Hungarian Peace Delegation, Paris, May 6, 1920, by A. Millerand,; Hungarian translation in Andras Gerö, ed., SORSDÖNTÉSEK (FATEFUL DECISIONS), (Budapest: Göncöl Kiadó, 1989), p. 163.

But even a cursory examination should reveal that Hungary was the least responsible of all the parties involved in causing the war. L. W. Cramer of Columbia University in his detailed study[104] finds enough blame to go around and ascribes some to all participants. Even the United States was drawn into the conflict through her own deliberate behavior that led to the sinking of the Lusitania. Cramer quotes then Senator laFollette:

> Four days before the Lusitania sailed, President Wilson was warned in person by Secretary of State Bryan that the Lusitania had six million rounds of ammunition aboard. Besides explosives and that the passengers who proposed to sail on that vessel were sailing in violation of a statute of this country, that no passengers shall travel upon a railroad train or sail upon a vessel that carries dangerous explosives. And Mr. Bryan appealed to President Wilson to stop passengers from sailing upon the Lusitania.[105]

Therefore it is tempting to conclude that civilian passengers were deliberately used on the Lusitania as a bait to trigger the American war machine to enter the war on the side of the Allies.

It is impossible to detail the complicated web of secret or semi-secret alliances and maneuvers in the three decades preceding the outbreak in 1914. Cramer first distinguished between "the more fundamental underlying causes [of the war] which reach far back into diplomacy and history of Europe"[106] that preceded the assassination, and immediate causes, the events following the assassination. He summarizes

the underlying causes in four categories:

1. the complex of secret alliances upon which the alleged 'Balance of Power' rested;

2. nationalism;

3. imperialism;

4. militarism.

...in respect to these four underlying causes the responsibility must be shared by all the powers in question.[107]

---

104 L. W. Cramer, THE....
105 Ibid., pp. 115-6.
106 Ibid., p. 7.
107 Idem.

54

In fact, he seems to suggest, based on the evidence, that in at least two if not all four causes, the Allied side was at least as, if not more guilty than the Central Powers.[108]

It is obvious that since the Franco-Prussian War which Germany won decisively in 1871, but at least since 1891 the two sides, including Germany, France, Russia and England, were lining up, waiting for a spark to start a war that each side expected to win.[109] In 1907 England joined France and Russia in what became the Triple Entente.

It seems the last of the series of steps in getting ready for a global conflict took place just months before the assassination. According to Admiral Horthy's memoirs in November 1913 the three Axis powers had entered into a secret agreement about convening their naval forces in the Naples (Italy) area, and "only a few months prior to this England and France concluded a similar agreement."[110]

Cramer presents evidence that seems to show that both before the outbreak of the war, and during the war, the Allied side was the more ruthless, cunning, and treacherous. For example, he quotes from a report of the Russian Ambassador in London to Sazonov, the Russian Minister of Foreign Affairs, a conversation on November 20, 1914 with Grey, the British Minister of Foreign Affairs:

> He (Grey) has told me enough to prove to us that under certain special conditions, England would enter the war. For this, in my opinion, two conditions are necessary: in the first place, the active intervention of France must make this war a general one; secondly, it is absolutely necessary that the responsibility for the aggression fall upon our opponents.... The question of who is to be the aggressor will be of greatest significance. Only under these circumstances would the British government have the support of the

---

108 Ibid., pp. 7-8; for evidence see Chapters 1, 2, pp. 7-59.
109 Details of this preparation for the coming war is best described and analyzed by Cramer, op.cit. Other reports and explanations, including several earlier assassination attempts against representatives of the monarchy, are found in several books quoted by Zoltán Bodolai, THE UNMAKING OF PEACE, The Fragmentation and Subsequent Destruction of Central Europe After World War One by the Peace Treaty of Trianon (Cleveland, Arpad Publishing, 1984) pp. 14-18; Sources include Z. Bodolai, TIMELESS NATION, (Sidney, 1977), Oscar Jaszi, THE DISSOLUTION OF THE HABSBURG MONARCHY (1929), S.B. Vardy HISTORY OF THE HUNGARIAN NATION (USA, 1971), Sandor Szilassy REVOLUTIONARY HUNGARY 1918-21 (USA, 1971),
110 Miklos Horthy, EMLEKIRATAIM (MEMOIRS), 2nd ed. (Toronto: Weller Publishing, 1974) p. 75.

public opinion which the government needs for energetic action....[111]

In other words, all they have to do is to provoke and trick Germany and/or Austria to strike the first blow, get France into the conflict and the English public will be misled into supporting a war their government was itching to get into. Both tasks were easy. Because of Germany's central geographic position between the two hostile nations, France and Russia, Germany could not fight on two fronts at the same time. So to defend herself she had to rely on a plan of preemptive strike against France first, before Russia completes its mobilization, so they can then concentrate their forces on the Eastern Front, according to the Schlieffen Plan that was known to the French. It was named after Graf Alfred von Schlieffen, chief of the German General Staff.

This plan had provided the loop-hole the Allied Powers needed. They could instigate the hostilities and still pin the blame for aggression on Germany, as long as Russia only mobilized but did not attack.[112] But the French government's behavior also belies a high degree of callousness toward their own people. They knew that the Schlieffen Plan calls for the immediate overrun of France and the full defeat of the French army, yet, in the hope of ultimate victory, they were ready to accept it.

As for involving France, it was no great problem. In fact, France almost insisted on being part of any major conflict since the "rigorously secret" Franco-Russian Military Convention of 1894 has tied the two countries military action close together. Again, the only condition was that it had to look like Germany was the aggressor to trigger the treaty. "The terms of the treaty were not published until 1918. Even the French parliament, when it declared war on Germany, did not fully know the exact nature of the obligations which the French government had assumed toward Russia."[113]

France took another major step toward coaxing Russia into eventual military action when in 1911 France signed a convention with Russia

> to allow Russia to float annual loans of between four hundred and five hundred million francs on the Paris market for railway construction, on condition that Russia immediately undertake to build strategic railways agreed upon between the Military Staffs and that the peace-time effectiveness of the Russian army be notably increased.[114]

---

111 Cramer., pp. 57-8.
112 Ibid., pp. 67-8.
113 Ibid., p. 20. For details see Ibid., pp. 18-20.
114 Ibid., p. 56.

France was just as supportive of making the war as general as possible even after the assassination. Instead of cautioning and urging moderation in light of the almost certain attack on Serbia,

> France assured Russia of her support in accordance with the obligations of the Franco-Russian alliance.... This was the equivalent of a "blank check" whereby France would support Russia whatever steps she took to prevent Austria from carrying out her plans against Serbia.[115]

In light of the Schlieffen plan, this meant that Russia's mobilization would draw Germany into the conflict, and Germany would be forced to attack France. While the French government continued to instigate the outbreak of the war through the Russian and Serbian governments, the Austrian Crown Council (in which Hungary had one single vote, which was cast by Prime Minister Kalman Tisza against the hard-liner position while the representatives of all the other minorities supported the hard line all along), voted on July 7th for a strong response,[116] demanding the surrender of those responsible for the assassination. Due to Tisza's objection,[117] the plan was shelved, however, at this time. On July 14, "irritated perhaps by the provocative attitude of Serbian governmental officials and newspapers, and impressed by the considerations put forward by Brechtold, Tisza finally gave way in the a Cabinet meeting and agreed that the terms of the Serbian ultimatum should intentionally be made unacceptable."[118]

But Tisza still wasn't through. When on July 19 the Cabinet decided on the final draft, before Tisza would give his consent to the adoption of the ultimatum, he forced the Cabinet, in a futile effort to localize the war, to unanimously agree "that immediately upon the outbreak of the war a declaration would be made to the Powers that the Monarchy was not conducting a war of conquest and did not intend to incorporate the Kingdom of Serbia...."[119]

The ultimatum was delivered on July 23, with a 48 hour time limit to respond. The Serbian government responded with mobilization, and the Serbs refused to turn over the assassin.

---

115 Ibid., p. 67.

116 One must wonder in retrospect if they were in on the plot to lure the Monarchy into provoking the war!?

117 Tisza wrote to the Emperor on July 8, 1914, objecting to forcing the war on Serbia, concluding with the following statement: "... in spite of my sincere service to you, or, rather, because of it, I could not share the responsibility for a war as the exclusive and aggressive solution." Letter of Hungarian Prime Minister Tisza to Ferenc Jozsef Emperor, king of Hungary. Letter printed in Ernö Raffay, MAGYAR TRAGÉDIA; TRIANON 75 ÉVE --The Hungarian Tragedy; the 75 years of Trianon (Budapest: Pusky Kiado, 1995) p. 220.

118 Ibid., p. 64.

119 Ibid, p. 68.

Horthy's Memoirs also give an interesting insight into the Austrian thinking that contributed to the aggressive stand of Austria, and explains Hungary's reluctance to support the Austrian stand. After the assassination Horthy was summoned by Crown Prince Charles, the new heir to the crown after Ferdinand's assassination, and asked Horthy "Well, what can we expect?" "A world war," Horthy responded, to which Charles explained that he had just been assured by the Austrian Foreign Minister that the war will be confined to Serbia. When Horthy explained why the war would spread beyond Serbia, the astonished crown prince cried out "how awful it would be!"[120] It seems the Hungarians had a better awareness of the international situation than the Austrians.

Austria-Hungary itself had been a minor power in this configuration, but unfortunately, within the Monarchy Hungary had little to do with foreign policy. After the death of Ferdinand, neither the Monarchy, nor Hungary had any territorial claims or imperialistic aspirations. So why would Hungary be the aggressor?

In spite of basing their verdict on the charge that Hungary was chiefly responsible for the war, the Allied and Associated Powers sitting in judgment in Trianon never examined the question. So let us do, belatedly, their homework for them. In a metaphysical and dictionary sense, the aggressor is one who first disturbs peace or makes an unprovoked attack. Hugo Grotius, a 16th century Dutchman, who is considered the father of international law, gives a similar definition: "the breakers of the peace are not those who resist violence with violence, but those who use violence first."[121]

In this sense Serbia and the Panslav interests in Russia behind her, along with France behind Russia that had encouraged terrorist acts against the Monarchy for at least ten years prior to the successful assassination at Sarajevo were the obvious aggressors. The assassination of the Crown Prince and his wife was only the most spectacular act of at least seven acts of terror in four years trying to spark a war. But was Serbia responsible for the act? According to Grotius again,

> if the subjects commit an act of armed violence without orders from their state, it will be necessary to discover whether the act of private individuals can be called officially approved? ... Three things are needed to constitute such approval: knowledge of the acts, power

---

120 Ibid., p. 74.
121 Hugo Grotius 3, XX, 28. Grotius derives his norms from the common sense approach, that without some rules there can be no stable international system.

to punish them, and negligence to do so.... Such negligence is equal to command.[122]

There is little doubt that all three elements were present in the case of the Sarajevo murders. Aside from the Serbian army providing the bombs and revolvers and arranging to smuggle the assassins into Bosnia, "members of the cabinet, including Pashitch, the Premier, knew of the plot a month beforehand but took no effective measures to prevent its execution or to properly notify Austria," other than "a vague hint that the presence of Francis-Ferdinand at the army maneuvers in Bosnia might lead disaffected Serbian youths in the Austrian army to attempt his life."[123] So on account of the murder, Serbia was the immediate aggressor, with Russia and France right behind Serbia.

But what about responsibility for spreading the war beyond Serbia? Granted, the Note from the Monarchy was a severe one. But does that constitute aggression? The 1894 Franco-Russian military alliance specified that "the aggressor is the one who mobilizes first." Under this criteria the verdict is easy: Serbia mobilized her forces first, on July 25, 1914, nine hours before the Austrian ultimatum expired. Austria-Hungary announced mobilization only six hours after the Serbs. Russia also mobilized secretly the same day. Thus, no matter how one twists it, Hungary was not the aggressor and was in no way responsible for World War I.

National Self-Determination

The second pretense used at Trianon was the right of the nationalities in Hungary to self-determination. But according to Clyde Eagleton, writing in 1953, thirty five years after Trianon, in the prestigious Foreign Affairs, the publication of the Council on Foreign Relations,

> (T)he concept of self determination is not a simple one, and it has always defied definition. It is a two-edged concept which can disintegrate as well as unify; consider the Austro-Hungarian Empire. There has never been a judge to pass upon its claims; indeed, there has never been a law by which judgment could be issued. The textbooks of international law do not recognize any legal right of self-determination, nor do they know any standards for determining which groups are entitled to independence; on the contrary, international law holds that a state which intervenes to aid a rebellious group to break away from another state is itself

---

122 Ibid., 3, XX, 30.
123 Cramer, pp. 59-60

committing an illegal act. Furthermore, if and when a group has factually established itself, other states have no obligation to recognize it as a legal power, a sovereign state. The emphasis has been upon the word "self"; the group itself must fight through to what it wanted. Secession or revolution could not be recognized as a legal right. There was no community law, or judge, or machinery, to uphold a claim of self-determination.[124]

While there has been some evolution in the role of the UN in the matter of self-determination since this was written in 1953, Eagleton's position certainly was valid in 1920! This means that since "international law holds that a state which intervenes to aid a rebellious group to break away from another state is itself committing an illegal act," the signatories of the Trianon peace treaties breaking up Austria-Hungary and assisting Hungary's minorities to break away from Hungary in the name of national self-determination, the case Eagleton uses to illustrate his point, had violated international law.

The real reason for breaking up Hungary was the existence of secret agreements entered into during the war to reward certain countries to stay out of the war, or to enter it on the allied side. There are also conspiracy theories that suggest, without any credible evidence yet quite persuasively that since Hungary was punished more severely than any of the principals in the conflict, there might be some anti-Hungarian conspiracy at work.

As for the lack of the right to rebel, it means only that every government has both the right (to protect the leadership) and the responsibility (to protect stability) to defend itself. Thus, there can be no contrary right (to rebellion, that is) within the same legal system. Therefore governments may take appropriate steps to prevent a revolution and to punish participants in a failed revolution. On the other hand, this should not be viewed to give governments absolute right to oppress people. De facto successful revolutions and secessions become legitimized after the fact, and the revolutionary or secessionist government may be recognized as legitimate by the international community.

The recent developments in the concept of self-determination and related international law will be discussed later. At this point we shall focus on this issue only as much as necessary to place Trianon in the full context of international law as it was enunciated by Grotius.

---

124 Clyde Eagleton, "Excesses of Self-Determination" (FOREIGN AFFAIRS, July 1953). Reprinted by special permission in Robert A. Goldwin, READINGS IN WORLD POLITICS (New York: Oxford University Press, 1959, 304-316) p. 305-6.

To understand the reasoning behind Eagleton's argument one must go back to Grotius again, who derives his norms from the common sense approach and suggests that without some rules there can be no stable international system: "It is in the interest of human society that governments should be firmly established, beyond the hazards of controversy, and all presumptions that help promote such a state of things should be favorably considered."[125] Sovereign equality and the concept of territorial integrity has been universally recognized since Grotius as the basis of international law.

Grotius distinguishes between private ownership and assertion of sovereignty. Both are "forms of taking possession of things that belong to no one." Sovereignty is supreme power or jurisdiction by a central government over people or territory.[126] "Sovereignty is not on a level with other things; instead, it far surpasses them in the nobility of its purpose."[127] Taking possession over a territory, however, even for a length of time, is not sufficient to establish sovereign possession. Even undeclared intention is not sufficient, according to Grotius. Sovereign intentions must be "disclosed by some outward sign,"[128] like planting a flag or some equivalent symbol. Therefore, it would be inappropriate to apply the principle of sovereignty to nomadic or migrating populations temporarily occupying a territory without a central government.

Private ownership also starts by taking property that does not belong to anyone, and it has to be marked or staked out (and registered to an owner) and can be alienated, but in civilized countries it is subject to certain laws established by the sovereign.

Once sovereignty is established, it can be alienated by conquest, but then there is nothing to prevent the previous sovereign to regain, by force if necessary, the lost territory: "Sovereignty won by force can be overthrown by force."[129] Sovereign possession can also be abandoned, freely or voluntarily surrendered, or exchanged for consideration, like sovereign rights over Alaska was purchased from the Russian sovereign by the sovereign United States of America. It should be noted that on the one hand, alienation of sovereignty does not affect private property rights, which are an entirely different (though similar) issue. In other words, the purchase of Alaska did not affect any private ownership rights on the territory of Alaska. On the other hand, owning, purchasing, or taking private property does not change, nor does it give one the right to change sovereignty. If the Cubans would

---

125 Grotius, 2, IV, 8.
126 Ibid., 2, III, 4.
127 Ibid., 2, IV, 12.
128 Ibid., 2, IV, 3.
129 Ibid., 2, V, 14.

purchase half, or even the entire state of Florida, it would still remain US territory, until the US would cede it, through a treaty, to the sovereign state of Cuba, or Cuba conquers it from the United States with military force, or the new residents in Florida would stage a successful revolution against the United States and establish the sovereign country of Florida.

In the case of Quebec Province, sovereignty over Canada was transferred peacefully from England to the multi-ethnic Canadian provinces as a unit. Although most of the property is owned by French speaking Canadians, the private property ownership rights of French Canadians does not automatically translate into sovereign rights for Quebec.

Because sovereignty is so special, it is protected above other considerations, as Eagleton suggested. Revolutions are domestic matters of a country (this is why the Soviet Union has violated international law in entering Czechoslovakia in 1968, and intervening in the Hungarian Revolution of 1956, justifying the UN investigation). As for the issue of self-determination, Eagleton is right. There is no such positive right--as yet, although one may argue that it is included in the general concept of basic human rights. But the lack of positive international law does not mean that it cannot be accomplished voluntarily or forced out by violent means. In Grotius the question of self-determination comes up discussing "Public Good Faith in the Ending of War; in Particular, Treaties of Peace" in Chapter XX, Article 5 which deals with the subject of treaties. According to Grotius again,

> [I]n order that any part of the sovereignty may be alienated validly, there must be two consents, the consent of the whole body, and, in particular, the consent of the body in question, which cannot be rent away against its will from the body to which it has belonged. [130]

In other words, treaties can create new sovereignty only with the approval of the population of both the mother country and of the proposed new sovereignty. This was implied in Wilson's fourteen points, but denied by the makers of the Treaty of Trianon. A. Millerand, in the name of the Allied and Associated Powers, dismisses the Hungarian demand for a plebiscite with some self-serving, unproved and undocumented remarks. In his cover letter to the Treaty, A. Millerand wrote the following:

> It is true that the Hungarian Peace Delegation argues that the Conditions of Peace never ordered popular referendum. If the Allied and Associated Powers considered it unnecessary to proceed with such a survey of the population, it was because they were convinced that if such a survey was based on conditions guaranteeing sincere

---

130 Ibid., 3, XX, 5.

expression of opinion, it would not lead to substantially different results, than what the Powers concluded, based on careful analysis of Central Europe's ethnographic relationships and national aspirations.[131]

This is nonsense, of course. First, there is no such assumption allowed by Grotius or any other expert on International Law. Second, Millerand confuses referendum with survey. The Hungarian government requested, according to international law, a binding referendum, and Millerand talks about an information gathering survey. Third, if one looks at the statistics given above showing that out of 13.3 million, a total of 3.7 million, less than thirty per cent were truly "liberated" from under foreign domination, while 9.6 million people were forced to live under a different foreign rule, the conclusion of the Allied and Associated powers seems absurd! Let us look at the ethnic composition of the new states. In the newly formed multi-national state of Czechoslovakia,

> in a total population of 13 million, Czechs comprised only 6.3 million or 48.4%; with 25% Germans; 16% Slovaks; 9% Hungarians; and the rest divided between Ruthenians, Poles and others. In Yugoslavia there were only 54% Serbs; in Rumania 67% Rumanians; but in Transylvania there were only 54% Rumanians.[132]

It was only a small, unrepresentative sample of extreme nationalist leaders, most of them refugees, residing abroad, who had made the secret deals among themselves and politicians of the Allied Powers during the war, and convinced the delegations of the Allied and Associated Powers to partition Hungary. Thus they had created a political situation where they have satisfied their own personal aspirations to assume power over and at the expense of their own and other nationalities in newly created or enlarged multi-national states. So, at best, the Allied and Associated Powers were misled and hoodwinked by a group of Rumanian and Czech political émigrés led by Edward Benes and Thomas Masaryk. Masaryk had an American wife assisted him in carrying out his propaganda and his plans to create a "Democratic Czech Republic."

Benes, during the last phase of the war "urged the great powers: "Detruisez l'Autriche-Hongroie (Destroy Austria-Hungary). This slogan was adopted by the French Premier Clemenceau and became one of the dominant principles of the Paris Peace Conference of 1919."[133]

---

131 Cover Letter, in Gerö, pp. 163-5.
132 Miroslav Lazarovich, "Regional Federalism or a New Cataclysm," in Francis Wagner, ed., TOWARD A NEW CENTRAL EUROPE A Symposium on the Problems of the Danubian Nations (Astor Park, FL: Danubian Press, 1970) p. 149.
133 Idem.

Thus, national self-determination had nothing, or very little to do with the territorial decisions during the Peace Conference. But if it had, Grotius's rule would still apply. He makes an exception to the rule requiring two plebiscites: "In case of extreme or other ways inevitable necessity, a part may by itself transfer to other hands the sovereignty over itself without consent of all the people."[134]

This means, on the one hand, that the majority of a state has no inherent right to oppress a sizable minority and the international community may assist in freeing such oppressed people to gain independence. On the other hand, this creates the classical definition of self-determination: "transfer to other hands the sovereignty over itself without consent of all the people" or their government, and sets the perfect justification for self-determination: "extreme or other ways inevitable necessity."

Therefore the international community would not violate international law to recognize a unilateral determination to secede in extreme situations. But the terms of the Treaty of Trianon transferring sovereignty were not based on claiming such extreme or other wise inevitable necessity, therefore both referendums, one in the mother country, and one in the affected territory should have been held. But even in a case of extreme or other ways inevitable necessity, only the referendum all the people, i.e. the people in the mother country can be dispensed with; a referendum should have been held at least in the affected territory.

Therefore no argument will validate the false claim that the carving up of Hungary at Trianon was based on international law! In fact, Trianon was illegal!

A good case can be made today in light of this requirement that the Bosnian conflict could be resolved peacefully by breaking up Bosnia only if both the entire population of Bosnia and each of its three constituent nationalities, if they can be identified and separated for voting purposes, would approve in a referendum the separation and creation of three independent sovereignties that can decide their future after the separation. But if one nation, let us say the Serbs of Bosnia or the Albanians of Kosovo would decide in a referendum, based on obvious and reasonable claim of extreme or other ways inevitable necessity, they should have the right to secede and any international rule prohibiting it violates Grotius's principle.

The well documented oppressive and obstinate attitude (including forced assimilation and even the threat of genocide) of the Rumanian, Serbian or the former Slovak governments elected and aided by certain ultra-nationalist

---

134 Grotius, 3, XX, 5.

groups in those countries, leading the massive protests from the oppressed minorities, could be considered extreme and other ways inevitable necessity to justify and provide sufficient reason to consider allowing a referendum in the affected regions about the separation from their current sovereign and create their own sovereign or hand it over to another sovereign.

On the other hand, in the dispute between Quebec and the rest of Canada, there has been no extreme or other ways inevitable necessity alleged. At the same time the secession of Quebec would break up Canada not into two but three parts, geographically severing Eastern and Western Canada, with the most serious economic and other consequences for English speaking Canada. Therefore, it would seem that to maintain good order, both referendums should be required. It should also be noted that the separatists are not demanding more rights, since Canada not only has one of the worlds most progressive minority policies, but Quebec already has considerable autonomy in domestic and economic matters. Many oppressed minorities would be glad to have half as much rights and autonomy as the people of Quebec have. Quebec separatists just want separation, not more rights.

Therefore in the absence of both referendums, the Ottawa government has the right (and obligation) to protect the unity of Canada, and to punish any rebels. Also, no foreign government should recognize a break-away group as Quebec's legitimate and sovereign government unless they have succeeded in a revolution, or alternatively, they have proven to the international community or the World Court a case of extreme or other ways inevitable necessity. Because of geography, the third alternative allowed by Grotius, that is, France or any other country conquering Quebec by force, is not a realistic alternative. Where geographically feasible, however, countries conquering contiguous regions of neighboring countries where their co-nationals resided is another option that has been used to solve minority problems. In this case, however, Grotius warns that "(S)overeignty won by force can be overthrown by force."[135]

This standard, as suggested by Grotius, is pretty vague in itself and needs further definition. It seems that the distinction made by Pope Pius XI can be helpful in this matter: "there is ... room for fair and moderate nationalism, which is the breeding ground of many virtues, but beware of exaggerated nationalism as of a veritable curse."[136] The suggested standard is this, then: is the effort to secede motivated and driven by a desire to protect the survival of moderate nationalism and to obtain the right to continue in their language and culture or life-style against attacks from exaggerated nationalism, and every other, more moderate effort, including demands for autonomy, has

---

135 Ibid., 2, V, 14.
136 see # 9 above

failed, or is it an effort by exaggerated nationalists to disrupt social cooperation among peaceful ethnic communities? Without passing judgment at this point over any secessionist movement, it is obvious that there are some such movements where survival of the national identity is not in danger, and therefore those movements would not meet Grotius', or any other criteria, by the Pope's standard.

Thus, the matter of self-determination is not a dead issue. As far as international law is concerned, it applies to any situation, including Central Europe, and more specifically the Carpathian Basin and the Hungarian minorities in the countries surrounding Hungary. Unilateral secession could be approved only if extreme necessity is proven. If it is proven, then it would be up to the World Community and the UN to order and supervise such a referendum in the affected areas.

Creating autonomous regions with shared sovereignty, as will be argued later as a more moderate compromise solution, designed to eliminate the need for the more radical secession, should be handled the same way, since it involves re-taking some sovereign functions over their own affairs from the current sovereign, while leaving other sovereign functions to the central government of the country. In case of extreme necessity, the international community should allow the people of the affected area to have a referendum and proclaim, and if necessary, order or force the majority nation to negotiate or accept such autonomy for the minority.

Is the Minority Issue a Domestic concern?

Although this question is not really a part of the diagnosis, it is a relevant part of the history of the region and places the countries with Hungarian minorities in a somewhat unique situation.

The only substantive argument that can be made against raising the issue of self-determination is insistence that the question of minorities is an internal matter for the countries involved. But in the countries under discussion the change of sovereign possession was accomplished by treaties that included certain restrictions and conditions, making the relevant internal matters subject to international jurisdiction and control. Thus, in addition to the international provisions that one might suggest in cases of extreme or otherwise inevitable necessity, this situation is also controlled by international treaties!

66

M. Millerand, in his cover letter, specifically talks about the issue of protecting minority rights and tries to assuage the Hungarian government: "As for the Hungarian ethnic islands falling under such (alien) sovereignty, Rumania and the Serb-Croat-Slovene state has already signed, and the Czech-Slovak state has ratified treaties to assure the protection of the minorities, fully guaranteeing their interests."[137]

Interestingly, even some Rumanians admit that international protection of the minorities was a condition, albeit an unwelcome one, of receiving the territories with Hungarian population by the Treaty of Trianon. In a book published in 1971 by the Academy of the Socialist Republic of Rumania, intended as Rumanian propaganda to justify their behavior, the authors admit that

> (T)he Trianon Treaty includes some causes which affected to some extent the independence and sovereignty of the Rumanian State; the Rumanian delegation at the Peace Conference accepted these clauses under pressure from the representatives of the Great Powers. Such was the clause providing for the protection of the national minorities from the outside...
>
> The protests of the Rumanian delegation against these clauses ... were ignored by the Great Powers. Article 47 was included in the Treaty , stipulating that Rumania pledges itself to Hungary to include in a Treaty concluded with the Chief Allied and Associated Powers such provisions as these powers may consider necessary to protect in Rumania the interests of citizens who differ from the majority of the population in respect of race, language or religion.
>
> Undoubtedly, by such provisions the Big Powers reserved their right to interfere in Rumania's internal affairs.[138]

While factually accurate, the implication of the above quote is false. It seems to imply that the clauses were forced upon Rumania. This is false, of course. Unlike the Hungarian government, that was forced to ratify the loss of her territory and population without gaining anything in return, there was no force exercised upon Rumania to accept the deal that gave Rumania Hungarian and German inhabited territories in Transylvania for guarantees of minority rights. The clauses were part of a contractual agreement: if Rumania

---

137 Cover letter... published in Hungarian translation in SORSDÖNTÉSEK, p. 165.
138 Quoted in GENOCIDE IN TRANSYLVANIA: A NATION ON DEATH ROW; a documentary compiled by The Transylvanian World Federation and the Danubian Research and Information Center (Astor, FL: The Danubian Press, 1985) p. 137, from The Academy of the Socialist Republic of Rumania, UNIFICATION OF THE RUMANIAN STATE (1971) p. 314. The word *of* in the last line of par. two probably is a mis-print and should read *or*.

wanted the territories, they had to ratify (and carry out) the clauses. Once the contract was ratified and the transfer of the territory was consummated, the clauses were to be binding, like it or not! And if the Rumanian state refuses to honor one part of the contract, according to basic legal principles, the other part also becomes invalid and the entire contract becomes null and void. Therefore, if the discrimination, oppression and forced assimilation of the Hungarian population continues and Rumania refuses to honor the protective part of the treaties and fails to grant at least shared sovereignty in the form of autonomy, Transylvanian Hungarians should be justified to reclaim the sovereignty over themselves, and if they wish, to return to Hungary. Furthermore, the Great Powers that made the decision to turn millions of Hungarians over to these countries, should feel obligated to assist the Hungarian minority to free itself from the oppressive regimes. The same principles apply, of course, to the other affected countries, Czechoslovakia and Yugoslavia and their successor states, Slovakia and rump Yugoslavia.

The Treaty of Paris (1947) concluded with Rumania after World War II also contains protection for the minorities under international guarantee. Right after Articles 1 and 2 which deal with and restore Rumania's boundaries with Hungary to the Trianon boundaries, Art. 3 prohibits legal discrimination and requires Rumania to guarantee equal protection based on "race, sex, language or religion." Article 5 requires that Rumania dissolve and prohibit "in the future the existence and activities of organizations of that nature which have as their aim denial of the people of their democratic rights." But what is most important, the Treaty also contains a provision making the minority issue subject of international supervision without time limit in Art. 38.1:

> Except where another procedure is specifically provided under any Article of the present Treaty, any dispute concerning interpretation or execution of the Treaty, which is not settled by direct diplomatic negotiations, shall be referred to the Three Heads of Mission acting under Article 37, except in this case the Heads of Mission will not be restricted by the time limit provided in that Article...

This makes the minority issue in Rumania a legitimate concern of the Allied and Associated Powers and specifically, the Three Heads of Mission (i.e. the Heads of the Diplomatic Missions of the Soviet Union, the United Kingdom, and the United States of America in Bucharest; see Art. 37). As for the time limit, while Article 37 limits the authority of the Heads of Mission to "a period not to exceed eighteen months," it must be obvious that the nature of protection afforded in Articles 3 and 5 were not meant for only a period of 18 months but as permanent protections, therefore the provision of "no time limit," expressed in Art. 38 is the relevant rule.

Thus, the main argument Rumania uses in defense of its minority policies is that it is their own internal matter, has never been valid, and the Paris Treaty of 1947 only re-enforced the previous situation. According to Lazarovich,

> (T)he danger of allotting millions of other nationalities to the newly created micro-states was foreseen at the [Trianon] Peace Conference for which reason signing of a "Treaty for the Protection of Minorities" was required when accepting the peace treaties. Some representatives of the newly created states refused to sign it. This revolt was led by Rumanian Bratinau.[139]

This should have been a sufficient warning for the major powers to think it over twice granting sovereignty over millions of national minorities to these politicians, and especially makes it obvious that Millerand's above quoted statement in his cover letter was not quite justified.

But the point is made perhaps most forcefully by President Wilson. In response to Bratinau, the President stated the obvious:

> Mr. Bratinau suggested that we could not, so to say, invade the sovereignty of Rumania, an ancient sovereignty, and make certain prescriptions with regard to the rights of minorities. But I beg him to observe that he is overlooking the fact that he is asking the sanction of the Allied and Associated Powers for great additions of territory which came to Rumania by the common victory of arms, and therefore we are entitled to say: "If we agree to these additions of territory we have the right to insist upon certain guarantees of peace."[140]

Under tremendous pressure, Czechoslovakia signed the Minority Treaty on September 10, 1919, and the treaty is known as the Treaty of Saint-Germain-an-Laye. Article 1 of the Treaty required that its Articles 2-8 be "recognized as fundamental laws and that no law, regulation or official action will conflict or interfere with these stipulations, nor shall any law, regulation or official action prevail over them." These Articles guarantee equal treatment to every citizen of the new Czechoslovakia "without distinction of birth, nationality, language, race or religion."[141]

---

139 Miroslav Lazarovich, p. 149.
140 Ibid., p. 150. Quoted from Col. E.M. House and Charles Seymour, editors, WHAT REALLY HAPPENED AT PARIS, The Story of the Peace Conference 1918-19 (New York: Scribner, 1921) p. 214.
141 For excerpts see Charles Wojatsek, FROM TRIANON TO THE FIRST VIENNA ARBITRAL AWARD (Montreal: Institute of Comparative Civilizations, 1980) and Edward Chászár DECISION IN VIENNA (Astor, FL: Danubian Press, 1978). pp. 187-90.

Seeing the pressure to protect minorities, in his eagerness to please the great powers, Benes went so far that he had presented a "Protocol on Behalf of Czechoslovakia to the Commission for the New States" at the peace conference, on May 20, 1919, which begins with the following declaration of intent:

> 1. The Czechoslovak Government intends to organize its state by taking as the bases of the rights of the nationalities the principles applied in the constitution of the Swiss Republic, that is to say, the Government designs to make of the Czechoslovak Republic a sort of Switzerland, while paying regard, of course, to the special conditions in Bohemia."[142]

While such a declaration sounds great, it is more than strange that it mentions only the Czechs and Germans, and fails to mention Hungarians and even Slovaks who will live in this New Switzerland. From this, and from their reluctance to sign the minority treaties, especially the Rumanians, the Associated Powers should have been suspicious enough not to entrust millions of ethnics to their domination without stronger and enforceable guarantees, unless some of the Associated Powers had some hidden interests or agenda..

It took less than a decade to make it obvious that Benes's promises were empty words and that the reluctance of the Rumanians to accept any restriction on their treatment of the minorities were the true indicators of things to come. Oszkar Jaszi, an expert on minority affairs, Minister of Minority Affairs in the Karolyi Government, and a supporter of regional autonomy and a federal solution to Hungary's minority problems, wrote a prophetic work in the 1920's while Professor of Political Science at Oberlin College in the United States.

Although many consider some of Jaszi's work anti-Hungarian, hurting, or at least not too favorable to the Hungarian cause, as it is shown even in the following quotes, in the last chapter of his work on the collapse of the Hapsburg Monarchy he summarizes the post World War I situation in Central Europe quite accurately. His overall evaluation of the monarchy, he believes also applies to the successor states, is expressed in the statement: "The collapse of the Hapsburg Empire is not surprising at all; what is surprising is that this mixture of people, based on the constituent nationalities mutual hatred and lack of trust in each other, lacking a common state ideal, could have survived for so long.[143]

---

142 Ibid., p. 191.
143 Oscar Jaszi, THE DISSOLUTION OF THE HABSBURG MONARCHY (Chicago: The University of Chicago Press, 1929; from Hungarian translation in SZAZADUNK ;

He finds the same lack of a common ideal and mutual hatred in the newly created or enlarged states and warns that

> although many the old irredentists (of the Monarchy) have disappeared, several new ones surfaced that endangers the situation of Europe, unless the new states use better methods than the old Hapsburg empire used....

> The dangers of the newly created states face are the same as the dangers of the now defunct monarchy: over-centralization and forced assimilation. The local, ethnic, cultural, and often religious differences are not able to be expressed in appropriate public forms, and the dominant nationalities apply the same political and cultural means that were used before the war by the Germans, Hungarians and Poles to maintain their hegemony over the peoples under their rule.... some of the victorious nations did not learn from the tragic fate of the Hapsburg Empire and continues the old procedures in the field of public education and government. Here and there the worse fever of nationalism poisons the public atmosphere....

> The dangers of nationalism and new irredentism are great.[144]

Many believe that Jaszi is wrong in comparing the oppression under the new regimes with the alleged oppression under the Hungarian rule. But even if it were true, there is still a lesson: "you fellows better watch out! You do not want the same thing that happened to Hungary to happen to you! Do you?" If Hungary was carved up for its minority policies, is there any good reason why Rumania, Slovakia or Serbia should not suffer the same fate?

Jaszi also faults the West: "Unfortunately, the Western public opinion does not understand this sufficiently. Many believe that a mere legal pacifism and peaceful, humanistic propaganda will be sufficient to mitigate the arrogance of the victors and the revenge of the victim."[145]

Jaszi's understanding and indictment of the West has been proven by the fact that his five-point recommendation has been completely dismissed[146] by those responsible for the creation of this situation and who have also accepted responsibility for eventual correction of the wrongs committed by

---

Tarsadalomtudomanyi Szemle (OUR CENTURY; a Social Science Review) 1929 November, p. 546.

144 Ibid., pp. 548.

145 Ibid., p. 549.

146 Although it will be seen later that the U.S. Committee responsible for plans for East Central Europe after World War II had studied his work we have just quoted from--but unfortunately, it did not help to produce a better solution.

the Treaty. Jaszi ends his work with five recommendations that would have solved the problem if carried out, and a warning:

1. Border revision in every case where homogeneous national minorities can be re-attached to their ethnic co-nationals;

2. organize the ethnic minorities into public institutions that would be able to provide their own cultural and educational facilities that would be limited only by the required loyalty to the state;

3. decentralization in the spirit of local self-government of the over-centralized and bureaucratic state machinery;

4. removal of restrictions on commerce and increase economic and cultural cooperation;

5. destruction of intellectual and civic education representing intolerant attitudes as indicated by several quotes above (in the original text).

And finally, according to Jaszi, "(I)f the League of Nations would be unable to carry through with these radical reforms, every legal and educational work would be useless. The harmful work of the defunct Monarchy will be carried on by other nations.[147]

It should be obvious by now that Jaszi's prophetic warning was realistic, and if it was heeded in time, even after the conclusion of the Second World War, there would be no minority problem endangering peace in Central Europe today, and no cold war in which western military presence is needed to stop and prevent returning to a shooting war in Bosnia. It is not stretching the point too far to argue that even World War II could have been avoided if the nationality issue creating the conflict between Germany and Poland over the Danzig Corridor, along with other stress points along ethnic and cultural fault lines would have been solved in time.

Thus, Jaszi's warning demonstrates that minority issues do have international consequences, and the international community has a right if not an obligation to intervene to eliminate ethnic conflict.

This much was even admitted by the United States during the Second World War. Toward the end, when the allied victory seemed inevitable, the United States created an Inter-Divisional Committee[148] on the Balkan-Danubian

---

147 Jaszi., p. 550.
148 See Ignac Romsics, editor WARTIME AMERICAN PLANS FOR A NEW HUNGARY, Documents from the US Department of State, 1942-44 (New York: Columbia University Press, 1992) p. 256. It should be interesting to note that the Committee in its considerations concerning Hungary's "Political Reconstruction: Nature of a Permanent Government," among other sources had relied on Jaszi's just quoted work, THE DISSOLUTION OF THE

Region. On May 1, 1944 the Committee prepared and discussed a secret background report on the "Treatment of Enemy States: Hungary."[149] The report states that

> (T)he United States is not committed to any specific boundaries in this area, although it has denounced territorial changes effected by force. It would look with favor upon territorial adjustments which would contribute to the development of more friendly relations among the peoples of Central and South Eastern Europe and which would contribute to the peace and stability of Europe as a whole. Hungary's claims for territorial adjustment, in so far as they are based on ethnic considerations, should receive sympathetic consideration, although care should be taken to avoid the appearance of rewarding Hungary for acts of aggression against its neighbors.[150]

The Committee fails to consider that the alleged "acts of aggression" were reactions to the unjust and illegal Trianon Peace Treaties. Thus, instead of correcting the acknowledged errors and injustices of Trianon, they further seem to condemn Hungary for reacting to the injustices. Still the overall tone of the recommendation seems fair and sincere.

The report then goes into detailed discussion of the border situation concerning each of Hungary's neighboring countries. A follow-up "Summary of Recommendations, Treatment of Enemy States: Hungary" was prepared on July 26, 1944. This Summary makes a distinction between the U.S. opposition to forceful boundary changes (and it incorrectly considers the Vienna Arbitrals forceful, or at least done by hostile forces, even if both parties accepted it at the time) and on this basis states, without ever mentioning justice, minority rights or national self-determination,[151] that

> the United States should in principle, favor the restoration of the 1937 Slovak-Hungarian frontier. In the interest of the peace and stability of the Danubian region, however, consideration should be given to the ethnic claims of Hungary in the area of Grosse Schuett and the Little Hungarian Plain. The United States should be

---

HABSBURG MONARCHY, along with Rustem Vambery, THE HUNGARIAN PROBLEM, C.A. Macartney, HUNGARY AND HER SUCCESSORS, and A. J. Taylor, THE HABSBURG MONARCHY.

149 Romsics, pp. 269-280; Document is identified as PWC-151, CAC 142b.

150 Ibid., p. 271.

151 It should be also noted that in earlier discussions the self-determination issue was discussed in the context of Point 2. Of the Atlantic Declaration that states: "(T)hey desire to see no territorial changes that do not accord with the freely expressed wishes of the peoples concerned" (Ibid., p. 92)

prepared to look with favor upon any settlement of these claims reached through free and direct negotiations between Czechoslovakia and Hungary or through other peaceful procedures.[152]

In a series of discussions during the summer and fall of 1944 the same point has been repeated. The September 1, 1944 "Progress Report" states: "In the interest of the peace and stability of the Danubian Region, consideration should be given to the ethnic claims of Hungary..."[153] An undated secret "Briefing Paper," submitted by Secretary of State Hull to the President on September 6, 1944, states that "we do not regard the pre-Munich boundaries as unchangeable and believe certain changes to be desirable in the interest of a stable settlement."[154]

Thus, while Hungary was treated as an enemy state, even the government of the United States had recognized that there is not only merit in the Hungarian claim to territorial changes, but international peace and stable settlement require to undertake those adjustments. Yet, nothing has happened in more than fifty years since the end of the war to restore these conditions of peace, except applying pressure on Hungary to renounce any claim to border adjustment, and even to renounce its right to protect ethnic Hungarians who have been suffering under modern Europe's most inhumane dual dictatorships: being ruled by Soviet style communism, and at the same time oppressed by chauvinistic fascists.

It is ironic that in 1944 the US believed that border changes are necessary foundations of international peace and stability, thereby implying on the one hand, Trianon was wrong and a threat to peace since it did not follow the proposed principle of national self-determination in drawing the borders, on the other hand did not see any violation of international law in re-drawing frontiers. Yet, today the same US insists on the sanctity of borders in the interest of international peace and stability.

---

152 Ibid., p 281.
153 Ibid., p. 284.
154 "Department of States Briefing Paper: American Policy toward Hungary." Ibid., p. 287.

IV.

THE SOLUTION

Solutions that have failed.

We saw a list of Jaszi's proposed reforms, and it is hard to argue with it, but before one would accept any proposed remedy, we should review them, and some of the arguments behind them, in some detail.

It is obvious that if the international community takes the development of human rights during the last half century seriously, something must be done to protect the millions of innocent indigenous minorities in the heart of Europe before another Bosnia-type situation breaks out. There are several suggestions, from the radical demand to undo the Treaty of Trianon completely and restore the thousand year old boundaries of both Austria and Hungary and to dismantle the then created and already disintegrated states, to the equally radical (in its implications and potential Bosnia-like consequences) do nothing approach and wait for the "spiritualization" of the borders.

Then there are the minimalists who demand only equal treatment for individuals, and oppose any demand for more than individual human rights. This position can be summarized as human rights only. These people are not only naive about the political process in general, and the situation in Central Europe in particular, but their position seems to have been carved in stone from the 1970's. Since then there has been a serious movement by international law experts and serious observes into the direction of autonomy in cases where the human rights only approach has failed to produce results! The human rights only approach is stuck on level 2 of the minority situation as categorized by Hannum, unwilling to realize when the situation requires level three or higher solution.[155]

A peaceful solution of any problem must be a political solution. The essence of the political process is deal-making. Each side has to start with a bargaining position so they can make a deal. But if one starts with the attitude that one wants only equal treatment for the minorities and does not

---

155 see notes 195-7 below. It should be noted that the problem is not with seeking a level two solution, The problem is if one or both sides become rigid and refuse to cooperate with other groups and create division and conflict between the minority group itself. Such a divided minority has much less chance of gaining recognition of their rights, even level two, than if they are flexible and cooperate to get as much as possible.

get it, there is no room for bargaining. In fact, I am convinced that this attitude caused more harm than good, because it gave the other parties freedom to reject any human rights demand. One certainly would not want people with this attitude as diplomats or one's union negotiators! But if one starts with a more radical demand, like the demand that Hungary wants the old borders back (even if one does not expect it back), there is room for bargaining and in the process one might end up with equal treatment. The danger with this strategy is that instead of sitting down to serious negotiation, the majority would use it (as it in fact did) as an example of how radical and irrational the minority's demands are. So one should not make such a demand in advance, only at the start of the negotiation, and even then, only privately, least one box oneself in and be treated by one's own people as a traitor if one is forced to compromise.

Even if the human rights only approach would succeed in creating laws and constitutional provisions, given the depth of anti-Hungarian feelings, often amounting to paranoia among the majority population of the countries around Hungary, in all likelihood, it would not be enforced. One must doubt, based on past experience, that this approach would work. In fact, this might even feed their paranoia, suggesting that Hungary really wants to throw them out of their "sacred homeland" and the anti-minority pogroms could dramatically increase and cause more hardship for the minorities. Normal bargaining strategy can work only among rational people.

A sort of compromise between the two positions was proposed by Zsolt Zétényi, a former member of the Hungarian Parliament and chairman of its Judiciary Committee. He proposed to the Antall government the so called golden ring solution. If one would offer you a golden ring for a couple dollars, according to Zétényi, you would be suspicious and would not buy it for the fear that it might be fake, stolen, or somehow dangerous. But if one would offer you one just below the fair market value, you would be less suspicious and might be talked into making the deal.

Similarly, according to Zétényi, unconditional statements by the Antall and the subsequent Horn governments that we do not want border corrections, might sound even to a normal person, let alone a paranoid one, as a dangerous or insincere ploy, because a rational person would not just give away the right to a territory, unless there is a trick somewhere, or unless they have some ulterior motive. The Basic Treaty signed by Hungary with Rumania (and later with the Ukraine and with Slovakia), at the urging of some western countries, including the United States, has such a ring to it: Hungary offered, under obvious western pressure, border guarantees without the Hungarian minority effectively receiving anything in return. So, according to Zétényi's theory, to our paranoid neighbors Hungary must be insincere and dangerous. The result: the situation of Hungarians in Rumania (at least before the elections following the signing of the treaty), and in Slovakia as well as in the Sub-Carpathian region (which was originally given to Czechoslovakia by the Trianon Treaty, became autonomous region within Czechoslovakia on October 9, 1938, was transferred from Czechoslovakia to the Soviet Union after the war, and finally to the Ukraine after the collapse of the USSR, changing sovereignty three times in seventy years) became worse than it was before the treaties were signed.

As for the Serbs, who had suffered through a bloody conflict in Bosnia and one might think that as the result they have become less chauvinistic, in Serbia's parliamentary elections in September (1997) the Milosevic led pro-Communist Socialist Party lost its majority, but instead of the more democratic parties picking up those seats, according to the AP story[156], the "anti-Western Radical Party, led by extreme nationalist Vojislav Seselj, made major gains and took 82 (out of 250) seats" behind the 110 seats which went to the Socialist Party. Seselj, "the Radical Party leader known for virulent 'Serbia for Serbs only' rhetoric" also came in second behind Milosevic's hand-picked successor in the presidential race, forcing a run-off election. The pro-democracy forces of Vuk Draskovic, the Renewal Movement, received 46 seats, less than 20%, and Draskovic came in third for the presidency with 21% of the votes. So the choice of 80% of Serbia's population voted for Milosevic's chauvinistic pro-Communist Socialist Party and the ultra-nationalist Radical Party. The "Serbia for Serbs only" slogan is a code phrase for continued ethnic cleansing, that will undoubtedly turn again against the Hungarians living in Serbia, once the conflicts in Bosnia and Kosovo will be settled.

As has been indicated already, informal international pressure does not work either. In 1989 the UN's Human Rights Commission passed a Swedish draft, co-sponsored by six other nations, to send a special envoy to investigate the human rights situation in Rumania. The Resolution was passed 21 to 7, with 10 abstentions. Yet, no subsequent UN action was taken to remedy the Rumanian human rights violations. Neither did the withholding of Most Favored Nation (MFN) status or denial of the invitation to join NATO temper the radical minority policies of Rumania and Slovakia. Against all rational expectation, even the threat of prosecution as war criminals failed to prevent some Serbs to commit atrocities and war crimes against innocent population in Bosnia in an effort of ethnic cleansing.

Change of regimes will not help the minorities either. The NEW YORK TIMES documented in two articles with Bucharest by-lines in March 1990[157]

---

156 Albany TIMES UNION, Sep. 26, 1997.
157 Celestine Bohlen, "The Romanian Revolution is Over, It's Back to Old Hatreds in Transylvania" NEW YORK TIMES, March 21, 1990, reporting from Cluj, a major Hungarian

how the situation remained the same after the ouster of the dreaded dictator, Ceausescu, because anti-Hungarian attitude is so deeply rooted in the population of Rumania, especially among the masses of Rumanians who have been transported from other regions of Rumania to Transylvania, mainly under Ceausescu, to change the ethnic balance of Hungarian populated cities and regions.

In Slovakia we have witnessed an even greater change when Czechoslovakia broke up and Slovakia separated from the Czechs to set up their own republic. For the Hungarian minority if anything, the change made their situation worse. At least the Czechs were a moderating force, but now, in spite of the bi-lateral basic agreement that was signed recently, the situation is getting worse by the day, as we shall see. The source of the problem is deeper and more complex.

In Serbia, the 1997 elections do not bode well for minority relations either: Serbian nationalism is just as alive, and just as dangerous, as it was when Crown Prince Ferdinand was assassinated, or when greater Yugoslavia was created by the Peace Treaty of Trianon. Unfortunately, as current efforts to defuse the Bosnian conflict indicates, Serb nationalism is still disregarded by the Western Leaders, including President Clinton. Had they been more aware of the importance of political culture, the whole Bosnian situation could have been prevented, and the world would be much more peaceful today.

Some people hope that an eventual spiritualization of the borders will solve the problem. The idea is that eventually border crossing will be just as easy and just as common as border crossing between say Germany and France, once bitter enemies. But this expectation is unrealistic, since the majority nationalities in the Carpathian basin will never allow such a spiritualization, because in their paranoia. The masses have been brainwashed by their intellectuals, educators, orthodox clergymen, newspapers and politicians to expect that spiritualization of their border would lead to eventual surrender of their sovereignty and would restore Hungarian rule. But even if the spriritualization of the border was possible, without a radical change in the majority attitude it would not solve the discrimination and persecution of minorities. It would only make it easier for the Hungarians to abandon their old home and escape to Hungary, which they clearly do not want to do and should not be forced to do.

---

populated city called Kolozsvár in Hungarian, often considered the Capital of Transylvania, now under the domination of radical Rumanians, and John Kifner "Fighting Abates in Transylvania but Not the Anger" NEW YORK TIMES, March 27, 1990, reporting from Tirgu Mures (Marosvásárhely), another Hungarian populated city.

In an unpublished essay[158] Istvan Sebestyen-Teleki documents that even in western countries where the borders are "spiritualized," like in the Jura Canton in Switzerland, in Quebec, a Canadian province, among the Basques in Spain, and in Ireland, the minority problem has not disappeared. Therefore he argues that the Hungarian government's "border spiritualization" strategy is a facade to hide their inability and unwillingness to tackle the minority problem involving several millions of Hungarians, whom Prime Minister Antall claimed in his constituency when he announced that he considers himself the prime minister of 15 million Hungarians, which includes all Hungarians, living not only in the Carpathian Basin but throughout the West, from Austria to Australia.

The most radical proposal is to reverse the mistakes of Trianon by returning to the old boundaries, which would attach masses of radical Serbs, Romanians, Slovaks and even Ukrainians to Hungary. While one could make a good legal and perhaps even a moral argument that if Trianon was unjust, as it was, the way to remedy it and do justice is to return to the old, thousand year old boundaries. In a perfect world this would be the perfect solution: in a greater Hungary, independent of the Austrian rule, and under the doctrine of the Holy Crown all the peoples could be considered as equal partners with equal rights. Ideally, in a greater Hungary the Crown doctrine would protect all minorities and the minority problem would be solved by one swoop unless demagogues would continue to stir up anti-Hungarian sentiment among the minorities.

On the other hand, the successor states, including Rumania, which was called by President Wilson an "ancient sovereignty,"[159] gained full independence only at the Congress of Berlin in 1878, are not old enough to have developed their own western style common symbols like the Holy Crown of Hungary, as a protector of all citizens. Instead of the western style Crown concept they show raw chauvinism and a hatred of all "foreigners" residing in "their" land, fully deserving the "Balkan" characterization. In addition, they also lack the centuries old experience and patience in nation building. They want to develop their narrow, exclusive nation state overnight, by forced assimilation and violence.

Therefore, given the circumstances today, returning to the pre-Trianon boundaries would only repeat the mistakes of Trianon in reverse. It would disregard not so much the ethnic and cultural diversity of the people inhabiting the region, but the intensity of the current anti-foreign paranoia of

---

158   Sebestyen-Teleki Istvan, "Mi. Magunk! Az onrendelkezes trendjei a nyugati democraciakban" (Only Ourselves; Trends of self-determination in Western Democracies) Zurich, Switzerland, 1993.
159 See #139 above.

a large portion of the population and would create a multi-ethnic Hungarian state with major fault lines criss-crossing the country.

Even Ernö Raffay, a renowned Hungarian historian and author, admits that the old slogan, "Everything back" ("Mindent vissza!") would not work any more due to the many changes during the past seventy five years. The main, and most tragic change has been the whipping up of emotions, mainly hatred, against everything that is foreign, by some irresponsible politicians, acting as protectors of the right of the minorities like the Rumanians, Serbs and the Slovaks who were allegedly oppressed by Hungarians before Trianon. Another major problem would be the changed composition of the population which has taken place as the result of officially encouraged, and often even forced population transfer: sending Hungarians into the Regat, and giving incentives to Rumanians of the Regat to move to Transylvania, to dilute the population ratio favoring Rumanians.

It should be noted, however, that most of those demanding back the traditional territory of Hungary are fighting for a principle that is still being observed by countries like Great Britain. England went to war for the Falkland Islands a few years ago to protect a basically useless territory belonging to the Crown. According to Myers,[160] the western concept of the Crown includes territorial integrity. Thus, the argument goes, the Crown is compromised by the loss of its territory. Hungary has a similar Crown doctrine that includes provisions for the territorial integrity of "the countries of the Holy Crown."[161].

The willingness to accept less that the historic territories of Hungary does not mean to give up the old boundaries and the territories of the Hungarian Crown. All that is suggested is that there is room for compromise. If the world's policy makers decided, and the Hungarian people were given a chance to vote for boundaries that follow the traditional ethnic enclaves, returning as many Hungarians as possible, and, in a true sense of national self-determination, keeping as many Rumanians, Serbs and Slovaks as possible in their current state united with their own brethren, along the lines of the two Vienna Arbitrals during World War II. Hungarians probably would accept it in a referendum as final Hungarian boundary.

In the first Vienna Decision on October 26, 1938, Czechoslovakia, instead of permitting a popular referendum on the border issue, accepted the arbitration of Italy and Germany of the disputed territory that returned the Hungarian

---

160 see # 74 above.
161 Kocsis, p. 142.

populated regions of Czechoslovakia to Hungary.[162] The Second Vienna Award was at the expense of Rumania, ordered by Hitler, who acted at the request of King Carol of Rumania,[163] without either side having any say about the actual details. In fact, "thoughtful Hungarians," including Prime Minister Teleki, "were alarmed" by Hitler's decision to consider the request at all. As for Czechoslovakia and Rumania, the two Vienna Decisions could be interpreted that by requesting German arbitration, they had voluntarily relinquished the Hungarian populated areas to Hungary. It should be mentioned, that the Vienna Arbitrals were nullified without giving the changes a chance to prove if they would have advanced peace in the region. Thus, it is unforgivable for the Allieds to return after the war in the Paris treaties those territories to the pre-war owners.

Such a border adjustment sounds good, but while after the war it was not only possible but it had been already accomplished, today it would require extraordinary pressure from the international community to arrange it without violence. Also, the mixing of ethnic groups over the centuries have created such a crazy quilt that it is impossible to draw fair boundaries without forced exchange of tens or perhaps hundreds of thousands of people, causing untold human misery and suffering that politicians and statesmen in the past were all too willing to overlook. Those people have suffered enough already, and any correction of past mistakes should be as painless as possible.

Another solution would be secession, creating independent, sovereign entities without joining any other neighboring states. This solution also has its proponents, arguing that given the existence of an intolerant majority, exercising dictatorship and forced assimilation, this is the only effective solution. There is little chance, however, given the existing international legal structure, that is could be accomplished without violence. At least this is the lesson one can learn from the events in Bosnia and Kosovo.

Istvan Sebestyen-Teleki introduces his unpublished essay with a quote from Arend Lijphart: "(T)he violence during processes of separatism is not the result of the separatist efforts but of the attempts to stop it."[164] One may not like the violence and the logic, and the statement oversimplifies the process, but it is obvious that "it takes two to tango." All too often illegal acts of terror are responses by the powerless to legitimized acts of terror by a

---

162 Cf. Montgomery, pp. 120-1; also Charles Wojatsek, FROM TRIANON TO THE FIRST VIENNA ARBITRAL AWARD (Montreal: Institute of Comparative Civilizations, 1980) and Edward Cháazár DECISION IN VIENNA (Astor, FL: Danubian Press, 1978).
163 Following the August 28, 1940 Axis Conference, between the leaders of Germany and Italy, they decided to return somewhat less than half of Transylvania to Hungary, pretty much following the ethnic lines, as they did in the First Vienna Arbital. Cf. Montgomery, pp. 139-40.
164 Sebestyen-Teleki, p. 1.

violent, oppressive majority. This is not to justify terrorism but to explain that to blame violence on one party only is often unjust. When condemning terror, both the official and the unofficial kinds must be condemned equally.

The genesis of ethnic violence is complex. The process (and the conflict) usually starts with creating a heterogeneous situation where an intolerant majority, be it ethnic, religious, cultural or economic, is determined to assimilate a minority and denies certain rights to them. The minority usually first responds with demands for legal and constitutional protection of their rights. When this fails, the next step is demand for legal autonomy. The American planners for the post war world have often included autonomy in their discussions, considering it as an alternative solution to changing borders.[165] Although the proposal has been criticized as not fully satisfactory, the principle was looked upon with favor--it if would only work. It was felt that "autonomy could probably be maintained only by outside pressure."[166] But it might still be better than the current situation, with no effective outside pressure.

When the demand, including appeals to the international community, for some form of minority autonomy is met with more oppression instead of granting equal rights and equal treatment, the demand escalates into separatism and ultimately into violence when peaceful political means fail and oppression continues. Violence, just like war, is used when other means fail. Therefore to judge the situation and assign blame one must ask: was the demand just or unjust. In the modern world asking for the right to fair and equal treatment and to resist forced assimilation is recognized as a fundamental human right. Therefore it is the oppressor who must be blamed and forced, by peaceful international intervention, if necessary, to grant, at a minimum, equal treatment and cultural rights.

The Concept of Self-Determination in International Law:

Recent Developments

The evolution of the concept of human rights and of self-determination is illustrated by Hurst Hannum, who summarizes in a recent issue of FOREIGN AFFAIRS the current state of the concept of and solutions for national self-determination and makes some very sensible suggestions. According to

---

165 See Romsics, pp. 131 ff., 149-160, etc.
166 Ibid., p. 167.

Hannum "self-determination should be concerned with people, not territory."[167]

Claims of secession had always been permitted by international law under the rule of Grotius, but there has been some important development in recent literature by international law experts on self-determination, autonomy and secession.

For lawful and peaceful transfer of teritory between sovereign states Grotius requires two referendums, one in the mother country and one in the territory to be detached. There is only one situation where Grotius dispenses with the required referendums to secede:

> In case of extreme or in other ways inevitable necessity a part may, by itself transfer to other hands the sovereignty over itself without the consent of all the people, because it reserved that power, we may believe, when civil society was formed.[168]

In other words, Grotius believed in the Social Contract theory, and assumed that people may hand over part of their freedom necessary for a civil society, but did not, and could not, give others the power to oppress them as a group, in an civil society!

As for the territorial argument for secession, Grotius makes three points:

1. territory can be lost irretrievably by abandoning it[169] or

2. by conquest, but here he notes that "sovereignty won by force can be overthrown by force."[170]

3. Finally, "a party who had fought a lawful war should receive what he fought for and be recompensed for his losses and expenses, but should not be awarded anything on the score of punishment, for that creates more hatred."[171]

That is, territory of one country can be won in war, and it can be re-conquered in a new war, but cannot be awarded to another by treaty, as a form of punishment, as it had been done at Trianon after W. W. I.

There have been two areas of recent progress in the thinking of international law experts. On the one hand, two distinct lines of approach and argument were developed concerning secession in recent literature: the human rights

---

167 Hurst Hannum, "The Specter of Secession," FOREIGN AFFAIRS (March-April, 1998) p.15.
168 Grotius, 3, XX, 5.
169 Ibid., 2, IV. 4.
170 Ibid., 2, IV. 14.
171 Ibid., 3, XX., 11.

approach and the territorial approach. While the territorial approach deals only with secession, followers of the human rights approach developed a sharper distinction between the two forms of self-determination, autonomy and secession.

Let us consider the human rights argument first. According to the human rights approach the foundation of the claimed right of self-determination, whether autonomy or secession, is massive violations of human rights of certain minorities. When the violation escalates to a certain level, the minority, in the name of national self-determination, may demand autonomy, or even secede from their current state. The creation of the United States of America is an example when the perceived violation of the colonists rights reached an intolerable level, they had issued a revolutionary Declaration of Independence.

Over the centuries the power of the authoritarian state was the dominant force, until in the American Declaration of Independence self-determination was claimed as a God-given right and successfully achieved in the American War of Independence, which only the Americans call the American Revolution. The conflict had started as a struggle for "the rights of the Englishman," and the Declaration included both the collective rights of the people, and the inalienable, God given rights of each individual. President Woodrow Wilson, a political scientist, also based his concept of national self-determination on both the metaphysical concept of individual freedom[172] but in his statements he spoke of "self-government," or that "every people has a right to choose the sovereignty under which they shall live."[173] Thus, the emphasis came to be on "people." President Wilson, in an address to Congress also stated that "no right anywhere exists to hand people about from sovereignty to sovereignty as if they were property."[174] Thus, since Trianon handed millions of people from one sovereignty to another, with the stroke of a few pens, it is an excellent example of a specific territorial grievance, violating the rules and standards laid down by both Grotius and Wilson. But we shall discuss it later.

Other problems further complicate the issue of the right to self-determination.

---

172 Michla Pomerance, "The United States and Self-Determination: Perspectives on the Wilsonian conception," AMERICAN JOURNAL OF INTERNATIONAL LAW, vol. 70, 1976, pp. 1-2.
173 Idem.
174 64 Cong. Rec. 1741-42 (1917; address by President Wilson, US Senate) quoted in Kolodner, p.155 Eric Kolodner, "The Future of the Right to Self-Determination" in CONNECTICUT JOURNAL OF INTERNATIONAL LAW, vol. 10:155.

Although "people" are made up of individuals, and the American Revolution was fought by the colonists as a people, this shift in emphasis from individual to group rights had tremendously weakened the concept since while individuals can claim God-given, inviolable rights versus the oppressive state, the group had no such metaphysical or religious claim. Although the individual dignity is still recognized and serves, or at least is paid lip service to, as the basis of human rights, it has much less weight in the international order against the sovereign state. It is only the last ten or so years that collective rights began to be recognized by experts and some international organizations. Few would admit, of course, that behind the noble concept of sovereign state in practice there are fallible human politicians and administrators who are expected to carry out even ill-advised demands of the majority. They often do not deserve the kind of prestige and authority accorded to sovereign countries and governments.

The case for self-determination also had been weakened by the fact that once group rights started to be discussed, experts, politicians and statesmen cannot agree even on the definition of the "self" i.e. the "people" or "minority" part of the concept, as several recent authors indicate.[175] First, most experts would agree that recent immigrants and refugees should not be considered people that are entitled with the right of self-determination. Also, the term people goes beyond a collection of individuals, and the group is not as a clear-cut metaphysical entity as the individual.

Several definitions of minority group have been suggested. First, the term minority primarily implies a numeric relationship: any group of less than 50% can be considered as minority. In recent socio-political literature, however, the term often refers to a state of being oppressed, regardless of the numeric relationship. Thus, the large Hutu tribe in Burundi, oppressed by the smaller Tutsi tribe who happen to be in power, or the large Black population of South Africa that had been oppressed under apartheid by the small White minority, have often been considered minorities.[176]

Although there have been efforts to create a definition of the term minority, like the 1984 effort of the UN Sub-commission on Prevention of Discrimination and Protection of Minorities, it proved so controversial that the UN Human Rights Committee, the Sub-Commission's parent organization, in 1986 "postponed further consideration of the definition and

---

175 E.g. Pomerance, Ibid., pp. 21-23. Pomerance asks an interesting question; "In what way did the Masaryk-Benes committee represent the people of Czechoslovakia?" (p. 21). Of course, it would have been difficult because at the time they had claimed to speak for the Czechoslovak people, when there wasn't even a Czechoslovakia, and as we know now, the Slovak people wanted something different than the Czech or the Hungarian peoples.

176 Jan Robertson, SOCIOLOGY (New York: Worth Publishers, 1977), p. 286-7.

proceeded to elaborate the substantive articles of the draft declaration"[177] without clarifying who the subjects of the declaration are. The controversial definition stated that minority is

> a group of citizens of a state, constituting a numerical minority and in a non-dominant position in that state, endowed with ethnic, religious, or linguistic characteristics which differ from those of the majority of the population, having a sense of solidarity with each other, motivated, if only implicitly, by a collective will to survive and whose aim is to achieve equality with the majority in fact and in law.[178]

Hannum also quotes a definition from Sigler

> which specifically addresses the question of minority rights: a minority is deemed to be "any group category (sic) of people who can be identified by a sizable segment of the population as objects for prejudice or discrimination, or who, for reasons of deprivation, require the positive assistance of the state. A persistent nondominant position of the group in political, social and cultural matters is the common feature of the minority".[179]

Ian Robertson, summarizing the position of four authors lists the following criteria to establish minority status: (1) "members of a minority group suffer various disadvantages at the hands of another group"; (2) "A minority is identified by group characteristics that are socially visible" and important; (3) "A minority is a self-conscious group with a strong sense of 'oneness'"; (4) "People usually do not become members of a minority group voluntarily; they are born into it"; (5) By choice or necessity, members of a minority group generally marry within the group."[180]

In general, any of the above definitions would be satisfactory, but because of political reasons, is seems desirable to leave the term undefined so that minority rights can be easier violated and sanctions evaded by the sovereign governments that would have to define these terms. Therefore to this day there does not seem to be an authoritative definition and much of the protective language is just so much propaganda, without any real tooth..

There would be less of a problem with definitions if instead of the minority group the individual would be considered the depository of the right. But

---

177 Hannum, pp. 60-61.
178 Hannum, p. 60-61. Quoted from UN Document E?CN.4/Sub.2/1985/31 & Cor. 1 (`1985) at 30.
179 J.A Sigler, MINORITY RIGHTS, A Comparative Analysis (Westport, CT: Greenwood Press, 1983) quoted in Hannum, p. 61.
180 Robertson, p. 286.

this would be impractical in the political community, since individual self-determination could lead to anarchy. Even groups having the right to self-determination seems to scare many of our statesmen: according to Reuters News Service: "The big powers fear granting Kosovo independence would set off a disastrous chain reaction of demands for the same prize from disgruntled minorities nearby in the Balkans, especially Albanians in Macedonia."[181]

But is this fear justified? Ved P. Nanda mentions that there are some observers who seem to "fear that secessionist claims by various ethnic-nationalist groups will acerbate the existing fragile international order ... [and] call for placing severe limits on the scope of self-determination so as to regulate, control, and minimize its evil consequences," [182] and names Etzioni as one such writer. But instead of debating Etzioni, Nanda evades the answer dismissing Etzioni's ideas that "it may be argued that this hypothesis remains untested and lacks validity." So he changes the focus of the paper to "study the mechanism under which all these claims can be peacefully pursued and resolved."

Eric Kolodner takes a more effective approach: he argues that Etzioni's argument takes a very limited view of the concept of self-determination.[183] Kolodner distinguishes between internal and external self-determination, arguing that Etzioni's fear might apply to certain cases of external self-determination, but not to internal self-determination. External self-determination means complete independence, while internal self-determination means various forms and degrees of autonomy.[184]

Unfortunately, some authors who oppose self-determination, equate self-determination with secession, i.e. external self-determination, Kolodner's distinction notwithstanding. Disregarding autonomy as a form of (internal) self-determination creates problems, because external self-determination is much more difficult to achieve both administratively and politically. This allows many politicians to pay lip service to human rights and self-determination without effectively pursuing it, using yet another argument: they defend the sanctity of frontiers under the guise of defending peace and stability.

---

181 Reuters Report by Jovan Kovacic June 25, 1998
182 Hurst Hannum AUTONOMY, SOVEREIGNTY, AND SELF-DETERMINATION (Philadelphia: University of Pennsylvania Press, 1990) p 445; see also Amitai Etzioni, "The Evils of Self-Determination" (FOREIGN POLICY, Winter 1992-3, at 21,35.)
183 Eric Kolodner, "The Future of the Right to Self-Determination" in Connecticut Journal of International Law, vol. 10:153.
184 Ibid., p. 159-166.

In June 1998 President Clinton on his China trip conducted a dialogue with the Chinese leaders. He stood up for civil rights, and rejected the Chinese argument that violating civil rights and killing demonstrators and political opponents is justified in the interest of stability.

The Administration's unfortunate stand in the Serbian atrocities in Bosnia and Kosovo seems to echo the Chinese stand, rather than the President's voiced protest. The position of the Western world in the face of the mass murder of civilians in Kosovo by their own government seems to be that in the interest of stability we do not deny their right to do it, it is only the actual practice and the mass killing that we oppose!

In addition to the proliferation and the stability arguments, a third argument used at times to oppose self-determination and secession is that "it typically represents a remedy for past injustices."[185] Brilmayer, an apostle of the territorial approach, believes that only those minorities have the right to self-determination who have a territorial claim, and rejects all secessionist demands when there is only a "case of extreme or in other ways inevitable necessity," to quote Grotius, without territorial grievance. But should self-determination and secession demands be dismissed in human rights violations cases because of the lack of territorial grievance?[186]

This does not mean, that all experts are against secession. An "Editorial" in the American Journal of International Law[187] claims that certain CSCE and UN declarations concerning self-determination "are non-binding instruments, nevertheless, they purport to, and probably do reflect an 'opinio juris.' In the human rights fields a strong showing of opinio juris may overcome a weak demonstration of state practice to establish a customary rule." On this basis the editorial concludes that "from about 1970 on, there could be a right of 'peoples'--still not well defined--to secede from an established state that does not have a fully representative form of government ...."[188]

Kolodner's view also seems to be much more fair and realistic than those who fear that self-determination would cause instability:

---

185 Lea Brilmayer "Secession and Self-Determination: A Territorial Interpretation," YALE JOURNAL OF INTERNATIONAL LAW (Vol. 16, 1991), 177-202, p. 179.

186 It is on this basis that one can make a distinction between *irredentists* claims to territories a people once had occupied and ruled, and claims to secession because of current oppression. Not that the claims to formerly occupied territories are wrong, but at the present time they could not serve, in themselves, as the basis for the right to secession. They should be recognized, however, as one factor in determining the claim for secession. But even such claims have various weight. The Slovak claim for a greater Moravia sometime in the first millennia or the Rumanian claim to Transylvania as part of a Dacian empire are much less certain and proven than Hungary's claim of establishing sovereignty over the Carpathian basin eleven hundred years ago, in 895 AD

187 88:304, 1994

188 Ibid., p. 306.

(E)fforts to limit self-determination movements of today often foment the conflicts of tomorrow, [while] recognizing legitimate claims for self-determination might ensure world stability.

Rather than abandon this important right, the international community must readjust its conception of self-determination [as a threat to stability] to address the changing needs of the post-Cold War world....[189]

Therefore Kolodner, recognizing the complexities involved with secession, without excluding secession as an ultimate remedy, makes the following recommendation: (T)he international community, therefore, should attempt to resolve conflicts under principles of internal self-determination before supporting a people's right to external self-determination with its potentially disruptive consequences.[190] The problem with this recommendation is that he current international legal standard considers only actual but not potential consequences, so there is no legal provision to intervene. The standards must be adjusted first.

There are several similar statements in the various international law texts and journals. For example, according to Ved P. Nanda

... the international community should pay greater attention to internal aspects of self-determination [i.e. autonomy]... Whether self-determination takes the form of the creation of a state, or a confederation of states, ethnic power-sharing arrangements must be explored. ... In some situation cultural or linguistic autonomy should be considered adequate expression of self-determination. Promotion and protection of minority rights and means for redressing grievances regarding violation of human rights needs to be given greater consideration. The United Nations and regional organizations must play an active role.[191]

Nanda also gives a detailed explanation as to when would secession be appropriate remedy:

I reiterate that claims to secession must only be considered as a last resort when it is clear that ethnic groups cannot live together and it is equally clear that the group claiming secession makes a

---

189 Kolodner, p. 166.
190 Ibid., p. 162.
191 Ved P. Nanda, "Revisiting Self-Determination as an International Law Concept: A Major Challenge of the Post-Cold war Era" in ILSA JOURNAL OF INTERNATIONAL & COMPARATIVE LAW (1997, 3:443).

compelling case because of its perceived deprivation of human rights within the larger community. The claim that it is deprived of its right to participate in all value processes, power, wealth, and resources, respect and rectitude, enlightenment and skill, and affection and well-being should establish its right to secede. [192]

Hurst Hannum is one of the foremost authorities on self-determination. His basic principle is simple: when we talk about national self-determination, "our concern is with peoples rather than territories," so the effective equality of rights is the main concern. Therefore, "there is no reason to regard existing administrative or 'republic' boundaries within states as sacrosanct." [193]

It is not likely that Hurst Hannum was thinking of Trianon, but the following statement about majority attitudes could apply perfectly to the post-Trianon situation:

> Put simply, redressing historical grievances or responding to contemporary dissatisfactions cannot justify the dispossession of members of ethnic minorities who now live in the territory in question and whose ancestors may have lived there for generations. No group can claim exclusive control over a territory forever. It is morally impossible to decide which individuals should be forced to choose between emigrating or remaining under "alien" domination and which group should be rewarded with ethnically based political power in the form of a new state. [194]

This is exactly what had happened at Trianon: rewarding Hungary's minorities not only with the territory they had occupied, but by the opportunity to oppress millions of innocent ethnic Hungarians based partly on claims of past oppression by Hungary, partly on the dubious historic claim of prior occupation of areas that became sovereign Hungarian territory over eleven hundred years ago.

So, while Hannum seems to reject the purely territorial claim, he is also against oppression of minorities and would permit border changes under certain circumstances.

Hannum, in summarizing his almost five hundred page long study, puts the question of autonomy in a fair perspective; first, the minority issue is handled easiest on a demand by demand basis:

192Ibid., p. 452.
193 Hannum "The Specter..., p. 17.
194 Idem.

(M)any of the issues noted above [language, education, access to employment, ...] can best be resolved on an ad hoc basis, particularly where they involve recognized rights, such as language use or a free press. Even where it is difficult to identify a direct "right," e.g. to adequate representation on a police force, reasonably articulated demands may be satisfied by a responsive government that wishes to avoid exacerbating ethnic or regional tension. If conflicts have not become overly violent, various forms of administrative decentralization may offer solutions to complaints of geographical or economic marginalization.[195]

When these individual demands are not satisfied and

... most or all of these demands are at issue, however, the question then becomes one of autonomy or less-then-sovereign self-determination. It should first be underscored that a political demand for autonomy --even without assertion of an underlying right-- should be given serious consideration by any responsible government. State sovereignty does not imply retention of any particular political or economic system, and responsiveness to legitimate minority grievances is the hallmark of a government that respects the human rights of its entire population, as well as the principle of self-determination...

When demands for autonomy and self-determination are asserted as a matter of right, they are often founded on the illegitimacy of the government itself.[196]

When the situation escalates rapidly to this point and the legitimacy of the state is questioned, the state often treats the minority demand as rebellion, and uses weapons, including weapons of mass destruction, like it has been done in the case of Kosovo, to protect not only the territorial integrity of the state, but also the dominance of the Serbs over the minority Albanians. At this point, however, as refugees will cross the state's boundaries, foreign nationals might be harmed or at least inconvenienced by the refugee problem, neighboring countries might be tempted to intervene, and other unforeseen consequences may follow, so that the international community, i.e. the UN, might declare it a danger to regional stability and peace and decide to intervene. This can be done, of course, against the will of the majority and its

---

195 Hannum AUTONOMY..., p. 469. It should be noted that these points are not ratified international law but only the summary interpretation of current trends, the so called *opinio juris*, yet, they are important because they help to shape future law, and it also carries some weight with international community and thus tells both minorities and governments what is expected of them, and what can they expect from the international community.
196 . Hannum, "The Specter...", p. 17.

government. It should also be noted concerning secession that according to Grotius, in general two referendums are required in case of a peaceful secession, but in "extreme cases" the approval of the majority is not necessary.[197]

Unfortunately, however, there is no international forum that would judge the validity of the insurrectionist minority's claim of extreme necessity and denial of the legitimacy of the government or the state, or at least the legitimacy of the rule over the minority. The Hague International Court can judge individuals accused of genocide, but cannot convict governments who have ordered the genocide! But even if there was such an international body, to enforce secession might involve a great deal of diplomatic pressure, or even military intervention. Therefore it is imperative that the UN amend international law to force governments that are unable and/or unwilling to protect minority rights to consider and negotiate adequate autonomy for the minority and to provide sanctions. Such sanctions could include denial of the right of the government to govern the minority populated areas, i.e. to grant independence to the minority inhabited territories.[198]

Agreeing that boundaries may be changed for grave reason, Hannum essentially echoes Grotius in not allowing legal secession except when it is peaceful and voluntary, or in cases of extreme necessity. He repeats his already quoted position:

> In general, policy makers should continue to reject the notion that there is a legal right of secession.... On the other hand, central governments should no longer be allowed to hide behind the facade of national unity without explaining how minority rights are genuinely being protected.

> There are two instances in which secession should be supported by the international community. The first occurs when massive, discriminatory human rights violations, approaching the scale of genocide, are being perpetrated. If there is no likelihood of a change in the attitude of the central government, or if the majority population supports the repression, secession might be the only effective remedy by the besieged group....

> A second possible exception might find a right of secession if reasonable demands for local self-government or minority rights have been arbitrarily rejected by a central government--even without

---

197 See #133 above.
198 In Appendix I we shall present a Proposal for United Nations Resolution on Minority Issues

accompanying large scale violence. This exception, however, would come into play only when minimal demands are rejected...[199]

Although the basic principle when separation can be justified has been laid down in 1921 by the League of Nations, secession has never been a popular topic in international circles, and there has been only one case, according to Hannum, when the legitimacy of a government was denied on human rights grounds: the Somoza government of Nicaragua by the OAS. But even this was in response to general inhumane conduct, not to denial of minority demands.[200] Hannum also quotes a 1921 League report prepared concerning the Aaland Island dispute:

> The separation of a minority from the State of which it forms a part and its incorporation in another State can only be considered as an altogether exceptional solution, a last resort when the State lacks either the will or the power to enact and apply just and effective guarantees.[201]

This report was issued shortly after the dismemberment of Hungary at Trianon, and the creation of some new states that lacked both the will and the power to respect the minority rights guarantees that were required of them as the price of receiving the territories of Hungary. Thus, just one year after Trianon, the League of Nations clearly declared a standard and conditions for dismembering a country that were not met in the case of Hungary, making Trianon clearly a violation of international law. It should be noted that this was not a new legal standard but only a re-formulation of Grotius' rule about "extreme necessity. It also should be noted, that granting autonomy to the Aaland Islands prevented its breaking off from Finland, therefore the formula had worked.

It is not surprising in light of this principle, and the recent emphasis it has received from international law experts that a bipartisan demand has been issued to invoke this almost forgotten provision of the international law and sanction the Milosevic regime. A recent statement by "Helsinki Commission Leaders Call Milosevic Responsible for "Barbaric" Kosovo Massacre" and declare the Milosevic rule over Kosovo "illegitimate". On 21 Jan 1999 CSCE Commission Co-Chairman Rep. Christopher H. Smith (R-NJ) and Ranking Minority Rep. Steny H. Hoyer (D-MD) released the following statement on the situation in Kosovo:

---

199 Ibid., pp. 16-7.
200 Hannum, AUTONOMY, p. 470.
201 REPORT PRESENTED TO THE COUNCIL OF THE LEAGUE BY THE COMMISSION OF REPPORTEURS   (1921), note 87, at 28; emphasis added. Quoted in Hannum, AUTONOMY..., p. 472.

The massacre committed in the Kosovo village of Racak is nothing short of barbaric. The mutilation and killing of 45 villagers, including three women and at least one child, constitutes a crime against humanity, and units which participated in this gruesome act must be identified, as well as the chain of command. Ultimately, Slobodan Milosevic must himself be held accountable for the crimes committed in Kosovo and in Bosnia. The U.S. Congress has already stated its belief that Milosevic should be tried as a war criminal, and the recurrence of events like this massacre should remove all doubt as to the urgency of such a step.

The arrogant response of the Yugoslav and Serbian authorities to the incident-denying access to the site by the International Tribunal prosecutor and declaring the head of the OSCE Mission as persona non grata-cannot be tolerated. In fact, Serbia may well have lost Kosovo once and for all. No state has the right to exercise its authority in this manner, and we consider Serbian authority in Kosovo to be illegitimate. The international community should begin to treat it as such....[202]

The key sentence bears repeating: SERBIA MAY WELL HAVE LOST KOSOVO ONCE AND FOR ALL. NO STATE HAS THE RIGHT TO EXERCISE ITS AUTHORITY IN THIS MANNER, AND WE CONSIDER SERBIAN AUTHORITY IN KOSOVO TO BE ILLEGITIMATE. THE INTERNATIONAL COMMUNITY SHOULD BEGIN TO TREAT IT AS SUCH....

In other words, the two leaders of US Congress' Commission dealing with the Helsinki Process has declared that Kosovo situation has reached a point of such extreme necessity that the Belgrade government had lost its right to govern Kosovo, and this right has returned to the people of Kosovo. Therefore the international community should recognize the right of Kosovo to external self-determination, i.e., to independence. The extreme necessity provision does not require the approval of the majority group's or its government's approval.

This is an historic declaration by these two courageous Members of Congress. It is unfortunate that the media failed to publicize it and the administration has failed to act on it.

Although secession often is the only remedy like in the case of Kosovo, it should also be recognized that, like with armaments, the best armies are those that do not have to be used. The most important function of secession

---

202 CSCE NEWS RELEASE, Commission on Security and Cooperation in Europe, 1-21-'99

in international law should be to avoid the need to invoke it. Secession should be made quite difficult but not impossible so that recalcitrant majorities and small time dictators could not play the game of wasting time because time is on their side and they have nothing to loose, like Milosevic has been doing for years. If a sports team that is ahead has nothing to lose by stalling, it will stall. This is why they have clocks in football and basketball. There should be a shot clock in minority affairs also. If the government does not grant minority rights, of refuses to consider autonomy within a given time period, not more than one or two years after the demand has been made, it should risk loosing the territory occupied by the minorities. This should be done in a peaceful but firm manner, and military forces should be used on, again, in "cases of extreme necessity."

The most important goal of recognizing the right to secession should be not to change boundaries but to pressure states in the direction of democracy. Or, reversing the logic, according to modern international law theory, granting autonomy must be viewed not as the cause leading to secession, but as a solution preventing the need for secession.

So far we have discussed the right to autonomy and secession in terms of being oppressed. There is another approach to the problem: looking at the positive side of the issue.

According to Thomas M. Franck, there is an "emerging right to democratic governance" which may create an obligation for the international community to promote and protect democracy.[203]

Franck takes the idea from Immanuel Kant's essay, PERPETUAL PEACE,

> where Kant concluded that democracy in governance, while not a sufficient condition, is a necessary one to the prevention of breaches of the peace. Today it is becoming increasingly part of an emerging systemic consensus that people who feel themselves the legistlators of their governments through their participation as equals in a free, fair and regular democratic consultation are much less likely to take up arms either against other states or against their own state. In that as yet imperfect but emerging consensus self-determination is being re-defined and given a new life.[204]

Thus, we are back, in a full circle, at the idea of the social contract and the right of everybody to be treated according to the purposes for which the state had been created.

---

203 see T.M. Franck, "The Emerging Right to Democratic Governance," 86 AM.J.I. L. 46, 1992, pp. 57-77.
204 Franck, "Postmodern...", p. 21.

Eric Kolodner carries the idea a step further:

> Democratic governance can constitute a realistic compromise between an aggrieved people's demand for independent state and a government's unfettered oppression of that people. The international community should now apply the principles and structures... (and) ...(E)stablished principles regarding internal self-determination [that is, autonomy], ... [and should] attempt to usher in an era of global democracy and codify the emerging right to democratic governance.[205]

Going back to Hannum's three stages, in democratic governance the minority demands are discussed and taken care of at the first level, on a case by case basis, and would never lead to stage two and there will be no minority issue. The world will never learn that a certain minority had certain demands because it was resolved quietly, in a democratic manner, as a domestic issue and the minority can determine its fate and preserve its cultural self-identity without any noise or involvement by the international community. This is how democracy should work. In a truly democratic state everybody is equal, both individual and group rights are recognized, and even if there are minorities, there is no minority problem.

This concept has also received a tremendous boost at the Copenhagen Conference which was held from 5 to 29 June 1990, in accordance with the provisions relating to the Conference on the Human Dimension of the CSCE contained in the Concluding Document of the Vienna Follow-up Meeting of the CSCE. The Document has separate sections on democratic rights and on the rights of minorities. If this document had been passed by the UN and became binding international law, there would be no need for talking about secession, because people would live under "Democratic Governance" that Franck has proposed, in pluralistic, rainbow societies that the American approach tries to promote. But if democratic governance cannot be achieved in an ethnically or culturally pluralistic country, the only alternative for the minority to achieve this right is through secession

Dr. Mihaly Samu, a Professor at the Budapest Law Division of ELTE, Eotvos Lorant Tudomany Egyetem (Eotvos Lorant University) in Budapest makes an interesting point that has potentially great consequences for the entire autonomy debate in his study of minority issues:

> The earlier, liberal and socialist approaches assumed that the national minority problems must be solved with institutionalized cultural autonomy. The organizing principles of modern pluralist democracy

---

205 Kolodner, p. 166.

have passed this approach, and the ethnic minorities wide ranging participation in public life, and the development of their power base is emphasized (it does not narrow down to cultural autonomy...) In other words, in a pluralist democracy the emphasis is on developing the minority's self-organization in the general public arena, their self-governing institutions and "cultural autonomy" is realized in this framework.[206]

Professor Samu seems to suggest that conventional i.e. legalized cultural autonomy is too narrow concept to offer satisfactory solution for the minority problems. If it is true, minority autonomy should not be the final solution. Autonomy should be an interim or transitional solution leading either to achieving a pluralistic democracy where the minority members can achieve their equal and full participation not only in forming their own institutions, using their language, and maintain their customs and traditions without any hindrance, but move freely anywhere in the country, participate in the political life and the power structure of their country without any hindrance, discrimination or danger or to secession as the only other way to realize fulfillment of these rights in a separate country, under a separate sovereign.

Thus, autonomy can be viewed as a provisional solution leading to either democracy orto secession, depending on how the dominant majorities view it. Autonomy could be compared to a hot house where one grows and nurtures delicate plants until they are strong enough to be planted outside where they can stand on their own, withstand the vicissitudes of weather, just like any other plant. Or, to use another analogy, autonomy is like protective tariff designed to protect a new industry from the much stronger foreign competition until the industry is able to compete with the foreign imports in the free market.

Therefore the proper function of autonomy is eventual integration of the minority into the general society and to make it a "constituent nation," like the three ethnic group are treated as constituent groups in Switzerland. To realize this, of course, a sympathetic majority population willing to share power and to move in the direction of pluralistic democracy is required. If autonomy leads to acceptance of the minority as a constituent nation, or co-national group and to democratic governance, it becomes the strongest insurance against secession. On the other hand, the "One country one nation" slogan and the accompanying closed mind in a closed society a priory dooms any effort to achieve such integration. It prevents acceptance of the minority

---

206 Mihaly Samu, "Collective Rights and State-Constituent Qualities of the Minorities" in A MAGYAR KISEBBSEGI TORVENY (The Hungarian Minority Law), (Budapest: Puski, 1995), p. 41

as equal and forces autonomy to become a permanent institution, or to move in the direction of secession.

One of the major obstacle in the way of a peaceful resolution is that, as historian Erno Raffay[207] points out, that the successor states in the case of Hungary after they were created at Trianon, or enlarged, as Rumania, on the one hand had accepted an unproven and false mysticism as to their origin, like the Dako-Roam theory, and on the other have failed to develop an effective working national ideology, a nation forming principle that would incorporate the people of any nationality that came to them with the land. The only idea that holds them together is the hatred of not only Hungarians living in the same country (and also, by extension, in Hungary), but hatred of other-ness. Anything that is different, be it German, Jew, Roma, Muslim, Albanian, anything not Serb in Serbia, nor Rumanian in Rumania, and not Slovak in Slovakia. This pre-occupation prevents their economic development, handicaps them in the international relations by a rigid, oppressive human rights record, and makes democratic development extremely unlikely.

Raffay also points out that this hatred of all "otherness" is not only the common denominator of these countries, but it does not prevent them from forming an anti-Hungarian alliance with each other. They hate otherness only within their countries, but work with their neighbors against the common enemy. This hatred is coupled with a guilty conscience that makes some of them, the more aggressive and noisy ones, act like the thief who has stolen merchandise and is afraid that he will have to give it back. Until this element rules in these countries, there is little hope of either any successful accommodation or movement toward democratic governance. Such movement may come only either after an election, replacing the "old guard" by new, more democratically oriented leadership, or freeing their conscience by removing the cause of their psychosis, the "other" peoples from their midst, that is, allowing secession. If one follows Raffay's logic, on the long run, even those countries would be better off with a border revision. But it would take vision and a visionary, like President DeGaulle, who jettisoned Algeria to save France.

Because of the grave problems that secession involves, Lea Brilmayer proposes another criteria that would seem to fit another kind of minority demand.

The territorial argument, promoted by Brilmayer, addresses only the problem of secession. She seems to by-pass the less problematic issue of autonomy as

---

207 Raffay: "A Határkérdés Fölvetése", MAGYAR REZERVÁTUM (Raising the Border Issue," HUNGARIAN RESERVATUM) 1996. VI / Germany

a solution to current human rights abuses. Therefore one is free to conclude that in the absence of territorial grievance, and when no other solution seems to work, Brilmayer also would agree with Hannum and others in allowing autonomy as a proper solution as it would not involve territorial changes.

According to the territorial argument, secession, which is "territorial remedy for alien domination, must be justified by territorial arguments."[208] Supporters of his argument take the territorial integrity principle and apply it retroactively to former borders, therefore secession is restoring the status quo ante. According to this view the right to secession from the current state and return to independence or attachment to the original state from which it was detached must be based on "historical grievance" that came about as the result "of some unjustifiable historic event."[209] According to Brilmayer, "(S)ecessionist claims involve, first and foremost, disputed claims to territory. Ethnicity primarily identifies the people making the disputed territorial claim."[210] Here Brilmayer seems to contradict Hannum who interprets the concept of self-determination as "people's problem," while Brilmayer sees it as "territorial issue," i.e. a matter of which group is the lawful owner of a territory and who should exercise sovereign rights over it.

Since Brilmayer sees the problem in terms of "historic grievance," she emphasizes that it must be kept alive over generations.

> Ethnic identification keeps the historic grievance alive by passing it from one generation to the next. Old wrongs will not be forgotten so long as an existing group continues to experience the historical wrongs as its own, as part of its heritage. The usual modes of transmission of this shared sense of wrong are precisely the ones that typically define ethnic communities. Wrongs are passed down by recitation within the family, through educational and religious institutions and by way of shared culture, such as stories, myths, nationalistic songs, and the like. If at any one point an individual should ask, "why should I care about the past?" the answer follows that "These are your people who were wronged. You are one of us, and we all share this wrong and ought to struggle to make it right." ... Ethnicity answers the question, "why do people still care about something that had occurred such a long time ago?" It constitutes a barrier to assimilation and is a guarantee that historical grievances will continue to be relevant in the present day It gives the current

---

208 Brilmayer, p. 189.
209 Idem.
210 Ibid, p. 179.

claimants their standing in protest, not in a technical, but in an emotional sense.[211]

Human nature being what it is, the more the oppressive majority attempts to force assimilation, the more the minority, including its youth, will resent it. Thus discrimination and oppression creates exactly the opposite of the intended result. It forces the minority to adopt a siege mentality and to swear that they will never give in to the oppressor, and to cling to the memory of the territorial wrong they or their ancestors have suffered, and the grievance will continue until liberation comes. Thus, the territorial claim and the current human rights abuses re-enforce each other and make the case for secession even stronger.

Some secessionists movements, like the Jura separatists in the Swiss Jura canton, as we shall see, today base their claim exclusively on the territorial argument, without alleging any human rights violation by the Swiss. It should be noted, however, that Brilmayer does not seem to support such demands since she explains, that at least in non-colonial situations, secessionists "need additional arguments to support secessionist claims, such as the existence of widespread human rights abuses."[212]

Another interesting aspect of the territorial argument concerns forced population exchanges in a territory claimed by the minority.

> A third factor, also controversial, is the extent to which the territory has now been settled by members of the dominant group. It is a common strategy to attempt to solidify conquest by moving loyal citizens of the victorious state into the new territory.... I mentioned this strategy earlier as causing problems with plebiscites under the standard [i.e. human rights] account, but it also generates problems under a territorial analysis. From the point of view of separatists, such new settlement ought to have no significance whatsoever. They did not ask for these new inhabitants. Had the secessionists' territory not been improperly annexed, the newcomers could have been excluded entirely. Taking the newcomers' presence into account compounds the original injury. Yet, as a practical matter, the new settlers tend to legitimize the territorial status quo...[213]

Brilmayer makes an interesting point, and it should be important for the UN to prohibit or disregard such a population transfer in considering the minority's right to autonomy and secession. If allowed, this would be

---

211 Ibid., p. 192.
212 Hannum, The Specter..., p. 197.
213 Ibid., p. 200.

violating the legal principle that a perpetrator should not benefit from an illegal act.

While the two lines of argument seem to exclude each other, on closer examination the two in fact complement each other, or at least the territorial argument strengthens demand based on minority and human rights violations. According to Brilmayer, "the two supposedly competing principles of people and territory actually work in tandem."[214]

If a people constituting a minority in a state have never had independence or never had been part of another group, it is harder for them to justify and gain support for secession and independence and should be satisfied with autonomy. According to Brilmayer again, "the remedy for maltreatment [in these cases] is better treatment by the current government, not permission to set up a new state in the same location."[215]

But when a minority population can claim territorial grievance and is suffering widespread and serious human rights violations by a stubborn or incompetent government, after everything else failed, including attempts to gain autonomy, their right to secession should be recognized without forcing the minority to use violent means to create an international issue and a threat to peace. By the way, Brilmayer is also opposed to violence "such as bombing airplanes," as counterproductive way to gain publicity since "it might be undesirable to reward such activities."[216]

There is one more recent development in political theory that should be considered in discussing self-determination. Although political culture and the "political fault line"[217] is not directly related to self-determination and secession, in judging secessionist claims like Kosovo, it certainly should be considered. If the two populations in a state are separated by a cultural chasm as well as geography, the secessionist claims should be taken much more seriously since compromise and reconciliation would seem to be much more difficult and perhaps even impossible.

The Flip Side of De-Colonization

and the Lessons to be Learned for the UN

In order to protect both the current boundaries and human rights, in the 1960's the UN decided to end the colonial rule in the Third World (although

---

214 Ibid., p. 178.
215 Ibid., p. 188.
216 Ibid., p. 200.
217 See #50 above.

the term was not used). In their zeal, the authors of the UN Resolution to end colonial rule did not pay attention to the ethnic diversity existing in the soon-to-be-freed colonies.

The result was that on the one hand it was UN action that had accelerated the process of granting the right of self-determination to colonial peoples, and on the other hand the same action, quite ironically, had nailed the safety valve shut on ethnic minorities not only in the recently de-colonized countries but in other, older multi-ethnic states.

In the 1960's the Declaration on the Granting of Independence to Colonial Countries and Peoples stated that "all peoples have the right to self-determination; by virtue of that right they freely determine their political status and freely pursue their economic, social and cultural development." Yet, the same Declaration contained a clause prohibiting the disruption of the national unity and territorial integrity of the state. This could mean that not only secession but even the demand for territorial autonomy is prohibited.

It seems at first that this Declaration benefited the colonial peoples while not granting any rights to non-colonial peoples. But following de-colonization in most liberated countries ethnic conflicts flared up as the result of prohibition against border changes. When the colonial rulers had established their colonies, they had drawn the boundaries at their convenience, without any consideration of old ethnic lines dividing the colonial peoples. So, after the colonial powers that maintained peace and stability in their colonies were withdrawn, the conflict between the different ethnic groups that were forced into one state flared up, and today, according to a recent article in FOREIGN AFFAIRS there are about 10 million internal refugees in Africa, in Europe and Asia some 5 million each, and over 2 million in Latin America.[218] I have no statistics on the number of people killed in these conflicts, but I am sure it is also substantial.

Thus, the UN Declaration subjects the concept of national self-determination to two conflicting standards: on the one hand, seems to promise effective exercise of minority rights, on the other hand, it fails to support autonomy ("internal self-determination"), and explicitly prohibits secession ("external self-determination") or changing borders, the only effective means of guaranteeing self-determination against a hostile majority. This means that the UN Declaration on the long run created more conflict, suffering and violence than existed under the colonial regime and there are some peoples who were better off, or at least were more protected and lived more peacefully, during foreign colonial rule!

---

218 Roberta Cohen and Francis M. Deng, "Exodus within Borders," FOREIGN AFFAIRS (July-August 1998) p. 12.

The new UN rule went against centuries of tradition and international law,[219] the 1921 League ruling in the case of the Aaland Islands,[220] and current expert opinion.[221] All three allow not only autonomy but even secession in cases of extreme necessity. Thus, there are two possible solutions: either make the UN to amend its rule and explicitly allow secession in cases of extreme necessity, or interpret the current rule in light of the old rules and make the rule apply only to arbitrary secession efforts, but not prohibiting the traditional exception: extreme necessity. Congressmen Smith and Hoyer seems to interpret it this way, in not calling for a new UN Resolution.

Whichever approach one takes, the current situation is inadequate, since there is no authoritative international organ or court that could decide if extreme necessity is present or not. In the views of the two Congressmen such necessity has been present for quite some time, but in spite of their experience and learned opinion, it is still a private opinion that can be disregarded by not only the President of the United States but by Milosevic and his army too. So, ultimately the issue must be brought back to the UN to restore the extreme necessity rule with certain standards, and to set up an enforcement machinery.

The opinion of the International Court of Justice in the FRONTIER DISPUTE CASE, shows a great deal of self-deception in denying the right to change frontiers:

> (A)t first sight this principle [of territorial integrity/uti possidetis]conflicts outright with another one, the right of peoples to self-determination. In fact, however, the maintenance of the territorial status quo in Africa is often seen as the wisest course... The essential requirement of stability in order to survive, to develop and gradually consolidate their independence in all fields, has induced African States judiciously to consent to the respecting of colonial frontiers, and take into account the interpretation of the principle of self-determination of peoples.[222]

While the opinion is literally correct, the judges must have said it with tongue in cheek that the African States, whose governments were trying to protect the status quo which had elevated them into power, have "judiciously"

---

219 Cf. Grotius, # 134 above.
220 Cf. # 199 above.
221 Cf. authorities quoted in previous chapter.
222 Case concerning the *Frontier Dispute* (Burkina Faso vs. Republic of Mali), Judgment ICJ Rep. 1986, p. 554 at pp. 566-567; quoted in Thomas M. Franck "Postmodern Tribalism and the Right to Secede," in Brolman, Lefeber & Ziek, editors, PEOPLES AND MINORITIES IN INTERNATIONAL LAW [Dordrecht/Boston/London: Martinus Nijhoff Publ., 1993] p. 318) p. 5.

consented to the idea of territorial integrity, since the peoples, who were supposed to have the right of self-determination, were not asked, and have not consented! The court opinion shifts the subject of self-determination in its statement from peoples to states and governments, denying the rights of the peoples, in order to protect a hostile status quo that benefits governments. The opinion, and the position that it defends, has created a tremendous bed of Procrustes that all peoples must fit onto. This unfortunate situation could arise only because of the above outlined confusion about the definition of people. "People" could be the people of an entire state, the government of the state, and people of a minority. The UN Declaration should have been called "Granting of Independence to Colonial Countries and Enslaving Peoples" Declaration. Even if the politicians at the UN confused the situation, there is no excuse for the International Court of Justice which is supposed to be above politics for not clarifying the situation in the FRONTIER DISPUTE CASES. Without being familiar with the case, one might suspect that those arguing the right of the peoples to secede, were not familiar with Grotius and the 1921 League ruling.

As the above quoted statistics show, with 5 million internal refugees Europe is suffering from the same rigid requirement that prevents re-ordering the national borders enslaving minority peoples to reflect ethnic divisions that would end, or substantially reduce, local conflicts and would guarantee the right of self-determination. Therefore there is a growing movement to re-visit de-colonization and correct the two mistakes made in the first one: extend the same right to other continents, and remove the sanctity of borders concept from international law.

In this evolution of the concept of self-determination, according to Nanda, "as a marked departure from the past, there is no longer an international consensus today that the recognition of self-determination claims is to be limited to colonial and non-self-governing situations."[223] According to van Praag, general secretary of the Unrepresented Nations and Peoples Organization (UNPO),

> (A)ltough one form of decolonization has now almost been completed, the world is starting to experience what the Dutch Foreign Ministry spokesperson, J. T. Hoekema, described [in 1991] as the „second generation of decolonization." The international community must become aware of the inadequacy of the present legal order and its structures and must respond to this new situation. Change is needed both in the implementation of the right of self-determination and in the political and legal structures dealing with

---

223 Nanda, p. 444.

such questions. The vacuum in the law resulting from the refusal to recognize and apply, in a non-discriminatory manner, has been filled by the default notion that „might is right'. In this respect, law has become a mere tool to enforce actual power relations.[224]

Thus, the rigid International Court of Justice, UN and US positions, as applied in Bosnia and Kosovo, may have created the impression that they are unconditionally opposed to any frontier adjustment, and support the "might makes right" approach, making the principle of the inviolability of borders a "mere tool to enforce the actual power relations." We hope that this is not the case, but chauvinist oppressors in Serbia, Rumania or Slovakia, or anywhere else, for that matter, might think that it is, and use it as a license to oppress!

Therefore it is imperative to rectify the situation and correct the impression departed by the idea of the sanctity of the borders. To oppose autonomy in 1999 or 2000 is anachronism After at least a decade of effort, the turning point came as the result of the Yugoslavian wars of independence. Now the question is not if, but when and how? Peacefully or through bloody uprisings, under UN authority or against it? One must realize, as we are going into the next chapter that the name United Nations is misleading. The UN consists of representatives of governments, not peoples. The peoples have to exert tremendous pressure to move a body which, to paraphrase President Lincoln's Gettysburg address, is "of the government, by the governments, and for the governments." The governments are the constituency of the United Nations.

The next question should be asked, if the UN would have the will, does it have the authority to interfere in domestic problems and order autonomy or border adjustments? Or, in a broader context, does the "International Community" has the right to fix what is had broken? The answer should be not only a YES to this question, but a YES even to the statement suggesting that it in fact it has an OBLIGATION to fix what it had broken.

Self-Determination and UN Authority

The sovereignty of the state has been shrinking in the last century, giving rise to ever increasing role for international law. This trend at times have lead to considerable controversy, like the ex post facto application of laws at the Nuremberg and Tokyo trials as Justice William O. Douglas has suggested in

---

224 M.C. van Walt van Praag, "The Position of UNPO in the International Legal Order" in Brölman, p. 318.

his essay on the modern trends in the evolution of international law.[225] But ordinarily, law making precedes law enforcement even in international relations.

Thus when the UN had intervened in the Korean conflict, it interfered on the basis of its Charter that authorizes the United Nations to "take effective collective measures for the prevention and removal of threats to the peace, and for the suppression of acts of aggression or other breaches of the peace." As the consequence,

> the United Nations action in Korea was the first time outlawry of aggression was implemented by direct, military action by the community of nations.... This was noble, principled, responsible action that gave power and force to a newly forged tenet of international law[226]

by restricting the sovereignty of a member nation to peaceful, non-aggressive behavior towards her neighbors. Application of UN principles to non-member nations, if there were any, who did not voluntarily sign the UN Charter would be more controversial.

The international efforts to curb aggression has taken a new turn when the international community and the UN has decided to take preventive measures by prohibiting Iraq from producing chemical and biological warfare materials, and insisting on on-site inspection by an international group of experts. Such a step would have been considered highly offensive under the traditional concept of national sovereignty.

UN action might also enforce the right to self-determination by restricting the sovereignty of a member nation to peaceful, non-aggressive behavior towards her neighbors. Forcing subjects of a country to flee outside the country, if that is the case, should be deemed to disturb peace, so the UN could intervene in the domestic affairs of the offending nations. Perhaps less obvious international disturbance would be impeding the ability of minority members to interact freely and effectively with the outside world. Application of UN principles to non-member nations who did not volunteer to sign the UN Charter would be more controversial. But claims of breaches of peace would and should be only a pretense. Ideally, the UN members should resolve to enforce the right of self-determination based on the primacy of human rights over international boundaries or claims of sovereignty, whether it disturbs peace or not. Recognition among the membership of the international community is a privilege, with certain advantages, so, the state

---

225 William O. Douglas, THE RULE OF LAW IN WORLD AFFAIRS (Santa Barbara: Center for the Study of Democratic Institutions, 1961) p. 12.
226 See Ibid., p. 11.

owes certain things to the community of states, like respecting individual and minority rights.

Now, after years of aggressive Serbian behavior, the patience of the civilized world must have eroded to the point where in the interest of human rights and world peace, the United Nations will have to take effective action in the Balkan and develop a policy of not only promoting but demanding or if necessary, unilaterally granting and announcing autonomy rights, or in extreme cases, outright independence to oppressed minorities.

If the international community continues to stall, violence and various acts of terror may follow to call attention to the plight of an oppressed minority, as it has happened in many cases, even in the civilized Western Europe.[227]

Speaking of violence and its causes we should listen to Hannum again. Although Hannum rejects violence to achieve even a legitimate goal, he makes two points concerning violence, the second one being the lack of adequate and effective mechanism to settle minority issues.

> If neither international law nor politics offers a mechanism through which minorities trapped within a new ethnic state may rejoin their former state, or, at least, create an autonomous region within their new home, rejection of the border by force may be seen as the only alternative...
>
> ... the present lack of both normative and moral clarity may be responsible for at least some of the increased separatist violence of the post-Cold War years. Emboldened by the international community's acceptance of the dissolution of Yugoslavia... dissatisfied groups in all parts of the world are more likely to obtain meaningful outside support than low-keyed appeals for minority rights or autonomy.
>
> A more clearly formulated set of international norms, such as those suggested here, may discourage at least some questionable claims and the ready resort to violence that often accompanies them.... recognizing and accommodating conflicting rights is the only way in which the world can respond to diametrically opposed demands in a politically and morally disciplined manner.[228]

The oppressed minorities might learn from the Kosovo affair the wrong yet appropriate lesson: under the current international system sometimes one needs to cause violence, commit terror acts, otherwise nobody will listen.

---

227 E.g. the French minority of Jura in Switzerland.
228 Hannum, The Specter... ., pp. 17-8.

Once the conflict escalates and becomes violent, it will be viewed as terror by the majority, as justifiable freedom fight by the minority.

The international community could also learn from the example of Kosovo. They stood by silently when Serbia took away autonomy from Kosovo and from the Hungarian populated Voivodina, and the West refused to support autonomy demands while the conflict was on level two. When the conflict escalated to level three and the people of Kosovo denied the legitimacy of the Serbian government over Kosovo, about two years too late, President Clinton and the international community came up with a belated autonomy solution. However it is too little too late for the people of Kosovo, and too late for Milosevic, who have put everything on the Kosovo card. Giving autonomy now would mean that the people of Kosovo would be ruled with the assistance of their butchers, Milosevic could not keep what he had promised to the Serbs of Kosovo and would lose his hero status, and he just cannot afford that! The necessary good will to live within the same state under the same sovereign, and the necessary trust to expect that the terms of autonomy will be carried out once the attention of the world turns to other problems is just not there anymore, if it ever was. The international community backed both Kosovo and Milosevic into their respective corners so that peaceful solution other than full independence seems impossible at the time of this writing.

The obvious lesson is that if the minorities' reasonable demands are met and their rights are protected, or if autonomy is granted in time, it might make talk of separation obsolete. Granting autonomy in time would prevent the conflict from escalating to the stage when terror acts would seem the only hope to achieve equal rights. The reason is simple: although many would view various forms of autonomy as an imperfect solution, if the majority of the minority group is de facto satisfied with autonomy, they will neither support a costly and dangerous terrorist movement to achieve separation, nor would the majority want to face an uncertain future once secession is completed.!

This point is made quite eloquently by a team of experts of the European based Federal Union of Ethnic Groups, FUEN, who had issued an updated discussion document, PROTECTION OF ETHNIC MINORITIES, in 1994, including a draft for an additional Protocol to the ECHR, including a draft on Fundamental Rights of Persons belonging to Ethnic Groups in Europe, and a model proposal with an accompanying report on Autonomy Rights of Ethnic Groups in Europe. The aim of the documents is to urge "a comprehensive,

European-standardized protection of ethnic groups," that would complement the already existing rights of individuals within ethnic groups.[229]

Acceptance of these recommendations by the Council of Europe would bring group rights into the European system of protection, and would make the rights adopted "enforceable at the Council of Europe" level. But for global application and enforcement UN involvement is required.

The introductory report of the Autonomy Rights document analyzes "the strained relationship between the fundamental principle of sovereignty and territorial integrity of the State under international law and the fundamental principle of the rights of the national minorities." The principle of territorial integrity currently excludes the right of secession. Therefore the FUEN experts propose that

> (I)f an explicit right of secession is not given or--whatever the reason may be--is not desired or not desirable, a national minority has a right to a minimum of internal autonomy and to an optimum of autonomy, i.e. as much autonomy as possible, without endangering the national unity; the minimum of autonomy is in any case that extent which is necessary for the preservation of the existence and the identity of national minorities. In particular, cultural rights are a part of this minimum...

> ... Autonomy granted in time is the best precautionary measure against attempts of secession. (If) it is granted too late, i.e. at a moment when a powerful movement of secession has developed, it is possible that when it is granted it is no more credible, and then it is no longer suitable to stop the striving for secession."

The last paragraph bears repeating: "Autonomy granted in time is the best precautionary measure against attempts of secession," and one may add, of violence. Unfortunately, it is too late in Bosnia and Kosovo to prevent violence, but not too late in Voivodina, Slovakia or Transylvania, and in many other parts of the world!

The OSCE position on Self-Determination

The recent issue of OSCE Newsletter reports on the 7th Annual Session of the OSCE Parliamentary Assembly (PA) meeting held in Copenhagen in July, 1998. According to the report,

---

229 PROTECTION OF ETHNIC MINORITIES IN EUROPE, Updated FUEN-draft Convention; Bozen/Bolzano, 1994

A supplementary resolution on Kosovo was also approved. It appealed to all parties in the Kosovo conflict to return to the principles of non-violence and denounced the policies of the Government of the Federal Republic of Yugoslavia (FRY) for its military aggression against the Albanian population of Kosovo. While supporting the demands for strong autonomy for Kosovo, the Assembly reaffirmed the position that the principles of the international law with regard to the inviolability of frontiers and the territorial integrity of States, as enshrined in the Helsinki Final Act, should be respected in the case of the FRY and other States in the region.

It seems the PA Meeting was referring to the following provisions of the Helsinki Final Act (FA):

III. Inviolability of frontiers

The participating States regard as inviolable all one another's frontiers as well as the frontiers of all States in Europe and therefore they will refrain now and in the future from assaulting these frontiers.

Accordingly, they will also refrain from any demand for, or act of, seizure and usurpation of part or all of the territory of any participating State.

This provision is followed by one about the

IV. Territorial integrity of States

The participating States will respect the territorial integrity of each of the participating States.

Accordingly, they will refrain from any action inconsistent with the purposes and principles of the Charter of the United Nations against the territorial integrity, political independence or the unity of any participating State, and in particular from any such action constituting a threat or use of force.

The participating States will likewise refrain from making each other's territory the object of military occupation or other direct or indirect measures of force in contravention of international law, or the object of acquisition by means of such measures or the threat of them. No such occupation or acquisition will be recognized as legal.

And

VI. Non-intervention in internal affairs

The participating States will refrain from any intervention, direct or indirect, individual or collective, in the internal or external affairs falling within the domestic jurisdiction of another participating State, regardless of their mutual relations.

They will accordingly refrain from any form of armed intervention or threat of such intervention against another participating State.

But the FA also provides:

VII. Respect for human rights and fundamental freedoms, including the freedom of thought, conscience, religion or belief

The participating States will respect human rights and fundamental freedoms, including the freedom of thought, conscience, religion or belief, for all without distinction as to race, sex, language or religion.

They will promote and encourage the effective exercise of civil, political, economic, social, cultural and other rights and freedoms all of which derive from the inherent dignity of the human person and are essential for his free and full development.

Within this framework the participating States will recognize and respect the freedom of the individual to profess and practice, alone or in community with others, religion or belief acting in accordance with the dictates of his own conscience.

The participating States on whose territory national minorities exist will respect the right of persons belonging to such minorities to equality before the law, will afford them the full opportunity for the actual enjoyment of human rights and fundamental freedoms and will, in this manner, protect their legitimate interests in this sphere.

The participating States recognize the universal significance of human rights and fundamental freedoms, respect for which is an essential factor for the peace, justice and well-being necessary to ensure the development of friendly relations and co-operation among themselves as among all States.

They will constantly respect these rights and freedoms in their mutual relations and will endeavor jointly and separately, including in co-operation with the United Nations, to promote universal and effective respect for them.

They confirm the right of the individual to know and act upon his rights and duties in this field.

In the field of human rights and fundamental freedoms, the participating States will act in conformity with the purposes and principles of the Charter of the United Nations and with the Universal Declaration of Human Rights. They will also fulfill their obligations as set forth in the international declarations and agreements in this field, including inter alias the International Covenants on Human Rights, by which they may be bound.

VIII. Equal rights and self-determination of peoples

The participating States will respect the equal rights of peoples and their right to self-determination, acting at all times in conformity with the purposes and principles of the Charter of the United Nations and with the relevant norms of international law, including those relating to territorial integrity of States.

By virtue of the principle of equal rights and self-determination of peoples, all peoples always have the right, in full freedom, to determine, when and as they wish, their internal and external political status, without external interference, and to pursue as they wish their political, economic, social and cultural development.

The participating States reaffirm the universal significance of respect for and effective exercise of equal rights and self-determination of peoples for the development of friendly relations among themselves as among all States; they also recall the importance of the elimination of any form of violation of this principle.

It should be obvious from the above excerpts from the Final Act (FA) that there are serious conflicts in the principles of the FA and the structure of OSCE is built on a major fault line.

There is a conflict between the inviolability of the borders and the provision for human rights and self-determination, as has been proven by recent events in Kosovo and also in other parts of the world. Since the Milosevic government is protected by the provisions guaranteeing the inviolability of the borders, he can resist complying with the human rights provisions. Thus, in effect, the two provisions instead of complementing, they may mutually exclude each other.

In jurisprudence when two conflicting rights face each other, there are two principles: either the higher right prevails, or if the rights are equal, they are balanced against each other, calling for a compromise solution.

It should be also obvious that if there is any conflict between the two rights, the sovereign rights of states to "the inviolability of frontiers and the territorial integrity of States, as enshrined in the Helsinki Final Act," and the rights of individuals "which derive from the inherent dignity of the human being and are essential for his free and full development," the universally recognized human rights should prevail, at least in cases of extreme necessity to protect human rights, and human lives! The problem with the Helsinki Process that it also disregards Grotius' rule about extreme necessity, and OSCE will be unable to carry out its assigned mission until its hands are tied by the sanctity of borders rule.

The FA, unfortunately, leaves the protection of the minority rights to the good will of the governments that are in the hands of the dominant groups, and seems to exclude any means of outside pressure when it prohibits "external interference."[230]

It should be noted that in addition to giving priority to the inviolability of frontiers, the PA also used inappropriate language in the Copenhagen Declaration that may have helped it to come to the wrong substantive decision.

(a) As we have seen there are no "principles of the international law with regard to the inviolability of frontiers and the territorial integrity of States." There are only treaties and resolutions, passed by governments that often have an interest in the status quo. If there were such principles they would have to disregard how those boundaries came to be, and freeze forever the boundary situation, even those boundaries that might have been artificially created, like those imposed after World War One at Trianon, or when China occupied Tibet, or when Germany was divided into East and West Germany, or Tsarist Russia created an empire encompassing one and a half continents! The concept of the inviolability of borders was created as a cold war compromise to induce Russia to participate in the Helsinki process, and it is time to do away with it. If one wants to find true principles regarding frontiers one must go back to Grotius as we have done above.

(b) Therefore it is inappropriate, at least in this contexts, to use the term "enshrined." There is no fundamental right either to territorial integrity or to

---

230 A notable exception to this rule should be recalled: the three countries, Rumania, Serbia, and Slovakia, where there are sizable groups of Hungarian minorities, have treaty obligations to respect their rights, as explained above. So even under the current Helsinki accord, their treatment of minorities IS an international matter and foreign interference is actually demanded.

oppress a portion of population just because they belong to a different ethnic group, or profess a different religion than that of the majority, recognized for states and political systems. If anything is and should be "enshrined" by the FA, it is the inviolability of human rights "which derive from the inherent dignity of the human being and are essential for his free and full development"! If one wants to go back to the American Declaration of Independence, one may even claim that these inalienable rights are given by the Creator! There can be no right to territorial integrity or sanctity of borders that can go as high a source! Therefore OSCE policy must be based on the solid ground of the primacy of human rights over the rights of political regimes.

OSCE and the PA is on more solid ground when it seems to attempt at least some balancing, by supporting "strong autonomy for Kosovo." Unfortunately, however, it is not only too little too late in the case of Kosovo, but OSCE has no power or even authority to impose such autonomy. OSCE's hands are tied by the conflicting provisions of FA.

Looking back at the history of OSCE (CSCE then), it was formed at the height of the cold war, and it was necessary at that time to compromise with the Soviet bloc and trade border protection for human rights. But today the protection the FA guarantees states encourages small time dictators like the since then ousted Meciar the ousted Premier in Slovakia and Milosevic in Serbia, to continue their oppressive policies. The effort of OSCE to hold individuals liable for war crimes is commendable but is very insufficient to protect the rights of ethnic and religious minorities against military assault by their own government.

> The Assembly appealed to President Milosevic to speed up implementation of the commitments he entered into in the Moscow joint statement of 16 June 1998. The Assembly also called for the investigation and prosecution by the International Criminal Tribunal for Former Yugoslavia of crimes against humanity committed in Kosovo, the immediate withdrawal of Serbian special police units, and the end of operations against the civilian population.

It was quite naive for the Assembly to expect that such an "appeal" will have any concrete result. Their naiveté is further demonstrated by concluding that

> the Declaration "recognized that meeting the challenges of implementation of OSCE principles and commitments does not require the creation of new institutions and structures, but rather should involve a refinement of existing OSCE tools and resources in the pursuit of greater effectiveness."

Such naiveté will guarantee the inefficiency and eventual irrelevance of OSCE to make this planet a more peaceful place. "In the pursuit of greater effectiveness" the scope of the authority must be expanded, and only switching the emphasis from state rights to individual rights will make OSCE more effective. The rest of the PA's conclusion is also just so much verbiage that Milosevic will dismiss as he had dismissed even greater threats than monitoring and looking for early warning signs.

Also, the Assembly continued to call for revision of OSCE decision-making procedures and urged the OSCE Ministerial Council to "consider expanding those circumstances under which the existing consensus-minus-one decision-making mechanism is utilized to include, inter alias, approval of budgets, deployment of missions, and selection of senior personnel."

The Assembly also urged, "in particular, the establishment of continuous monitoring of compliance with OSCE principles and norms, so that implementation constitutes a basic and routine OSCE activity, including granting the Chairman-in-Office the power to invoke an appropriate review mechanism," and recommended

> that parliamentary institutions, including the OSCE Parliamentary Assembly, the Parliamentary Assembly of the Council of Europe, the European Parliament, and the North Atlantic Assembly, intensify their co-operation in election monitoring and that an appropriate division of labour be developed between the parliamentary and governmental institutions, including separation of responsibilities between assistance with the organization of elections and judgment of the quality and fairness of those elections.

The Assembly further recommended "taking concrete steps to set up the early warning system of social and economic indicators with a direct link to security, as proposed at the Prague meeting of the Economic Forum of 1996."

At the same PA US Congressman and former Chair, now House ranking member of CSCE, Mr. Hoyer also expressed concern and stated that "we must be prepared to intervene decisively--even if that means militarily."[231]

This is quite a bold statement within the existing parameters, but misses the point. Milosevic and the Serb leadership are willing to sacrifice more lives, preferably somebody else's, if necessary. But there is only one thing that would deter them: threat of losing Kosovo. Also, if we want to destroy Milosevic we can hurt him by taking away Kosovo and placing the blame on

---

231 Ron McNamara "Parliamentary Assembly Annual Session Focuses on OSCE, Institutions, Growing Crisis in Kosovo," CSCE DIGEST, vol. 21, #8, August 1988, p. 68.

his aggressive policies, making him a scapegoat instead of a hero or martyr. So, instead of more military threat, bring the issue before the UN to lift the prohibition on changing frontiers, and announce the independence of Kosovo. If Milosevic would then attack Kosovo, it would be war and then NATO or the UN would be justified to intervene militarily and decisively.

The Belgian Helsinki Committee proposes another project, which has had some success in Western Europe, but has been frustrated in Central Europe by the intensity of nationalistic feelings. Dr. Yvo J. D. Peeters reports in the Spring 1996 issue of OSCE/ODIHR Bulletin that instead of tinkering with borders, there are attempts to simply "make political borders obsolete."[232] Dr. Peeters observes that "the existence of political borders ... totally disregard the ethnic realities on the ground, and thus create the so called national minorities. One example of weakening political frontiers is the "cross-border co-operation" that allows members of the same ethnicity to cooperate with members of the same ethnic group across political borders. This would be especially useful in the Carpathian Basin where currently, with the dissolution of Yugoslavia, all six countries surrounding Hungary have sizable Hungarian population. Unfortunately, while there is a successful "Regional Forum" along the Austrian-Hungarian border, there is little interest by the other five governments of the dominant majorities in these countries in any cross-border co-operation of their ethnic minorities.

> The Euregion Carpatho-Tysa [Tisza in Hungarian] is without any doubt the most challenging transfrontier venture in Central Europe. It is formed by regions in Ukraine, South-East Poland, East Slovakia, East Hungary, and North-East Rumania. In this very sensitive area, ethnic problems are quite important. Some of the borders which are only from the post-war era are questioned. Proposals for regional autonomy are looked upon with great distrust by the several governments of the concerned states. Since the Hungarians make out the largest part of the minorities, some states are suspicious of hidden agendas from Budapest.[233]

The excuse is rather lame. Both Hungarian governments after the collapse of Communism have repeatedly renounced any intent to seek border changes, and in any case, there is little that Hungary could do to change the borders

---

232 Yvo Peeters, "The Contribution of 'Transfrontier Co-Operation and Institutions' to the Reduction of Ethnic Tension in Border Areas", OSCE/ODIHR BULLETIN, Vol. 4, #2, (Spring 1996), p. 6.
233 Ibid., p. 9.

peacefully. The excuse is presented only to justify their refusal of granting any rights to the Hungarian minority. If they would want to satisfy the rightful demands of the Hungarian minority, and are afraid of autonomy and any "hidden agenda from Budapest", following Hannum's arguments above, all they have to do is grant the minority adequate protection as it should be done in any decent democracy, and the demand for autonomy and the hidden agenda from Budapest will be dismantled.

But even if the governments would agree to transfrontier co-operation, that would not take care of most other needs of the minority. Yet, it could serve as an ice-breaker, as a first step toward meaningful reform, either granting minority rights on a case by case basis, or granting autonomy.

Considering everything in a global context, instead of recommending these almost meaningless and often quite useless regional half-measures, it is time to re-visit the concept of national self-determination, as a flood of articles in professional journals urges. It is time to strengthen the pro-human-rights provisions of OSCE and weaken the protection accorded to wayward states.

The US, Territorial Status Quo, and the Balkan Problem

Unfortunately, the US is not only committed to the principle of territorial status quo, but even criticizes others who call for changes in international policy and suggest border changes to alleviate the minority problem.

On November 20, 1997, Ms. Dorothy Douglas Taft, a member of the US delegation to the Warsaw OSCE Implementation Meeting, had issued, seemingly based on slanted information, a statement addressed to the Moderator which included the following statement:

> ... we do not believe that this concern [with human rights violations] is constructively manifested by calls to re-draw the borders in this region, as a member of the Hungarian Smallholders Party suggested two weeks ago. Accordingly, Mr. Moderator, we invite our Hungarian colleagues here to reiterate once again their respect for and commitment to its current borders, consistent with the Helsinki Final Act.[234]

Regardless of the fully inadequate reply by the Hungarian delegation[235] last year, the statement has been criticized by the National Federation of

---

234 Statement of Dorothy Douglas Taft, U.S. Delegation to the OSCE Implementation Meeting, November 20, 1997, in NATIONAL MINORITIES, p. 46.
235 see doc. # 214 of the Meeting

American Hungarians in a letter to the Honorable Senator Alfonse D'Amato, Chairman, and The Honorable Rep. Christopher H. Smith, Co-Chair of the American Congressional CSCE group, on the following grounds:

1. There does not seem to be anything in the Helsinki Final Act or the UN Charter that would prohibit a politician from making a remark about the desirability or necessity, under certain circumstances, of peaceful border changes.

2. In fact, US officials supported such adjustments as early as 1944, and

3. experts in international law increasingly support the idea of border adjustments, including the right to secede.

4. Therefore, the statement can be considered a one-sided interference in Hungarian domestic politics. The US CSCE delegation has yet to object publicly to statements by Mr. Funar or other chauvinistic Rumanian officials, or chauvinistic Slovak or Serb politicians.

Although the above quoted provisions of the Helsinki Final Act are quite ambiguous, they do not prohibit discussion, recommendation, or even request of peaceful border changes, or changes in the current international policy concerning border changes. Dr. Peeters in the official OSCE/ODIHR Bulletin pointed out that the various OSCE documents

contain some apparently contradictory statements about borders. On the one hand, the inviolability of existing borders is confirmed. On the other hand peaceful and negotiated change of borders is not excluded.

The experience of the last decade shows that most--if not all--participating states only stress the first principle. The second one has never been genuinely considered.[236]

The above quoted statement by Ms. Taft of the United States OSCE delegation is an example of how even the US, which does not seem to have any vested interest in the borders in Central Europe, overlooked the second alternative included in the OSCE provisions, not to mention that it also overlooked if not outright denied the applicability of the "extreme necessity" rule. Further, Ms Taft had overlooked, or was uninformed, that re-drawing the boundaries around Hungary, as long as peaceful means are advocated,

---

236 Peeters, p. 6.

has been recommended during the US. deliberations to prepare the US policy for the post WW II period.[237]

The Summary of these recommendations, prepared on July 26, 1944, after supporting changes along the Hungarian-Czechoslovak border, states: "7. The United States favors an adjustment of the Hungarian frontier in Transylvania along from North of Arad to Szatmar to Hungary,"[238]

If the recommendation had been followed in 1945, there would be no need now to raise the question of frontiers by the Hungarian Smallholders Party politician. By the way, it should be noted that the same party presently is a member of the governing coalition.

In addition, the right to self-determination, including secession is not only recognized in international law, but, as it has been shown, it is being increasingly promoted by international law experts as a means of preventing local conflicts when autonomy is not granted in time. Let me offer only one quote at this time. Thomas Franck wrote

> a minority within a state, especially if it occupies a discrete territory, may have a right to secede--roughly analogous to a decolonization right--if it is persistently and egregiously denied political and social equality as well as the opportunity to retain cultural identity.[239]

Many believe that such is the case in the countries that the Smallholders Party politician was referring to!

A similar attack on self-determination occurred in Congress some ten years earlier. The full House and the Senate Foreign Relations Committee already passed an amendment supporting autonomy for Hungarians in Transylvania. There was nothing in the amendment that would suggest that the purpose of the amendment was external autonomy, that is, secession. Yet, Bulcsu Veress, who was on Senator Dodd's staff at the time, interpreted it as a demand for territorial carving up of Rumania, wrote and circulated a list of "Talking Points" which attacked the concept and the Amendment, asserting that

> There is no law in international law that would give the right of self-determination to ethnic minorities... Whole nations, of course, have that right, such as the Polish or the Afghan nations even if they are temporarily deprived of its exercise. On the other hand, the very sentence in the Helsinki Agreement for example, that contains the

237 see Romsics, p. 271 (PWC-151,CAC-142b), p. 271, #148 ff. above.
238 Ibid., p. 281.
239 Thomas Franck, "Postmodern...", p. 13.

right of self-determination also reasserts the territorial integrity of states.[240]

Instead of attempting to limit the scope of the amendment and to clarify it, as Mr. Dornan explained on the House floor that the Amendment does not involve territorial changes, merely would assure free exercise and development of their national, cultural, and religious identity, the document misrepresents the aim of the Amendment.[241] If the author of the talking points was sincere in its support of the minority rights when he wrote that "the Dornan Amendment as written seems to give support to the Rumanian propaganda" i.e. that the effort to gain the right of self-determination is "only a pretext to conceal the real intentions of territorial revachists," he should have offered corrections, instead of recommending the "delete everything" that refers to autonomy. [242]

The author of the Talking Points also misrepresents international law. Although Mr. Veress should not be held responsible for the recent developments, as already outlined, there is no excuse for somebody who presents himself as an expert on international law, not to be aware of Grotius' rule which clearly establishes the right of even territorial self-determination, and the 1921 League of Nations rule in the case of the Aaland Islands. Both affirm that in extreme (and only in extreme) necessity, even territorial autonomy, without the consent of the majority population or its government, is justified!

The US defends its position that it is promoting a form of pluralism and supporting a form of "colorblind" society in the Balkan where people with different backgrounds will learn to live in peace within the same community. The hope is that in time Kosovo will turn into a beautiful and peaceful rainbow society of ethnic and religious groups. But this dream had been brutally destroyed by reality.

If one can learn anything from Balkan history is the lesson that ethnicity is more important than survival. People are willing to sacrifice not only their economic or physical well being but their (and others') very lives on the altar of blind ethnic hatred.

As President Clinton's own "race advisory board" reported, according to an AP story[243] the idea of a "colorblind society" does not work even here, in the

---

240 Talking points on the Dornan Amendment on the Hungarian minority in Transylvania (Section 190 of HR 1777, the State Department Authorization Bill)
241 Cf. correspondence, Dr. Zoltan Szaz to Sandor Csoori, Aug. 8, 1987.
242 see Talking Points.
243 July 8, 1998.

United States. According to John Hope Franklin, the Chairman of the advisory board,

> "the idea that we should aspire to a 'colorblind' society is an impediment to reducing racial stereotyping. ... Given that research has demonstrated that the best way to reduce racial stereotyping is to be conscious about racial differences, it is important to present thoughtful alternative to the 'colorblind society' concept."

Applying this to foreign policy, there is now scientific evidence, based on the board's research, that the consensus of the international community about forcing a diverse population live as next door neighbors, which is the foundation of the Dayton Agreement, is wrong, it is "an impediment" to regional peace. The best way to reduce ethnic hatred and achieve peace in the Balkan (and other areas) is to consider ethnicity as an important factor, and "present thoughtful alternative" policies, like separating them with international (secession) or at least internal (autonomy) boundaries to reduce if not eliminate the daily contact and thus much of the opportunity for conflict between diverse and often hostile groups.

This is not to suggest that those in charge of representing the US at international human rights forums are incompetent, but they should realize that aside from being locked into a paradigm that is outmoded and invites small time dictators to make a political career out of oppressing minorities, and those who deal with human rights problems abroad, need a wider perspective.

Therefore Hurst Hannum not only urges the statesmen and policy makers to create an appropriate mechanism to deal with minority issues and protections, but he wants to enlarge the focus of American politicians, and has a message to the lower level administrators who not only carry out policy but often also advise the policy makers. The message should not be limited to American personnel, of course, but should include even, or especially, the politicians, decision makers and advisors in states where there is a minority problem.

> The United States should recognize that minimum human rights and minority standards are expanding beyond the purely individualistic focus of America's own traditions, incorporating language, culture, and education. Potential mediators and advisers will need to become familiar with comparative arrangements for power sharing, devolution, federalism, confederalism, territorial and functional autonomy, self-government, special participation rights for

121

minorities or regional groups, proportional representation, and similar arrangements.[244]

But the problem is deeper than just ignorance or incompetence. The United States seems to give her full support to the policy of putting borders above people although it should be obvious that the policy is not working. The hopelessness of the Bosnian situation had been illustrated by Robert S. Gelbard, Special Representative of the President and the Secretary of State for Implementation of the Dayton Peace Accords in a Statement before the Senate Armed Services Committee on June 4, 1998.

Mr. Gelbard had admitted that "the [UN sponsored] peace process remains fragile, and without the security and confidence SFOR's presence provides, especially in light of conflict in the Federal Republic of Yugoslavia, Bosnia could well lose ground or, worse, slip back into war."

The SFOR forces are used as an artificial respirator that keeps a critical patient barely alive, and as soon as the plug is pulled, the patient dies. According to Gelbard,

> ... while we have brought tremendous political and economic pressure to bear on each of them over the course of the last 14 months, the best leverage we had with those hard-line Bosnians seeking to block arms control or police reform, refugee returns, or free elections was clearly the SFOR presence.

The public seems to blame the Serb politicians and military for the Bosnian crisis, but it is the international community that prevents a peaceful solution to the crisis. There is an excellent chronological account of the Yugoslav crisis provided by T.M. Franck which concludes that there is plenty of blame to go around.

> ...Finally, invited by the Serbian minorities in Bosnia-Herzegovina, the EC's Arbitral Commission established by the Hague Peace Conference process concluded that, whatever the extent of the right [of self-determination] it did not include the right to modify the borders as they existed at the moment of independence.[245]

Among others, it is these rulings that create the crisis in Bosnia as well as in Kosovo that doom not only the peace process but the innocent minorities

---

244 Hannum, The Specter ... , p. 17..

245 Quoted in Franck, "Postmodern...", Annex: The Yugoslav Crisis, p 27; AVIS, #2, 31 ILM 1992, p. 1489. Franck suggests that to the same effect see AVIS #3 which adopts the inviolability of the external borders of the seceding republics of the Federation which, it was said, was in the process of disintegrating (31 ILM 1992, p. 1499 at p. 15000).

who have been told over and over again that they have the right of self-determination!

If the investment of "tremendous political and economic pressure" without the troops could not buy peace in Bosnia, how do we expect to buy peace in Kosovo and in other areas of the world? Worse yet, how long are we going to keep our troops there? What if ethnic violence would erupt in neighboring Rumania or Slovakia, both countries with sizable ethnic minority population and a long history of ethnic cleansing?

Mr. Gelbard's statement is revealing evidence just how little our pressure has brought.

> We used that leverage and active United States diplomacy to persuade Milosevic finally last month to start negotiations on Kosovo's future status. Talks are continuing in Pristina -- the next round is set for tomorrow, but the process, initiated by Kosovo Albanian leader Dr. Rugova in a May 15 meeting with President Milosevic, is extremely fragile. It is seriously jeopardized by Belgrade's disproportionate and indiscriminate use of force in response to violence from Albanian extremists.

Less than a week after this statement William Cohen, our Secretary of Defense was lining up support in Brussels for military intervention in Kosovo. In September of 1998, amid some vicious attacks on the civilian population of Kosovo the US Congress had passed an almost unanimous resolution demanding the indictment and trial of Milosevic for war crimes.

While the action is commendable for standing up for human rights, it is done in the wrong place and the wrong time against the wrong person. The place should be the UN, clarifying the self-determination issue and resolve the conflict between territorial claims and human rights claims, and also by establishing its primacy of human rights over the state's rights to territorial integrity. The time should have been much earlier, at least during the Bosnia crisis, when Milosevic masterfully pushed the conflict to the breaking point and stopping when he met strong resistance, only to continue pushing as soon as the resistance had weakened. The wrong person in the sense that Milosevic has become a national hero to the nationalist Serbs and punishing him at this point only makes him martyr and an even greater national hero.

Milosevic is a textbook example of how the current international attitude allows dictators to operate. According to Julie Mertus,

> (M)ilosevic rekindled Serbian nationalism through Kosovo and the issue propelled him into power. Without Kosovo, Milosevic would not have the power base he needed to plunge into Bosnia and

123

Herzegovina and Croatia. Already a good Communist, Milosevic's deeds on Kosovo showed that he was a good nationalist as well. Milosevic's strategy on Kosovo became a defining and delimiting moment in Serbian politics. Once Milosevic had become the protector of Serbs in Kosovo, his role spread as the protector of Serbs everywhere. Without a Kosovo card, Milosevic would have had a far more difficult time implementing this strategy.[246]

It is the international community that dealt Milosevic the Kosovo card that he uses to trump now the international community. Against this understanding of Milosevic, when his entire future and influence is based on acting tough in Kosovo, it is more than naive to expect that he will negotiate peace in good faith or international observers will scare him. It is simply cynical to allow Milosevic to hold together and support his own power base by his Kosovo strategy of killing civilian population who have been told by the international community that they "shall not be denied the right, in community with the other members of their group, to enjoy their culture, to profess and practice their religion, or to use their own language"[247] or to select their own sovereign.

It should be noted that unfortunately, Milosevic is not the only one who plays the minority card to their political advantage. In Slovakia it was Meciar, the recently defeated Slovak premier, in Rumania the best known is Funar, the mayor of the ancient Hungarian city, Kolozsvar, now called Cluj, to name only the top ones. Below them there are entire political parties and hundreds if not thousands of radical politicians whose political future requires and thrives on ethnic conflict. In addition there are the educators, journalists and clergymen who have committed themselves to promote ethnic hatred and whose careers also depend on their ability to incite or fuel the fire of already existing ethnic conflicts.

Continuing the analogy, instead of indefinitely relying on the respirator, major surgery should be performed and the international community must cut Kosovo off the Serbian body politics to remove the Kosovo card from Milosevic's hand. At the same time we should not endanger the Hungarian minority in Voivodina, by forcing Milosevic to save face with his Serb constituency and stay in power by using the "Hungarian Card."

Fortunately, there is more and more support building in foreign policy circles both for autonomy as a form of national self determination, separating the

246 Julie Mertus, "Prospects for National Minorities under the Dayton Accords--Lessons from History: the Inter-War minorities schemes and the 'Yugoslav Nations,' in 23 BROOKLYN JOURNAL OF INTERNATIONAL LAW (1998) p. 827.
247 International Covenant of Civil and Political Rights (1966), Art. 27. Quoted in Franck, "Postmodern...", p. 11.

diverse ethnic groups to reduce the contact points and to eliminate, or at least substantially reduce the opportunity for violence, and for outright secession in extremely grievous situation that Grotius would call a "case of extreme or in other ways inevitable necessity," giving the aggrieved minority full independence and sovereignty. The Kosovo situation certainly qualifies as a "case of extreme or in other ways inevitable necessity."

The Dayton Accords concerning Bosnia are based on anachronistic principles in denying both autonomy and secession rights. Given the old hatreds and mistrust, only foreign, quasi occupational forces can maintain a temporary truce between the conflicting ethnic groups. The more the world--and the Clinton Administration waits, the more difficult it might be to avoid complete partition

In a recent issue of FOREIGN AFFAIRS two articles criticize the American policy in Bosnia, and seem to support all the experts, including Ervin Laszlo's views, and the FUEN experts recommendation. According to General Boyd, who was Deputy Commander in Chief, US European Command, from 1992 to 1995, the American insistence on forcing hostile ethnic groups with diverse political culture to live in peace within the same geographic area under one government is making things worse, instead of better and suggest that only dividing the three ethnic groups into "self-governing sub-states" with the central government handling only the most essential functions will bring peace and security to the area.[248]

The second article, written by Gideon Rose, Deputy Director of National Security Studies and Olin Fellow at the Council on Foreign Relations comes to similar conclusion. He proposes "a clear division and stable balance of power among different local factions--in other words, a partition."[249] The two authors' evaluation of US policy is not too flattering for the Administration. According to General Boyd, it is a matter of prestige and a fear of loss of credibility that prevents the Clinton Administration from accepting the facts and look for a solution,[250] while Rose calls the Administration's policy "delusion," and believes that the Administration is afraid that partition would "set a terrible example for the region."[251] The Administration was probably thinking of the Albanians in Kosovo and the Hungarians up North in Vojvodina, who had enjoyed autonomy within the former Yugoslavia, until the Serbs had eliminated it. After World War two for a period there also existed a Hungarian Autonomous Region in Rumania,

---

248 General USAF (Ret.) Charles G. Boyd, "Making Bosnia Work," in FOREIGN AFFAIRS (Jan-Feb. 1998) p. 46.
249 Gideon Rose, "The Exit Strategy Delusion" in FOREIGN AFFAIRS (Jan-Feb. 1998) p. 65.
250 Boyd, p. 44.
251 Rose, Idem.

with 78.8% Hungarian majority, which comprised almost 35% of the total number of Hungarians living in Rumania.

If one looks for a precedent for a sweeping change of attitudes in foreign policy, one needs to go no further than the 1960's, when Charles De Gaulle solved the long lasting fight to keep Algeria a French colony. According to Quigley, "the French army, after a series of defeats from 1940 (by the Germans) to Indochina in 1954, resolved not to be defeated in Algeria and was prepared to overthrow by civil war any French cabinet that wished to give independence to that area."[252] The crisis led to the collapse of the short lived Fourth Republic and the election of General De Gaulle, a military man perceived to be a hard-liner, and a new constitution inaugurating the Fifth Republic, that still exists today. De Gaulle promptly started negotiations and on March 18, 1962 reached a historic settlement granting Algeria her independence. It took a statesman and general of De Gaulle's stature to end the bitter fight that cost France over seven years, an estimated 250,000 lives and $20 billion.[253] Is there another De Gaulle in the US or Western Europe who would take the bull by the horn and get out of the current quagmire?

The irony is that instead of being afraid, the Administration should grab the opportunity to develop a new foreign policy doctrine centered on the concept of autonomy, and with one fell swoop solve the problems of minorities not only in Central Europe, from the Germans in the Czech Republic, the Hungarians in Slovakia, Rumania and Serbia, the Albanians in Kosovo, listing only those which seem to be geographically the closest to Bosnia, but in other areas of the world.

The Clinton Administration and other world leaders should recognize that autonomy has been applied successfully in several countries to solve the problem of ethnic conflict, so it is not an unknown and untried concept that we are recommending. Also, it seems to be the inevitable trend in the future. Zoltani and Koszorus quote Hurst Hannum on this issue, who pointed out that the

> reality of minorities and largely heterogeneous states in the contemporary world is also at odds with the theory of the nation state as it developed in the nineteenth century, and the rhetoric of one people/one state has carried over into the concept of self-determination in the post-1945 period.[254]

---

252 Quigley, p. 1179.
253 Ibid., 1180.
254 Zoltani and Koszorus, p. 137; cf. Hurst Hannum, AUTONOMY, SOVEREIGNTY, AND SELF-DETERMINATION (Philadelphia, PA: University of Pennsylvania Press, 1990) p. 71.

In other words, the heterogeneous unitary form of the state has become an oxymoron. The principle of national self-determination has made it outdated, in need of serious revision and reform by accepting the concept of autonomy as a solution of current ills and as the foundation of a peaceful new millennium.

Of course, as we shall see, the degree and exact form of autonomy recommended to protect the rights of culturally, ethnically or religiously diverse groups and communities would depend in each case on the local circumstances and should be determined by negotiation between the representatives of the minority population and the government that is dominated by the majority group. Outside forces, like the UN, OSCE, the European Community, etc., should only mediate (unless there is a case of extreme necessity), and provide the incentive, the carrot or the stick, if necessary, to improve life for the minorities of the several multi-ethnic countries, and to provide the human and minority rights that several international documents prescribe and seem to guarantee.

Thus, the situation in the former Yugoslavia is no less urgent than the Hungarian Revolution of 1956 was, and it demands no less urgent consideration by the UN, but hopefully with more success this time.

In the following we shall give some successful historic examples and current solutions, along with proposals to be applied in the Carpathian Basin, involving Hungarian and other ethnic minorities.

V.

SOVEREIGNTY, FEDERALISM,
AND THE THEORY OF AUTONOMY

Autonomy in Theory

Although there is an overlap between the right to external and to internal self-determination, much of the above discussion focused on secession.

Secession and autonomy rights have the same root: human dignity, but have quite different consequences. Unless secession involves joining another existing state, secession has grave international consequences, as gaining recognition and developing diplomatic relations with other countries, establishing sovereign presence in the world, including its own monetary system, new economic and commercial partners and disputes over old obligations, representation in international forums, organizing a separate and sovereign foreign policy with a separate defense system, etc. Therefore it is understandable that the international system is wary of secessionist efforts: if a new state cannot fulfill its international responsibilities, it can create chaos in the international arena.

Therefore it is time to turn our attention to autonomy rights. Autonomy does not involve any of these problems, and usually causes minimal interference within domestic affairs, since it usually affects only those who live in the newly autonomous system. The rest of the population does not lose anything but the opportunity to dominate another group, and on the long run the entire body politic stands to benefit from the elimination of the tension. But dominating over a minority group is not a God-given right, and a competent and democratic government, with a little good will, can overcome its loss.

If one considers Hannum's three stages of   asserting minority rights in evaluating any claim for self-determination, the first thing should be to determine at what stage is the situation. If the government is willing to sit down in good faith and satisfies most of the legitimate demands, it is the first stage.

As the unsatisfied reasonable demands keep growing, the situation more and more approaches the second stage, and autonomy might be the only solution and the two parties agree on a package deal: instead of discussing every demand separate, the minority takes all demands off the table, and demands a blanket authorization to handle its own affairs without unreasonable interference from the government or the majority population. According to Hannum, "(N)or is autonomy an end in itself--it is a tool to ensure that other rights and needs are appropriately addressed."[255]

Eva Maria Barki, in international law expert in Vienna, in an interview given in Rumania to a Hungarian paper about the popular issue of dual citizenship for Hungarians who live in Rumania, stated that

> the solution [of the minority problem in Rumania] is not the to be found in the dual citizenship.... the most important goal continues to be the autonomy.... With an adequate autonomy package every problem area, including the problem of citizenship can be resolved. Separate solutions for individual problems will never be successful. One package has to be placed on the table and discussed on the international level. There is no way to by-pass this, if one is serious about a solution. Much valuable time has been lost since 1990.... On the one hand, the past autonomy demands have to be filled with real content... most important is to have your own legislation, your own government, including the police, and your own judicial structure. On the other hand, I consider as a basic condition the creation of a federal system in Rumania.[256]

According to Barki's assessment, the Hungarian minority of Rumania is at the point where it is obvious that, in spite of vague promises and admitting the Democratic Federation Hungarians in Rumania, the political party that most Hungarians supported at the last election, to the coalition government with several portfolios, the individual Hungarian demands are not taken seriously by the government. So, according to Barki it is time to put everything aside, escalate the situation to the next stage and focus on demanding autonomy! Yet, the US attitude is (and was) that the Hungarian government should sign a bi-lateral "basic treaty" with Rumania that will sweep the problem under the rug, and will seemingly satisfy the Western leaders, without solving the problem. Unfortunately, the previous Hungarian government, under tremendous pressure by the US, did comply, but another treaty did not solve the minority problem in Transylvania. At the present time

---

255 Ibid., p. 474.
256 NAPI MAGYARORSZÁG (DAILY HUNGARY) Sept. 29, 1998, Istvan Pataky, "Schengen szíven szúrta a magyarokat, (Shengen Pierced the Hearts of Hungarians); interview with Eva Maria Barki about autonomy and dual citizenship.

they are at a point where responsible people start to talk about a future Kosovo in Transylvania.

According to the Rumanian daily, TRANSILVANIA JURNAL, Zsolt Lanyi, a Hungarian politician, stated in an interview that "only with the working together of Hungarians, Rumanians and Saxons can Transylvania flourish again; he also warned, if we don't move toward peace, a new Kosovo might develop which is not good for any ethnic group..."[257]

Lanyi did not want to create added tension, only stated the obvious. If the demands for autonomy go unanswered, the minority will begin to feel even more frustrated and betrayed, excluded from determining its own faith, might start to consider the existing government, or even the entire regime, as illegitimate from their perspective. If they can convince the international community of this, the road to independence should be open. "In the search for a means of determining whether a particular secessionist movement is legitimate or illegitimate, one common denominator is the violation of fundamental rights by the state; only where such violations occur can secession be justified.[258]

From this escalation of the demands it is obvious, as many commentators point out but the point bears repeating, that the best way to avoid the threat of secession is to listen and satisfy the demands and develop a mutually trusting relationship from the beginning. Since this did not happen in most of the disputed countries (if it did happen, there would be no dispute), in most cases at least autonomy (internal self-determination) seems inevitable. In fact, in spite of the advice given by Hannum that in situations when autonomy is demanded, "a kind of flexible intermediary [should be sought] which will enable the parties to negotiate solutions to particular grievances on the basis of pragmatic creativity,"[259] In this case Rumania, and in the case of Kosovo and Voivodina Serbia treats autonomy demands as hostile acts, almost on the level of treason.

Using an analogy from the medical field, some illnesses can be prevented, others can be treated if detected and medical care is sought in time, but if neglected it may require surgery or amputation, or will cause death!

Minority problems seem to follow the same pattern, and when stubborn and/or ignorant people refuse early treatment, eventually they may face the more serious alternatives.

---

257 RMDSz Press Watch, Nov. 17, 1998, V. 213.
258 Hannum, AUTONOMY...., p. 471.
259 Ibid., p. 465.

Therefore the parties should go back and see if the grievances can be handled on a case by case basis, that is, on level one, and if not, why not? Unfortunately, few states have the required flexibility, often because the minority card has been played far too long to advance political careers, people have dug themselves into a strong defensive position, and political careers would be broken if the government gave in to the minority. Thus, unfortunately, more often than not, once the conflict reached the level when autonomy is demanded, the process escalates rather than diminishes unless the hostile government is defeated and a more flexible government is elected, as it hopefully happened in Slovakia with the ouster of Meciar whose political career is based on anti-Hungarian chauvinism.

If autonomy is not granted in time, secession might be the only solution. The only way to nip the secessionist trend in the bud is by the international community (and I mean the UN, which alone has the authority and the means to make and carry out international law, and if necessary, can apply military sanctions) to make it clear at the outset that when it comes to the point, it will be most sympathetic to secessionist claims!

The already quoted bi-partisan leadership of the U.S. Congress's Helsinki Commission, explains why Serbia may have lost Kosovo: "Trying to coax Belgrade for an agreement on Kosovo has proven fruitless..." The Serbs have refused to accept a lower level solution, so they should be forced to pay the price!

The statement and the argument is in complete harmony with the views and conclusions of the experts. It is hoped that the international community, especially the United Nations, will heed the recommendation and act on it, as soon as possible, especially in light of the frustration caused by both sides at the Rambouilet (France) negotiations. After weeks of discussion, there has been no progress, and more than a month after the two Congressmen made the above quoted statement, the verification process not only failed to produce any result, but the verification team has been harassed and according to the latest news, have been detained by Serb border police.[260]

We have discussed autonomy as a legal concept and as a form of self-determination. Here we should discuss it from a practical perspective.

At one end of the spectrum one finds absolute collective autonomy as recognized by the international community and organizations. Absolute collective autonomy is called sovereignty, based on the essential characteristic of the modern statehood and international order. The state has ultimate and independent, i.e. sovereign authority over a people occupying a

---

260 AP story with Pristina, Yugoslavia by-line, February 27, 1999.

certain territory, with well defined boundaries. The people of the state are called citizens (which is unrelated to ethnicity) and its authority consists of making laws and enforcing them over the subjects, by having monopoly of sanctioned violence. Also, the state has the authority to maintain military forces sufficient to defend its territory and people, and to make war.

At other end of the spectrum is personal autonomy, which is a relatively recent concept in political theory and jurisprudence. Absolute personal autonomy, the idea that a human being is not subject to any superior rule or rule-maker exists only in the abstract. It is an ideal to which anarchists and some libertarians aspire. According to Saint Augustine (and Martin Luther), only if society would be populated by angels could we do away with law and authority on Earth. In practice, personal autonomy ranges from near zero for slaves, to near absolute for absolutist rulers. Personal autonomy has been curbed in various ways: by social customs and norms, including family roles and relationship, religious dogmas and precepts, jobs, business contracts and governmental authority by passing and enforcing criminal and civil laws.

If absolute or even near absolute autonomy would be practiced among humans, it would lead to chaos and a kind of state of nature about which Hobbes wrote in 1651 in LEVIATHAN that "life is a war of everyone against everyone," therefore "life short and brutish". Although this extreme situation has probably never existed in individual relationships, the family, the tribe and often religion being moderating influences, this kind of autonomy describes best the kind of relationship that existed among states in the international arena made up of sovereign states. until Hugo Grotius, the Father of International Law, brought some sense, order, and security into international relations.

Somewhere in the middle of the spectrum one finds different forms of autonomy which has to do with integration and division within a larger organization. Autonomy is a rather complex moral, social and political concept. According to Hannum, "personal and political autonomy is in some real sense the right to be different and to be left alone; to preserve, protect, and promote values that are beyond the reach of the rest of society."[261] Although many country's constitution and laws define autonomy, there is no legal definition of the term in international law. In other words, there is no legal responsibility mandated to respect the right to autonomy!

At the present time sovereign states can only be pressured to grant this right in a constitutional or legal form, but there is no set of recognized legal standards for these rights, nor can states be forced to grant autonomy. This situation hopefully will change soon, as the Kosovo stalemate might force the

---

261 Hannum, Autonomy, p. 4.

UN and the international community to bring some order into this chaos. Instead of prolonged and frustrating negotiations there should be some international court that would mandate autonomy or secession, and this decision should be backed by the full authority of the United Nations, including the threat and actual use of force, if necessary.

In terms of minority relations, there are several kinds of autonomy:

1. TERRITORIAL AUTONOMY, when in a large, contiguous area, people who have cultural, economic, or religious background that differs from that of the majority population of the country, are given the right to govern themselves (e.g. the Swedish population of Aaland Islands) as members of a minority. But the territorial autonomy would not solve the problem of minorities living in heterogeneous regions with significant majority and minority presence in various proportions. Based on the "shared space" concept,[262] they should share authority too.

2. SHARED AUTONOMY is based on the shared space concept, when two (or more) larger groups, often members of the country's majority population and a large minority, share a territory so that territorial autonomy is impossible, and personal autonomy is insufficient to accommodate the collective needs of the groups, with sufficient protections for each side from being dominated by the other group. In such arrangement the rights of proportionate participation in policy and law-making, execution, and enforcement are guaranteed to both groups. The arrangement should include the right to appeal to higher, perhaps international authorities, limited veto power in cases affecting their self-identity, separate educational facilities or programs, and legal protection of certain rights. For example, language rights could be guaranteed by extending the freedom of speech rights from the protection of the content to the protection of the form i.e. language of the speaker, and guaranteeing the use of minority languages in public transactions. Successful examples of shared autonomy include the German and Italian groups sharing power in Tyrol, Italy, under a Special Constitution of Trentino-Alto Adige.

3. LOCAL AUTONOMY when individual municipalities with large minority population exist in an otherwise majority populated region, and the local government has a degree of "home rule," allowing it to run the local government by and according to the values of the minority population but they exercise this authority under the laws and supervision of the higher, sovereign level of government.; and finally

4. PERSONAL AUTONOMY, which applies when minority individuals or small groups live amongst the majority population. In this case the

---

262 Ibid., p. 143.

minority members have the right to make some fundamental economic, cultural, religious and political choices effecting their personal lives, without interference, harassment, and discrimination from the government or the majority population. Personal autonomy differs from general individual human rights in that minority members should have the right not only to do what the majority does, but have the right to do it according to their own personal way and in their own language, according to their religion, culture, profession, etc. This includes the right to protect and maintain their language, culture and self-identity, including the right to form and join their own groups and organizations. Disregarding this difference between equal rights and minority rights can cause serious problems. When states proclaim that their minorities enjoy equal rights,[263] from the minority's perspective their situation is anything but "enjoyable." For example, if a country proclaims that its minority has equal rights to education with the majority, unless it specifies the right to have it in the minority language, it does not satisfies the minority's right to education according to the minorities needs. The point of personal autonomy is to have the right for their children to be educated in the minority's language, culture, traditions, etc., without any discrimination or harassment. It should be pointed out, however, that his right becomes meaningful only if there are minority schools and other institutions available near by, be it an autonomous territory, shared autonomy region, or available schools and institutions across the border if the minority lives near a border of a country where the appropriate institutions are available.

It should be noted that in working democracies personal autonomy includes the right to join groups and form organizations to practice your ethnic values along with others of the same ethnicity. Therefore in democracies, under "democratic governance," personal autonomy is not even mentioned: it is taken for granted, as a basic principle. Under democratic governance minority groups have the right not only to from their churches and organizations, but their schools, from elementary schools to universities, on an equal basis with other similar institutions catering to the majority population.

Concerning autonomy, some compromise could be worked out concerning the use of national symbols: the minority, instead of flying the colors of another sovereign, should be permitted to create their own official flag that is distinguished from the official flag of another country by including some regional or local symbols. This flag could be used in decals, buttons, etc., to

---

263 See Ibid., , p. 63.

indicate ethnic background, without being disloyal to the sovereign. With a little good will, even this touchy problem could be solved.

It is necessary to mention one more autonomy concept. On February 21, 1999 the Hungarian government organized a "Hungary and Hungarians beyond the Borders" conference, with the participation of representatives of minority political parties that have elected representatives in their own country. There was one person invited from the Hungarian community in the United States, who has been always hostile to the autonomy concept, and was working with Bulcsu Veress to delete the autonomy provision from the Dornan Amendment. In their Final Resolution the Conference contains a statement that seems to be a meaningless truism without promising or demanding anything or explaining how this desirable legislation and administrative action will come about. This is not a program point but a pious but meaningless, do-nothing declaration:

> 5. The goal of Hungarian national policy is the assurance of the personal and collective rights of Hungarians in the neighboring countries according to the successful practice of democratic countries of Western Europe. In the Central European region this requires further legislative and administrative action so that minority communities may conduct their affairs based on the subsidiarity principle.[264]

According to Grolier's 1999 multimedia dictionary, "subsidiary" means "serving to assist or supplement, secondary in importance." The subsidiarity principle in social sciences means that if something can be solved on a lower level, it should be solved there. This concept was made popular by the Catholic Church during the 1930, as part of its social program to reduce the power of the state over society. There is nothing in the concept that would refer to minority rights or issues. It merely means de-centralization.

For example, Italy has twenty administrative regions, all based on the subsidiarity principle, but only five has autonomous regions based on nationality considerations. The current county and local government structure of Rumania, Slovakia or Serbia completely satisfies the concept of subsidiarity. So the Final Resolution in using misleading wording, actually side-tracks the issue of national self-determination.

When the Hungarian Ambassador to Washington, the Honorable Dr. Geza Jeszenszky, former Minister of Foreign Affairs of Hungary, presented the Resolution to the United States government, in light of its anti-autonomy stance, nobody was surprised that they were very happy with this

---

264 Report of "Hungary and Hungarians beyond the Borders" conference, February 20, 1999.

meaningless statement,[265] The US had vehemently opposed and criticized the Closing Statement of the previous such meeting two years ago because autonomy was mentioned explicitly as one of the goals.

Autonomy and Unitary v. Federal Systems Of Government

The vast majority of the countries in the world have unitary forms of government, which means that all sovereign power is exercised by one government, with all branches exercising power on the same level. The federal system of government became somewhat popular after the American experiment succeeded.

In a federal system the sovereign powers are shared along functional lines on a territorial basis between a central government and several regional governments. In a typical federal system foreign affairs and defense, coining money, and some well defined areas of governance are in the hands of the central government, while other sovereign powers, usually police powers, i.e. maintaining domestic law and order, and some regulations of businesses and private affairs are in the hands of regional, autonomous governments. There are degrees of autonomy, and the federal system gives highest, constitutionally enshrined and protected sovereign authority to regional autonomous governments. . In such an arrangement the lower levels are constitutionally autonomous in legislating and carrying out the functions that are assigned to them.

Granting territorial autonomy to a minority differs from the federal system in that the areas inhabited by the dominant ethnic group are not further divided: there the central government governs in all aspects of government, and only the autonomous territory or the region(s) with shared autonomy are granted by constitutional provision quasi sovereign powers in certain relevant areas. A lesser degree of autonomy is when home rule is given to the regional governments by legislative enactment.

The basic rule of thumb in deciding which form of government is appropriate, other than historic i.e. arbitrary reasons, is that for a homogeneous population there is no need for a federal arrangement. On the other hand, if there are geographically identifiable heterogeneous groups without significant common ground, each group should constitute a state of its own. There are numerous micro-states that are viable. In cases of demands for secession this is another important concept to consider.

---

265 See open letter distributed on Internet, by Ambassador Jeszenszky, on February 25, 1999.

One needs geographically identifiable groups with some significant differences (ethnicity or race, language, religion of diverse cultural background) to justify territorial autonomy, and some significant common ground (again, similar ethnicity, race, language, or culture) to justify having a common sovereign in a federal system. Only when both conditions are met is regional autonomy and/or a federal system desirable. Ethnically, culturally or religiously heterogeneous states with important common features or interests are good candidates for federal system.

If one examines closely the American federal system, one will find that although there are regional differences, the existing state boundaries fail to reflect these differences. For example, New York City has more in common with the surrounding areas of New Jersey and Connecticut than with Upstate New York, and Upstate New York has more in common with Vermont and Massachusetts on the East and with North-West Pennsylvania and Ohio on the West. So the United States would be a poor example to imitate in drawing a federal system!

Another bad example of creating a federal state is the now near-defunct Yugoslavia. When Yugoslavia was created after World War I by the Allied and Associated Powers, they incorrectly assumed that having a Slavic background is sufficient to bind a population of three distinct religious backgrounds, Catholic, Orthodox, and Muslim, and of several nationality backgrounds together in a federal system. Recent events have proven that they were wrong! There was not enough binding power in the South Slav identity to keep Yugoslavia together. There isn't enough binding power even in Bosnia to keep it together as a peaceful federation of three ethnic and religious groups without the presence of international peacekeeping troops.

Many people believe that, according to the principle of subsidiarity, the least drastic yet potentially most effective solution for the minority problem would be full autonomy with a federal type of 0-0arrangement respectively, within many otherwise heterogeneous states. While this might be true in some cases, there are, and should be, different   kinds and degrees of autonomy considered in each case, as appropriate to the particular situation.

Zoltani and Koszorus distinguish three kinds of minority situations:

> first, there are crossborder ethnicities or communities, such as Hungarians in Slovakia; second, when the minority lives in compact communities at a distance from the state border and from its compatriots, as the Szeklers in Transylvania and the Csango of

Moldavia; third, when the minority is scattered throughout the region.[266]

We can add a fourth type, when there is a relatively balanced presence of two or more groups in the same region. Each of these types of situations would require a different form and different degree of autonomy. What would be practical for one, might be impractical for another situation: in some cases territorial autonomy might be feasible, others might require shared autonomy or local home rule, and in other cases personal autonomy or a combination of the different kinds would be the appropriate solution. Even in one country, if one finds instances of all four types of situations, like in Rumania, a combination of all four types of autonomy might be needed.

True national self-determination should include the right of a minority, especially if there is a "historic grievance," as Brilmayer suggested, to separate itself from a heterogeneous state dominated by a hostile majority with whom they have nothing significant or relevant in common. Such separation has happened in recent years peacefully in the case of Slovakia, and with considerable violence when Yugoslavia broke up. Under certain circumstances they may even have the right to join their motherland and instead of creating a different sovereign, change back to a sovereign under which they have existed previously and from which they have been cut off. As for joining a neighboring sovereign, it is the dream and desire of the Serbs in Bosnia, that the Dayton Agreement prohibited. Rumanians in Rumania also desire to be united with their brethren in Moldova, but the ethnic Rumanians of Moldova are not too eager to be united with them. The strongest case for such re-union could be made on behalf of the Hungarians who have been separated from the mother country for the arbitrary reason of using a railroad as the guide in drawing the new boundaries after Trianon, and the happened to fall on the wrong side of the tracks and as a consequence, have been divided initially into four, now at least six surrounding states.

As we have seen, in ethnically heterogeneous countries, if the regional boundaries can be drawn along ethnic and/or religious lines, the diversity requirement for a territorially based autonomy, and a federal system is satisfied.

It is somewhat harder, if not impossible, to find the necessary common ground, other than the history of eighty years of being victimized at the hands of the dominant ethnic majority in the minority's own homeland, between the Hungarian minorities and the Slovak, Rumanian, Serb and

---

266   Csaba K. Zoltani and Frank Koszorus, Jr., "group rights defuse tensions" in THE FLETCHER FORUM OF WORLD AFFAIRS, Vol. 20:2, Summer/Fall 1996, p. 143.

Ukrainian majorities in the respective countries to justify the federal arrangement even with the territorial autonomy to solve the minority problem. The majority's desire to hold on, for whatever reasons, to a certain territory inhabited by a minority and a perverse need of the majority to victimize the minority are even less adequate justifications for the maintenance of a unitary form of government and the denial of autonomy.

Thus, ideally, most minority problems should be solved by secession. In fact, however, state borders are still respected far too much and the international order is not yet ready to support separatism, [267] to make full separation a practical proposal, but seems to be moving in a direction to accept and support demands at least for minority autonomy.

The federal or a similar system would be ideal in providing the different degrees of autonomy. In larger regions with overwhelming minority presence the district could have full territorial autonomy. On the other hand, smaller minority populated regions along the border of neighboring countries could be given special rights to communicate and cooperate with their brethren across the border. Deliberate efforts of harassment, like when one has to wait up to 10 hours at a legal border crossing to visit a relative in the next village that is visible across the border[268] is not only undue harassment, but is a cause for demands of separation from the current sovereign in order to join the neighboring one. In some cases crossing the Rumanian border to visit relatives in a town just across the border was more complicated than crossing the famous Berlin Wall. As Dr. Peeters explains, the countries surrounding Hungary object to crossfrontier co-operation. The real reason seems to be that they see it as an effective tool to keep the minority on the defensive, and make them feel happy and grateful if and when the majority makes border crossing somewhat less onerous.

In this case a form of spiritualization of the borders, along with appropriate forms of autonomy or home rule, might make sense and eliminate, or at least lessen the conflict and the demand for separation. In these cases the minimum provisions for autonomy laws that one should expect would be, in addition to free border crossing to visit relatives and to attend religious services, permission to attend schools across the border and accepting the diplomas

---

267   unlike after World War One when the Trianon Treaties were drawn up; it would be impossible to draw the boundaries of Hungary where they were drawn in Trianon today, with so much emphasis on human rights and national self-determination.
268   Zoltani and Koszorus, p. 144.

earned in a neighboring country. Zoltani and Koszorus also refer to a proposal by Halperin for "trans-state self-determination"[269]

The problem of trans-state self-determination of Hungarian communities has become a much more complicated issue with NATO and eventual European Community (EC) membership for Hungary. It seems that all of Hungary's neighboring states with sizable Hungarian communities will remain outside of NATO and the EC, and the EC membership requires more stringent border controls as the frontiers of EC are extended to the East.

Such stringent controls would have a negative effect on this trans-state self-determination unless some accommodation was made to exempt ethnic Hungarian who are nationals of surrounding non-NATO or EC countries. Grant them either dual citizenship or give them special visa to make it easier to cross the borders back and forth, with the full co-operation of their respective states.

To summarize, the idea of autonomy, with different degrees of self government, from autonomous regions in a federal system to shared autonomy, home rule and personal autonomy, has been used successfully in a number of situations where ethnic or religious minorities have lived together with a majority in one country under one sovereign rule, as will be shown in the next chapter. In the countries in East Central Europe, however, the hatred against the minorities (not only Hungarians but anything foreign, as we have seen from the captured Vatra Romanesca document) and subsequent mutual distrust has reached such high proportions that any proposal would, and in fact, has aroused unjustified suspicions and fears on both sides. Therefore, it is felt by this author that an unusual step should be taken: provisional autonomy,[270] which would be reviewed after a few years.

Thus, it is suggested that when autonomy will be seriously discussed and negotiated, they should consider various forms of autonomy within the current respective states, with a time limit of five to ten years to see if it works, i.e., if it would solve the minority problems. This cooling off period would give a chance for the two sides to have some serious thinking and decision making concerning the future of the state and to move toward more genuine and effective democracy to eventually achieve "democratic governance." After five years the minority should be given a choice to determine their own future, in the spirit of true national self-determination, with the following two to four choices:

---

269   Ibid., p. 138; cf. M. H. Halperin, D. H. Scheffer, and P. L. Small, SELF-DETERMINATION IN THE NEW WORLD ORDER (Washington, DC:P Carnegie Endowment for International Peace, 1992).

270 According to recent reports a provisional solution has been suggested in the Kosovo conflict also.

1. keep and/or improve the autonomous arrangement for another five or ten years,

2. become independent, or

3. federate with a neighbor country whose ethnic background is the same, i.e. for the Hungarians it would be Hungary, or the Serbs in Eastern Croatia or Bosnia it would be Serbia, and so on.

4. abandon autonomy and freely return to a unitary form of government under the same sovereign.

During the trial period the autonomous regional governments and minority communities with home rule should have the right to refuse new settlers who would upset the ethnic balance, but should allow natural migration, i.e., allow people of different ethnic background to emigrate, and people of the same ethnic background to immigrate into the autonomous regions. Thus, at the end of the five year period the ethnic composition of both the autonomous region and the rest of the country could become more homogeneous by peaceful and free, voluntary migration. If they would decide to keep autonomy, perhaps every ten years thereafter, the same questions could be put up for referendum. Such an arrangement would provide an incentive for the majority to develop tolerance and to accept accommodation as a desirable form of pluralism and democratic governance.

Given the conservative nature of human beings, if their treatment by the majority people and protection by the government is satisfactory, I would expect that in a free referendum many, perhaps the majority of the minority group would vote to continue the autonomous arrangement and stay in the state they will have been used to, rather than become independent state or enter a new federation with their brethren across the border. Also, even if the situation will not be perfect in five or ten years, since human beings are basically conservative, they often prefer the bad they know to the uncertain, potentially worse future. Therefore, given a halfway decent effort from the majority population to accept peaceful accommodation instead of forcing assimilation, the minority would probably decide freely to remain within the state. Thus, this arrangement would be a good test of the sincerity and the ability of the anti-minority, chauvinistic majority groups to demonstrate that they can live with democratic rules and respect the minority's rights. In a sense, the outcome of the referendum would be determined by the treatment of the minorities by the majorities, so, the region's and the country's future would be in the majority's hands.

Also, there might there be strong family and perhaps economic ties between minority population and the rest of the country to justify an experiment giving the federal system a chance for a five or ten year period as proposed.

Last but not least, as Zoltani and Koszorus point out in connection with the Swiss arrangement that although concessions are mutual, they fall more heavily on the part of the majority, as can be expected, "but it provides the means for preserving a multiethnic state by ensuring that all have a stake in its future."[271] In other words, the choice for the majority is either concessions, or facing continued demands for separation, and perhaps the eventual fracturing of the multiethnic state. Why should the majority make more concessions? Because they are in the better, more privileged position, and they have more to concede and more to gain by making concessions than the minority that is being oppressed already!

If at the end of the period the ties prove too weak to sustain a federal union, the region should have an option to separate, or if the ties are sufficient to justify a federal arrangement in the eyes of the people, the only ones who can make the decision in a referendum, then the federation would stay! As for the entire country, putting the minority problem behind them would allow the people and the government to concentrate on economic development and the re-building of their country that invariably has been devastated by almost a half century of communist rule. So, instead of leading to secession, granting autonomy could be the first step toward democratic governance.

World Government, Sovereignty and

Minority Rights on Collision Course

Sovereignty has been gradually weakened by the growing concern about human and minority rights, as has been discussed already. U.S. Supreme Court Justice William Douglas, after mentioning several international agencies that work in areas formerly reserved to sovereign states, proclaimed in 1961:

> (T)he tools with which we can evolve a "rule of law" into a more mature system are at hand. There is only the will to use them. Why do nations hold back? Why are we not willing to take the lead in inaugurating a truly golden age of international law? We could, I think, do it, if we asserted the moral leadership of which we so often boast. We need more commitment and less lip service. World opinion is ready to be marshaled....World opinion on the side of a "rule of law" is powerful. Those who were forced to vote against it

---

271 Ibid., p. 138.

would lose prestige and influence. This force of world opinion must be mobilized.[272]

If world opinion was on the side of rule of law in 1961, it should be much more supportive after three and a half decades of frustration in the Middle East, the violent break up of Yugoslavia, ethnic cleansing and the continued maltreatment of minorities in several Central European countries, and the frustrating experience in Bosnia and Kosovo, where foreign troops are needed to maintain a fragile peace, not to mention the ethnic violence in Africa and Asia.

It is beyond the scope of this essay to discuss world government or international law in detail. It should be pointed out however that it would be easier to obtain majority support now for laws that are designed to prohibit and prevent conflict and violence. In other words, it would be easier to support an international organizing principle that Laszlo talks about than an actual government that would try to govern, with a single law, all the nations and peoples of the Earth as some early advocates of world government[273] seem to have suggested. World government will be acceptable only, if it becomes a "hinderer of hindrances," as the 16th century Levelers in England, corresponding to modern day libertarians, suggested as the only role of government.

Justice Douglas also quotes, with seeming approval, or at least as something that is worth consideration, Rosco Pound, who "observed in a chapter in Northrops Ideological Differences and World Order, 'all states need not be merged in a great world state, in which their personality is lost, in order that their conduct may be inquired into and ordered by authority of a world legal order'."[274]

World peace may, indeed, require a world legal system. But how individual nations and peoples conduct their lives, as long as they leave each other alone and do not threaten certain international standards of behavior, should be left up, to the individual states and their, hopefully democratically elected, governments. Under world government we should not exchange minority self-determination, or even majority self-determination for collective, global determination. In a truly democratic world order both the homogeneous states, and the dominant majorities along with ethnic minorities in heterogeneous states, are entitled to self-determination that a world government might jeopardize.

---

272 Ibid., pp. 27-8.
273 E.g. Arthur M. Schlesinger, above.
274 Douglas, p. 5.

As it has been pointed out above, the maltreatment of minorities has been deemed by both experts and several international organizations to be a potential threat to international order, therefore, it should be considered a valid subject for international law, inspection, and action, if the international organizations, like the UN, or the EC is to act as a "hinderer of hindrances," i.e., to protect peace from the would be aggressors..

Thus, the foregoing discussion of sovereignty and autonomy is relevant in three ways: First the trend is growing in the direction of the international community supervising the treatment of minorities, invading areas that traditionally had been considered domestic matters of a sovereign state. Second, since no other solution seems to work, the recommendation stated above calls for autonomy for ethnic groups within the state, with sufficient police power to protect and liberate the minority from an oppressive majority and possible efforts of ethnic cleansing. Third, as discussed above, according to Ervin Laszlo of the Club of Rome, world peace can be based only on a pluralistic basis, where, regardless of necessary political borders, culturally diverse groups, both in the majority and in minority, have sufficient autonomy to govern themselves and to maintain their ethnic or religious identity.

VI.

AUTONOMY IN PRACTICE

Autonomy and Collective Rights in Historic Hungary

Hungarians had been in both majority and minority position within the state. In the Austro-Hungarian dual monarchy Hungarians were treated by Austria as a minority, often oppressed and exploited just as any minority has been in history. At the same time, Hungary had her own minorities to deal with. So, studying Hungarian history, one had to acquire an awareness of being on both sides of the power relationship.

Jozsa Hevizi wrote an excellent essay about the role, position, and treatment of minorities in historic Hungary. Hevizi, in this privately published paper,[275] gives a challenging interpretation and an interesting history of autonomy for religious and ethnic groups (the two often coincided, since some ethnic groups also had their own religion different from that of the majority) in Hungary.

Hevizi starts out with a statement that sounds like a truism and one that surprises no one: "In several countries regional autonomy has been seen as fundamentally threatening to the concept of the unitary state." Of course, regional autonomy does weaken the dominant role of the majority and the unitary nature of the state. But as her study shows, there are compensating benefits for the loss of the unitary state. The unitary nature of the state has no particular value in itself, in fact, at times the unitary state as a goal can be an obstacle to peace and normal development. In some states defending the unitary form is a disguise for maintaining majority dictatorship. On the other hand, "it is anachronistic to suggest that the realization of regional autonomy in the age of economic integration is necessarily a prelude to full separation."[276] The point is illustrated with examples from Western Europe where autonomy does not threaten the integrity of the state. Such examples

---

275 Jozsa Hevizi, "Regional and ecclesiastical autonomy as an expression of collective rights in historic Hungary" (Budapest: Bird's Eye, 1996; ISBN 963047431X).
276 Ibid., p. 8.

include, as we shall see, the autonomies of various degrees in South Tyrol, Switzerland, Belgium, Alsace-Lorraine, in Finland for the Swedes, etc.[277]

The work proves that to run a multi-ethnic state requires an ability that the Hungarians have developed, following Saint Stephen's warning in his Admonitions to his son, Prince Emeric (Imre) about the advantages of having a multi-cultured and multi-ethnic state,[278] and conversely, granting autonomy judiciously made it possible for Hungary to survive a thousands years, despite her multi-ethnic population. There was a centuries old conflict within the Austro-Hungarian empire between the Hapsburg kings and the Hungarian nation. It was the Vienna Court's instigation, with the full support of the assassinated Crown Prince Ferdinand, of Hungary's minorities against the Hungarian state that created the fatal conflict with the nationalities, leading to the dismemberment of Hungary.

Hevizi explains that during the Middle Ages society was conceived of as a collection of groups, and individual members of the group were accorded rights based on their group affiliation. Within the group there were hierarchies, but to the outsiders all members of the group were more or less equal: there were no minorities as the term is used today. In those days "minority" was purely a statistical term without social and political connotations. There was only diversity without any ethnic discrimination. The discrimination that existed was based on the hierarchical structure of society that existed throughout Europe. This situation is well summarized by Kalman Benda:

> The Hungarian state did not make an issue of language usage: in local government they used the language of the group in the area, and in the Orthodox liturgy also preserved the popular language. Ethnic differences did not result in disadvantage and did not result in conflicts in the public arena. The population did not diversify based on ethnicity but on social privileges. The governing was in the hands of the nobility that included a good number of non-Hungarians, and in the 90% underprivileged population we finds together the Hungarian and non-Hungarian peasantry and serfs....

> Had it been different, had the Hungarians attempted a policy of assimilation when the rule was in Hungarian hands and Hungarians constituted about 80% of the population, the non-Hungarians would have assimilated.[279]

---

277 Idem.
278 Ibid., p. 10.
279 Samu, Introduction, p. 5-6.

148

If the feudal system lasted longer in Hungary than in western Europe, it was probably because the traditional order became part of the nation's self-defense against the Hapsburg oppression.

But under the influence of the slogans of the French Revolution the individual became viewed as the depository of all rights, thus, the old framework was shattered and the members of certain groups suddenly found themselves in a minority role. Sociologists distinguish between the two kinds of societies by calling them Gemellshaft and Gesellshaft, or organic and mechanistic societies, respectively. In the organic societies people were bound together with all kinds of social ties and traditions that does not exist in the mechanistic, urbanized society. While in the West the disadvantages of the new kind of society were offset or at least mitigated by economic prosperity, in the more backward countries of Central Europe and other regions of the world, economic stagnation, resulting from a pre-occupation with ethnic differences, prevented the development of peaceful accommodation between the ethnic groups, creating a catch 22 type situation.

According to Hevizi,

> The modern state, thus, replaced group privileges with individual rights and failed to recognize the limited assertion of rights of individuals who belong to a minority ethnic group when the latter had lost its ability to defend its interest by the weakening of its special institutions. The minority citizen became a tax-payer, yet did not secure the same rights in return for his taxes as members of the majority group to whom these rights were automatically granted because they held the levers of power. The interests of a member of a minority group coincide with those of the majority to an extent, yet, they diverge when the use of a minority tongue in schools is affected and the overall preservation of his own ethnic identity is imperiled.[280]

This is one of the most eloquent statements justifying minority autonomy that I have ever read! Also, it states the two conditions to justify the federal system: sufficient common ground and interest to justify unity, and sufficient diversity to justify autonomy! This is what Hungarians did understand, and the rulers along with the peoples of the newly created states after Trianon do not understand! This is the principle that the Hungarian born Ervin Laszlo of the Club of Rome is urging as the foundation of a new World Order, as it was quoted above! Laszlo seeks to return to the good old days when group rights were respected, and discrimination was largely unknown in Western

---

280 Ibid., p. 6.

149

societies. It is hoped that the statesmen deciding the future of the world for the 21st century will all read Hevizi's work as required reading. It is a veritable primer of a flexible treatment of minorities. It shows how Hungary was always able to be flexible and successful in maintaining a dynamic balance between the interests of the central government, mainly in the field of defense, and the needs of the minorities in taxation, religion, economic conditions and language education.

Throughout Hungary's history, beginning with the Szekely's (Szeklers) who had joined forces with the Hungarians even before they both have settled in the present day Hungary in 896, minorities had enjoyed considerable autonomy. The Hungarian nation has occupied the central regions of the Carpathian Basin, while the Szeklers occupied the Easternmost part of Transylvania. The Hungarian kings have granted regional autonomy to the Szeklers from the beginning.[281]

As other groups migrated to Hungary, like the Besenyo-s (Pechenegs),[282] between the 10th and 12th centuries, the Kun-s (Cumans) and the Jasz-s (Jazygians)[283] in the 13th century, and the Saxons in two waves in the 12th and 13th centuries,[284] they all received not only autonomy but often special privileges, to attract even more settlers to the sparsely populated country.

Similarly, when the neighboring Croat's ruling dynasty died out in 1091, the widow of the last Croatian king requested King Laszlo of Hungary to govern Croatia, the country's separate entity was preserved and the two governments had never merged![285]

Hungary's other minorities received their autonomy and privileges under another mechanism: religious tolerance and ecclesiastic autonomy. The Rumanians[286] and the Serbs[287], although they arrived into Hungary at different times and resided in different areas, had much in common. They both brought with them the Orthodox faith and as such enjoyed numerous privileges: they were independent of the Roman Catholic hierarchy, were allowed the use of their language in both the liturgy and education, while the Rumanian Uniate Church (that remained loyal to the Pope) had enjoyed the same privileges as the Catholic Church. Hungarians provided the Rumanian Orthodox Church with bibles and textbooks in Rumanian language. The

---

281 Ibid., pp. 11-13.
282 Ibid., pp. 13-14.
283 Ibid., pp. 14-16.
284 Ibid., pp. 16-21.
285 Ibid., pp. 21-22.
286 Ibid., pp. 26-31.
287 Ibid., pp. 31-34.

leaders of the Rumanian nationalist movement between 1848 and 1867 all came from the clergy of the two Rumanian Churches.

After 1868, during the most crucial era of the upsurge of nationalism, the Orthodox Church also had a distinct advantage over the Catholics. While the Catholic bishops were appointed, the Orthodox bishops were elected by their own nationalistic clergy. In this and many other ways Rumanians were the beneficiaries of reverse discrimination at the expense of the Catholic or Protestant Hungarians. Also, the Hungarian Diet in 1868 gave the status of national church to the Rumanian Orthodox Church. They had also received state grants from moneys collected from Catholic and other sources to cover most of their expenses.

Thus, in Rumanian villages, "shielded by their Church," Rumanian became the official language and the language of all instruction. Hungarian, if taught at all before it was made a requirement in 1907, provoking a great furor, was taught as a second language a few hours a week. In exchange, schooling became free of charge and the teachers received increased salaries. All official and school records were in Rumanian, names of places were unified for postal use, but otherwise Rumanian names could be used and family names were never changed.

The Serbs also obtained special privileges from the Hapsburg rulers and in the 18th century they have enjoyed more privileges than the Hungarian serfs. Little wonder that most Serbs had fought on the Hapsburg side against the Hungarians in the 1703-1711 Rákoczy War of Liberty. By this time they had enjoyed de facto ecclesiastic autonomy over religious, educational, language and cultural matters and quasi regional autonomy in the frontier region, being removed from the authority of the Hungarian state and were direct under Vienna's rule. Although the Hapsburgs had taken back some privileges on account of aggressive proselytizing by the Orthodox Church, they were still in a favored position. Yet, the Orthodox synod was not satisfied: in 1790 they demanded political reforms, including full regional autonomy. The same demands were reiterated in 1848. After the Agreement of 1867, when some of Hungary's sovereign rights were restored to the Hungarian Parliament, in 1868 the Rumanian Orthodox Church and the Serbs were granted full authority over education and textbook selection or recommendation, and in Serbian elementary schools the language of instruction was Serbian.

As for the economic condition, both nationalities have enjoyed equal protection with Hungarians, they had numerous banks, and were well represented among the landholders.

The situation of the Slovaks[288] was quite different. Although some of their ancestors had lived in the Carpathian basin when the Hungarians arrived at the end of the 9th century, others have migrated to the area they presently occupy from Bohemia, Moravia and Poland at the invitation of King Bela IV who gave them various concessions following the devastating Tartar invasion in the 13th century, and again many came after the Turkish occupation of Hungary ended centuries later.

The Slovak residents of Hungary who came before the Reformation were mostly Catholic and they, unlike the other nationalities already discussed, have not acquired special privileges. The new-comers, however, were granted the freedom to practice the Lutheran faith, and use their own language. It was important to note that through their religious affiliation the Slovaks have developed close ties with the Czechs. On the other hand, during the Counter-reformation movement to counter the Lutheran influence, Cardinal Pazmany of Hungary made important concession to the Slovak Catholics in the use of the Slovak language in Catholic liturgy and in the education of Slovak priests. This greatly promoted the spread of the Slovak language and its development as a literary language, and contributed to the development of the Slovak intelligentsia and the Slovak nationalist movement first in Pest, Hungary, then in Pozsony (Bratislava).

In 1848 the Slovaks have petitioned the Emperor demanding territorial autonomy directly under Vienna. The demand was reiterated in 1881, demanding a clearly defined Slovak region in Northern Hungary. It seems the Slovak intelligentsia always had an anti-Hungarian and pro Slav and Russian attitude and although only 7% of Slovaks in the Northern region spoke any Hungarian around the turn of the century, they had a fear of losing their Slav identity.

It greatly strengthened the position of the minorities in the Monarchy that the Slovak, Serb and Rumanian nationalist had frequent meetings after 1893 to coordinate their demands. The coordination of these demands along with the publication of inflammatory manifestos and anti-Hungarian sentiments created a fear of separatism in the Hungarian government and led to some ineffective counter measures and restrictions on the minorities.

Hevizi finally discusses briefly the Ruthenians[289] inhabiting the north-eastern part of Hungary, whose ethnicity is mixed although there is a Ruthenian language. There is also a sizable Hungarian population in Ruthenia. They settled in the region gradually, between the 13th and 17th centuries. Over the centuries they have also received numerous privileges from various kings

---

288 Ibid., pp. 34-37.
289 Ibid., pp. 38-41.

152

regarding the payment of the tithe. Their religion was Orthodox, and later, under pressure from Vienna, many changed to the pro-western Uniate church. In addition, they were subject not only to Slovak pressure to use Slovak language but also from the Russian Orthodox Church. They were more pro-Hungarian, yet, in the spring of 1848 they demanded the establishment of a special Ruthenian Crown Province. But since they were fighting on the Hungarian side during the uprising, they were punished by Vienna and some 30 cartful of Ruthenian prisoners were carried off to Austrian prisons. Of all the regions of Hungary this region seems to have been the poorest.

This study by Hevizi has been discussed in some detail to give the reader an idea of the complexities of the ethnic situation in the Carpathian Basin. There are two especially interesting conclusions that can be drawn from the above.

Hevizi's first conclusion is that these demands did not come from the people who had enjoyed many privileges, at times more than what the Hungarians themselves had enjoyed. The demand for autonomy and eventual separation came from politically motivated radical intellectuals who did it out of national pride and conviction, or personal desire for power, or under the influence of foreign, often Pan-Slav interests.[290] This point is well illustrated by the fact that Ferdinand was assassinated not by a dissatisfied Bosnian, but a radical Serb, who was dissatisfied with the promise of more political influence for Serbia within the Monarchy, and actually wanted to prevent an autonomous Serbia and to promote Pan-Slav interests under Russian influence.

Second, as Hevizi has pointed out, all the countries with Hungarian minorities now oppose regional autonomy, yet, when the shoe was on the other foot, and they had enjoyed considerable ecclesiastic privileges, autonomy was one of their main demands! If autonomy was desirable and justifiable for the minorities then, why do the same groups oppose it now for the truly oppressed Hungarians who are not protected even by similar ecclesiastic privileges?

In fact, the Hungarian Catholics in Slovakia are treated as second class citizens and are deprived even by their own Church of their rights under Canon Law to liturgy and the sacraments in their native language. While the minority churches throughout history, including the United States, acted as shields of nationality rights, allowing their language and culture to flourish, now the Slovak Catholic Church and hierarchy is one of the main supporters of forced assimilation of the more than half million Hungarian Catholics in Slovakia, disregarding both Canon Law and the strong tradition and statements of the popes supporting linguistic autonomy! Bishop Wright of

---

290 Hevizi, p. 7.

153

Worcester, Mass. Wrote in 1956, based on the teachings of Pope Leo XIII that

> ... those invested with the civil sovereignty of the State have the obligation to respect the characteristic good of any national group which may, lacking political autonomy, exist within the confines of their administrative jurisdiction, an obligation to which there exists on the part of the national community thus subordinated a corresponding right to demand of the civil order respect for its patriotic heritage....

> ...Hence language rights are to be given the favor of the law not merely as protecting a people's heritage, but as being the medium of those highest elements of it which are identified with the religious traditions of one's ancestors. At least since the Lateran Council (215) ... it has been the explicit policy of the Church, reflecting its own respect for national usages, in any State or diocese in which there is a mixed population, to appoint priests to minister to each national group in its language and according to its own rites.[291]

The Concordat that the Holy See concluded with Italy also provides that in addition to Italian, Church communications, including church bulletins, could be published in minority languages and clergy should be provided to administer to the faithful in their native tongues.[292]

It is ironic that of the two kinds of nationalism distinguished by His Holiness Pope Pius XI, "fair and moderate nationalism, which is the breeding ground of many virtues," and "exaggerated nationalism, ... a veritable curse," the Slovak Catholic Church seems to be on the side of the "veritable curse."

Autonomy in Other Countries

The 1996 GROLIER Multimedia Encyclopedia under Autonomy lists several cases on political and governmental autonomy, from Argentina to Yugoslavia. Some of them are historic, others had existed in recent history, and some political or linguistic autonomies are still in existence today. Also, some of them are cities or city states, other regions and parts of a country, but the point is that regional autonomy is not a rare case or a modern invention.

---

291 Most Reverend John J. Wright, D.D. NATIONAL PATRIOTISM IN PAPAL TEACHING (Westminster, MD: The Newman Press, 1956) pp. 143, 145.
292 Ibid., p. 145.

In Belgium, for example,

> (F)or many years the Flemish and Walloon (French-speaking) communities were in conflict over whether French or Dutch should be used in the schools, in the courts, for business, and for administration. French, being the language of the upper classes, had traditionally been dominant, a situation greatly resented by Dutch-speakers. In 1966 the country was divided into four linguistic areas. Dutch, which in Belgium includes the Flemish, Brabant, and Limburg dialects, became the official language north of a line running from east to west just south of Brussels. French, which in Belgium includes the Picardic, Walloon, and Lorraine dialects, became official south of the line. German became official in the Eastern Cantons, and the Brussels area was designated as bilingual. Each of the three language communities has autonomy in its own linguistic region over cultural affairs, language use, local social issues, and in national and international cultural relations.[293]

While Belgium is a small country, India, one of the world's largest countries, also has a federal system.

> India gained its independence from the British on Aug. 15, 1947, at which time two predominantly Muslim regions in the northwestern and northeastern corners of the subcontinent became the separate state of Pakistan. In 1956 the map of India was largely redrawn as provisions were made for reorganization of the states along linguistic lines, with the goal of preserving regional cultures and aspirations. A policy of "democratic decentralization" provides states with a large measure of self-government. Thus, the modern country of India is a union of 25 states and 7 union territories.[294]

Slovakia is also listed under Autonomy, and it is ironic that "(I)n its Memorandum of 1861, the Slovak National party of Bishop Stefan Moyses, one of Slovakia's national heroes petitioned Emperor Francis Joseph to grant the Slovaks territorial, linguistic and political rights, but to no avail,"[295] yet, when Hungarians request similar autonomy in Slovakia now, it is similarly "to no avail." How fast people forget when the shoe is on the other foot!

Putting majorities in ethnically heterogeneous countries at ease is very important, because they have a fear (or at least, use fear as an excuse for

---

293 "Belgium," in 1996 GROLIER MULTIMEDIA ENCYCLOPEDIA. Please note that in this and several subsequent quotes from GROLIER irrelevant material has been omitted, without changing the meaning or context of the material.
294 "India," Ibid.
295 "Slovakia," Ibid.

continued domination of minorities) of instability and eventual secession, loss of territory. Rudolf Chmel, a Slovak nationalist politician, as an invited speaker at a Budapest forum discussing Autonomy, unabashedly expressed this excuse: "(W)hen a Slovak politician (irrespective of his or her political beliefs and affiliations) hears the word autonomy, he or she automatically suspects a source of danger."[296] It is hoped that the following diverse examples of autonomy will dispel most of these irrational fears.

Chmer seems to suggest that the problem with autonomy is that it may lead to border changes:

> The question of borders is another sore issue and is not only a matter of minority but of international importance. It would be essential to find a solution that could be reassuring for both sides. I do not think we should treat the minority issue and the border issue as one single question, but unfortunately, they cannot be completely separated. If we could solve the border issue in a reassuring way, in accordance with the international agreements in force, I am sure we could have greater prospects of finding a better solution in the minority issue as well.[297]

So, he wants Hungary give guarantees of border stability "in accordance with the international agreements in force" in good faith, but they refuse to honor the same international agreements in force regarding minority rights in good faith. Autonomy would be a middle ground, and at the same time, it would de-fuse the border issue, since the minority issue, which fuels the border issue, would be eliminated. So Chmer and his nationalist friends face the alternative: autonomy now or continued demands and eventual border changes later. To eliminate the border issue, they should be willing to discuss and grant autonomy. To alleviate their fear of the word autonomy, let us start with an examination of one of the most extreme and most successful cases on record.

The Aaland Islands and the Majority's Fears

The Aaland Islands are a Swedish speaking autonomous province of Finland with a population of about twenty five thousand. Aaland Islands is first in alphabetical order, but it is discussed first because it shows how much

296   Rudolf Chmel, "A Debate with Empathy," in Vilmos Agoston, ed., AUTONOMY--Challenge and/or solution. Lectures held at the Conference on Autonomy, organized by the Hungarian Alliance of Free Democrats, the Dutch Liberal Party, and the German Friedrich Naumann Foundation; November 18-20, 1993 (Buffalo-Toronto: Matthias Corvinus Publishing Co., 1995) p. 88.
297 Ibid., p. 90.

autonomy can be provided without breaking the country in two, if there is trust, good will, patience and cooperation on both sides. Although some of their rights and practices might sound radical, and nobody would expect that the Aaland situation would be copied for any new autonomous region in Central Europe. While the Aaland Islands autonomy could not be used as a model in most minority situations,[298] it could at least be a starting point in discussions and negotiations for new autonomous regions in other multi-cultural countries not only in Central Europe but perhaps in other parts of the world.

Let us start the analysis of the Aaland Islands situation with a brief historical review.[299] Beginning in the 12th century, Sweden gradually conquered the area of today's Finland, consolidating its authority in the 16th century. During the 18th century a growing separatist movement in Finland demanded independence. As a result of the war of 1808-09, Sweden surrendered Finland to Russia. Finland became an autonomous grand duchy with the czar assuming the title grand duke of Finland. The Russian governor-general represented the supreme executive power, and Finland was allowed to retain its old constitution. It had its own parliament, government, civil service, law and courts, postal services, army (until 1904), and currency. In 1906 the Finnish diet was replaced by the unicameral parliament, and simultaneously universal suffrage was adopted.

At times, strong attempts were made to Russianize Finland, provoking a growing desire for complete independence. After the Russian Revolution of November 1917, Finland declared its independence on Dec. 6, 1917. Civil war broke out in 1918, with Soviet-supported Communist troops fighting German-supported non-Communists, the latter led by Carl Gustaf Emil MANNHEIM. In 1920 peace was concluded with the USSR following a territorial war over KARELIA, but relations between the two countries remained cool.

Aaland Islands were contested by Sweden on linguistic grounds when Finland became independent in 1920, and Finland claimed the Islands for "historical and geographical reasons." The League of Nations, in one its more successful decisions, left Aaland under the sovereignty of Finland, as

---

298 Lauri Hannikkainen, CULTURAL AND EDUCATIONAL RIGHTS IN THE AALAND ISLANDS. An Analysis in International Law. Publication No 5, of The Advisory Board for International Human Rights (Helsinki, 1992) p. 67. The booklet contains a detailed analysis of the situation, and the complete English text of the ACT ON THE AUTONOMY OF AALAND, 16 August, 1991/1144.
299 The following two paragraphs are based on "Finland" in 1996 GROLIER MULTIMEDIA ENCYCLOPEDIA

an autonomous province, requiring respect for the Swedish character of the Island population and their culture.

The first acts of autonomy (1920 and 1922) have been greatly modified and modernized by the 1951 Act and last time by the 1991 Act, each subsequent act strengthening the autonomy and the Swedish character of the islanders. Each act had been negotiated and mutually accepted by both the Finnish Parliament and the Aaland Provincial Parliament (the new official translation of the 1991 Act uses the term Aaland Legislative Assembly, dropping the term "Provincial"). The federal status of Aaland is regulated by the 1991 Act, providing in Chapter 4 detailed lists of sovereign powers exercised by Aaland, and in Chapter 5 for the sovereign powers to be exercised by the State, along with shared powers and delegated powers of the Aaland Legislature.

It should also be noted that Aaland Islands is a neutral and demilitarized territory, with no military obligation of its residents in the Finnish Armed Forces, but they may be required to serve in other capacity instead of military service. The Islands' neutral status is also protected by international agreements.

The current law establishes Aaland as a monolingual (Swedish) province: the use of Finnish language is not required and most islanders do not speak Finnish. Instruction in all schools on the Islands is in Swedish, while all pupils in Finnish schools in Finland must study Swedish![300] The required second language on the Islands is English, and Finnish is available as an elective course. But with limited opportunity to practice, they do not learn enough to be able to use Finnish for communication.[301] Since Aaland, due to the small size of its population, does not have its own university, degrees earned in Iceland, Norway, Sweden or Denmark, in addition to Finland, are accepted when such requirement exists.

A related requirement in the current law governing gaining the right to domicile is that the immigrant/applicant have a working knowledge of Swedish. Given the fact that all Finnish schools teach Swedish as a required course, according to the author of the study, this is not an unreasonable or impossible requirement, and is consistent with the principle that the Swedish

---

300 Ibid., p. 15. It should be noted that before Finland became occupied by Russia, which occupation ended with Finnish independence, Finland had been a territory of Sweden and the official language was Swedish. But the study of Swedish could also be justified because of Finland's close economic ties to Sweden. Imagine all students in Transylvania or Slovakia studying Hungarian, because both were at one time Hungarian territory, and because of the importance of economic ties with Hungary, while Hungarian students would not study Rumanian or Slovakian!

301 Ibid., p. 31.

character of the Islands should be maintained and guaranteed by the Finnish state.[302] It should be noted, that the Swedish and Finnish peoples are recognized as having different ethnic origin.[303]

The Aaland Islands have lively cultural life with festivals, art exhibits, a number of excellent museums,[304] and its own flag, with blue, yellow and red colors. The Aaland flag flies daily on school buildings and government offices, and on ships that are registered in Aaland. Since 1992 Aaland issues its own passport. The Aaland Island's Legislature also has the power to levy "additional tax on income" and other taxes for Aaland and municipal tax for municipalities.

There had been considerable discussion, and even conflict, over the language of television when it was first introduced, but now both channels are completely Swedish, just as five of the Island's six radio stations. The two Island newspapers are Swedish, of course, and while they accept advertising and announcements in German or English, they refuse anything but obituaries in Finnish. And this is all under Finnish sovereignty!

The Finnish author of the study summarizes the value and applicability of the Aaland model of autonomy in his concluding paragraph:

> How well would the Aaland model--autonomy, legal safeguards for its national character and demilitarization--suit other islands and minority territories? It seems that autonomy and demilitarization could be suitable and welcome for many other islands and ethnic territories. On the other hand, the safeguards for the national character of the Aaland Islands is so stringent that they can hardly serve as a generally suitable model for other minority territories.[305]

The Rhaetians in Switzerland

Michael Kosztarab, a "Hungarian-American" entomologist from Transylvania, in his autobiography calls the attention of the Rumanian

---

302 "To conclude (this chapter), the requirement that Finnish speaking residents in the Aaland Islands have an adequate knowledge of Swedish as a condition of the right of domicile has a legitimate aim, is reasonable, and there is proportionality between the means employed and the aim sought. The requirement is relatively mild but in the long run it may be an important guarantee for the preservation of the Swedish character of the Aaland Islands " See Ibid., p. 56.
303 Ibid., p. 19. It should also be mentioned that Hungarians, Slovaks and Rumanians also are recognized as having different ethnic origin.
304 the Aaland Museum won the Council of Europe award for the best kept museum in 1982; p. 17.
305 Ibid., p. 67.

government, "striving toward integration into the European Community,"[306] to the Swiss example, so they could meet the ethnic and minority entry requirements of the EC.

A good example for the Romanian government, in treating their ethnic minorities, is provided by Switzerland with regard to the Rhaetian ethnic minority.[307] These people, less than 1% of the Swiss population, speak Romansch, an ancient language derived from vernacular Latin. Most of the Rhaetians live in the mountainous Canton of Graubünden. The Census of 1970 listed only 50,339 people who spoke the Romansh language in all Switzerland. But already in 1938 the Swiss Federal Constitution had been amended to include Romansch as one of the four national languages, and in the Canton of Graubünden, where 23.4% of the population spoke Romansch in 1970, it is one of the three official languages. In Graubünden, the civil servants are required to master at least two of the three official languages of Switzerland, plus Romansch. In the district where Romansch is the principal language, it is also the medium of instruction in the primary schools. Romansch is taught at four Swiss universities and their teachers are trained at Chur.

Laws and regulations are published in Romansch at Federal expense. Official business can be transacted in Romansch, and defendants have the right to be tried in their own language. Communities with bi-national population have the right to use Romansch, together with German, on place names and street signs. The 1990 pogrom in Tirgu Mures against the Hungarians started because a local pharmacy put up a bi-lingual sign "Farmacie-Patika" in Romanian and Hungarian. The city until recently had been inhabited by a Hungarian-speaking majority.

The Romansch language benefits from federal subsidies, including publication of textbooks and other cultural means. Radio programs of Studio Zurich since 1972 include daily news bulletins and weekly features broadcast in Romansch, and the Romansch Radio Corporation has its own program. Since 1963, Swiss television has been broadcasting in Romansch, and in 1976 began the inclusion of thrice weekly current affairs program, with other weekly features.

---

306 Michael Kosztarab, TRANSYLVANIAN ROOTS, The True Life Adventures of a Hungarian-American (Blacksburg, VA: Pocahontas Press, Inc., 1997) p.199.
307 see M. Stephens, LINGUISTIC MINORITIES IN WESTERN EUROPE (Llandysul, Wales: Gomer Press, 1976).

The Rhaetian people are respected by their Federal Government, and are allowed to develop and strengthen their culture as they choose. A proverb much quoted in Graubünden is: "An ounce of Goodwill outweighs a ton of Good Reason" (Stephens).[308]

While the Aaland example illustrates what the FUEN experts refer to as optimum autonomy, protection of the Romansch language and culture provides more than the minimum internal autonomy. It should be noted that both types have successfully prevented calls for secession. On the other hand, forcing the lid on the brewing dissatisfaction with the status quo can lead only to violent explosion, like it has happened in Bosnia.

Gagauzian Autonomy in Moldova

One of the most surprising development in East Central Europe in the 1990's was the granting of autonomy to the some one hundred and fifty thousand strong Gagauz population by the Rumanian speaking majority of the Republic of Moldavia, a former Soviet Republic. The Council of Europe has declared the new constitutional structure "exemplary."

At the same time, it has provoked an angry reaction from the Rumanian government stating that "the (new) law encourages separatism, leads toward a federal arrangement, and fails to protect the rights of the majority of Moldova."[309]

Moldova was coveted by Rumania after the break up of the Soviet Union, to create a Greater Rumania uniting all Rumanian speaking peoples, but in a 1993 referendum 83% of the Moldavians refused to unite. Instead, they even granted autonomy to their own minority, the Gagauz. This establishes a precedent whereby the Rumanian majority of Moldova gave up its right to dominate, oppress and forcefully assimilate a minority. On the other hand, even the post Ceausescu government of Rumania considers a federal arrangement taboo, and would not willingly give up or change her own oppressive minority policies. In their blind hatred the Rumanian response even fails to get the real meaning of the situation. Instead of "encouraging separatism," the solution has put an end to the separatist argument by the Gagauz, and should serve as a precedent for Rumania, if they want to end any Hungarian separatist movement in Transylvania.

The Gagauz people are Orthodox Christian Turks, who escaped the Ottoman Empire during the 19th Century and settled in the southern part of Moldova.

---

308 Kosztarab, Ibid.
309 Quoted in article :Nemzeti Autonom terulet Moldovaban", ("National Autonomy in Moldova") by Csaba Skultery (Budapest); source and date unavailable.

After the break up of the Soviet Union, the Gagauz wanted independence and they were at the brink of a bloody civil war that was averted by a settlement granting wide ranging autonomy to Gagauzia at the end of 1994.

The Introductory Statement to the law expresses good will and tolerance, and emphasizes human rights so eloquently that it could be quoted in every text about autonomy. After defining Gagauzia as an autonomous territorial unit of Moldova and outlining the general terms of their rights, it makes an interesting provision: "(I)n case the status of the Republic of Moldova as an independent state is subject to changes, the people of Gagauzia has the right to external self-determination."[310] In other words, if Moldova would unite with Rumania in the future, Gagauzia is free to become independent: it would not have to join Moldova in a Greater Rumania.

The law also guarantees the right to use Gagauzian language along with the Moldovan and Russian in official capacity within the territory. Local communities with Gagauz majority would comprise the Autonom Territory, and where Gagauz are in a minority, 1/3 of the electorate might demand a referendum about joining the Autonom Territory, retaining their right to secede with another referendum, if the decision turned out to be a mistake. Gagauzia also has a People's Assembly, elected for a two year period in election districts, based on universal, equal, direct, secret and free ballot.

The People's Assembly in addition to setting up the local governmental structure and public administrative system, is competent to adopt local laws in the following spheres:
1. science, culture, education;
2. housing and communal services...;
3. health care, physical culture and sports;
4. local budgetary, financial and fiscal activities;
5. economy and ecology;
6. labor relations and social security.[311]

In addition, the officials of Gagauzia are members of the Executive Branch of Moldova, and there is close, organic relationship between the central government and the territorial government. Article 25 states that "The Republic of Moldova is guarantor of a thorough and unconditional realization of Gagauzia's powers established by the present Law." No minority can expect more (or should expect less!) than provided in this Law.

It is interesting to note that Gagauzia has a great deal more than just language autonomy, while the Rumanian majority and its government refuses

---

310 Law On the Special Legal Status of Gagauzia (Gagauz Yery), December 23, 1994; Art. 1 (4).
311 Ibid., Art. 12 (2).

to consider even free use of Hungarian language in education, without any form of autonomy!

The Basque minority and Catalonia in Spain

There is another case of autonomy in Western Europe where the Basques, once an autonomous people, had to resort to violence and terrorist acts to re-gain at least partial autonomy for the region belonging to Spain.

> The Basques are a people whose homeland is the westernmost part of the Pyrenees Mountains and the immediately surrounding regions. This area comprises four provinces in Spain (Guipuzcoa, Vizcaya, Alava, and Navarra) and three provinces in the department of Pyrenees-Atlantique in France (Soule, Labourd, and Basse-Navarre). Known to the Spanish as vascos and to the French as Basques, the Basques call themselves Euskaldu and their homeland Euskadi. Basque speakers number about 890,000 in Spain and 80,000 in France (1987 est.), but a larger number identify themselves as Basques in each country.
>
> Their language is Basque, or Euskara. Although attempts have been made to link it to ancient Iberian, a Hamito-Semitic group, and Caucasian, its origins remain uncertain. The sound pattern resembles that of Spanish.... In spite of this, and the presence of numerous Latinate loan-words, Basque has maintained its distinctiveness throughout two millennia of external contacts....
>
> Basque is the only language remaining of those spoken in southwestern Europe before the Roman conquest. Since the 10th century, it has gradually been supplanted by Castilian Spanish, and under the Franco regime its use in Spain was outlawed altogether. The ethnic insularity of the Basques, however, has fostered revivals. Attempts are now being made to standardize the orthography.[312]
>
> The origins of the Basques are still a mystery. (Not only is) their language unrelated to any Indo-European language, (and) although they look much like their French and Spanish neighbors, Basques possess the lowest frequency of blood-type B and the highest frequencies of types O and Rh-negative of any population in Europe. They are staunchly Roman Catholic and noted for their distinctive folklore, folk theater, games, music, and a light-footed, acrobatic form of dancing.

---

312 "Basque Language" in GROLIER.

Traditionally a fiercely independent peasant and fishing people, they were known as early as the Middle Ages as skilled boat makers and courageous whale hunters and cod fishermen who often ranged far into the Atlantic. Their characteristic settlement is the isolated farm. The growth of villages is a relatively recent response to increased industry and trade in the Basque region.

A large number of Basques have migrated to North and South America. Historically, this migration has been the result partly of adverse political circumstances (most Basques opposed the Franco regime in Spain) and partly of the inheritance rule known as primogeniture, by which the oldest son inherits the family farm. Younger sons generally have either sought employment in coastal settlements as industrial workers or fishermen, or they have migrated to the New World, frequently finding work as sheepherders.

Isolated in their mountainous homeland, the Basques repulsed incursions by Romans, Germanic tribes, Moors, and others until the 1700s. They lost their autonomy in France after the French Revolution (1789) and in Spain by the early 1800s. A movement for Basque separatism rose in the 19th and 20th centuries, which since 1959 has been led by the militant separatist organization ETA (a Basque acronym for "Basqueland and Freedom"). Spain's Basques were granted home rule in 1980, but ETA violence continued. Basque separatists won about 16% of the vote in regional elections in October 1990.[313]

Currently the relationship between the Basques residing in Spain and the Government of Spain is regulated by THE STATUTE OF AUTONOMY OF THE BASQUE COUNTRY.

The Law establishes the "Autonomous Community within the Spanish State under the name of 'Euskadi' or the Basque Country."[314] The Basque Country consists of three "historic Territories,' with the province of Navarra eligible to join if it so chooses.

The flag of Euskadi (Basque Country), along with the flags of the historic territories are recognized by the Statute. "Euskera", the language of Basque people, has the status of official language in Euskadi. Provisions are made for the teaching, maintaining, researching and further developing the Euskera. But their autonomy extends to far beyond mere linguistic autonomy.

---

313 "Basques" Ibid.
314 STATUTE..., Article 1.

The Basque public authorities, in the areas lying within their jurisdiction, shall:

- Watch over and guarantee the proper exercise of the citizens fundamental rights and duties.

- Lay particular emphasis on a policy aimed at improving living and working conditions.

- Adopt measures that will help to promote higher employment and economic stability.

- Adopt measures aimed at promoting favourable conditions and removing obstacles in such a way that the freedom and equality of the individual and of the groups of which he is part, may be effective and real.

- Make possible the participation of all citizens in the political, economic and social life of the Basque Country.[315]

Next, Article 10 lists 39 subject matters in which the Euskadi has sole jurisdiction within the autonomous region, sometimes in harmony with the relevant State statutes. The subject matter includes internal procedural matters and governmental housekeeping chores, right of public domain (i.e. exercise a degree of sovereignty), fishing; hydraulic projects; social welfare; educational, cultural artistic, charitable or similar Foundations and Associations; scientific and technical research; culture; fine art institutions and the handicraft industry; historic, artistic, monumental, archeological and scientific heritage; archives, libraries and museums not in state (Spanish) ownership; economic planning, internal trade; institutions of corporate, public and territorial credit and savings banks, commodity exchanges; industry; transfer of foreign technology; railways, transport by land, sea, river and cable, ports, heliports and airports, and the Meteorological Service; Public Works; roads and thoroughfares; casinos, gaming and betting; tourism and sport; statistics; and finally, # 39 deals with community development, condition of women, policy regarding children, youth and old people.[316]

"The Basque Country may (also) regulate, set up and maintain its own television, radio and press, and in general, all the social communications media..."[317] The Basque government is also charged with executing and enforcing certain state policies. It also has an almost fully autonomous judiciary system, set up by the Basque legislature, and only a few types of

---

315 Ibid., Art. 9.-2

316 Ibid., Art. 10.

317 Ibid., Art. 19.-3.

cases can be appealed to the State's highest court.[318] They also have their own independent police force.[319]

While TITLE I deals with the jurisdiction and powers of the Basque government, TITLE II sets up the government itself, consisting of an elected Parliament, Government, Administration of Justice, local and municipal system, and exercise of constitutional overview and settling of conflicts of jurisdiction.

TITLE III deals with Finance and Property. The Basque Country government essentially establishes its own taxes, and pays in one sum a certain amount to the State "as a contribution towards all State burdens (as established by a Joint Commission)[320] that are not directly taken up by the Autonomous Country."[321]

TITLE IV provides for amending the Statute. This gives the obvious advantage to the Basque Parliament, since only they can initiate amendment, even if the Spanish Parliament wants changes. Once a proposal is before the Basque Parliament, it has to be approved by an absolute majority, then the Spanish State Parliament has to approve it by means of an Organic Law, and finally, the electors must approve it in a referendum.[322]

Another provision states that "no treaty or agreement may affect the powers and jurisdiction of the Basque Country except by the means of [certain constitutional] procedures."[323] This provides additional protection, making it almost impossible to whittle away at the powers of the autonomous government by using international agreements. Even the United States Constitution does not give the states this rigth not to have their powers curtailed by international treaties.

The last unnumbered provision is a grandfather clause, protecting all pre-existing rights.

Spain has another region that has obtained autonomy recently: Catalonia.

> Beginning in the 9th century, Catalonia was ruled by the counts of Barcelona. In 1137, Catalonia was united with the kingdom of ARAGON, but it preserved considerable autonomy. During the 13th and 14th centuries, Catalonia reached a peak of influence as it dominated Mediterranean trade and Catalan art and literature

---

318 Ibid., Art. 13, 14. Also, Art. 34-35.
319 Ibid., Art. 17. Also, Art. 36.
320 Ibid., Art. 41.-1.e).
321 Ibid., Art. 41-1.d).
322 Ibid., Art. 46.
323 Ibid., Art. 20.-3.

flourished. The region's prosperity declined under Castilian domination in the 16th and 17th centuries. From 1640 to 1659, Catalonia allied itself with France against Philip IV of Spain, and in 1714 its autonomy was abolished. Separatism revived in the 19th century. A Catalan Republic was recognized in 1932, but an attempt to secure total independence was suppressed in 1934. With its autonomy restored in 1936, Catalonia was heavily Loyalist during the SPANISH CIVIL WAR. After the Nationalist victory (1939), however, it again lost its autonomy, and Franco's government adopted a repressive policy toward it. The region regained its autonomy in Spain's 1978 Constitution, and in 1980 Catalonia's voters elected their first legislative assembly.[324]

Thus, for Catalonia it took the death of Franco and a new Spanish regime to re-gain their much fought for autonomy.

Autonomous Regions in Italy

This particular case is especially interesting, since during the peace conference following World war II this was mentioned in connection with the fate of the Hungarian minority. The foreign ministers were discussing territorial and minority issues, and James F. Byrne, the American Secretary of State wrote:

> (I)n the midst of all these claims and counterclaims, Italy and Austria provided the conference with a timely demonstration of statesmanship by working out an enlightened agreement insuring basic human rights for the German speaking peoples in South Tyrol, which remained with Italy. We have tried to use this as an example of reasonable bilateral negotiations to help solve such problems as Czechoslovakia's desire to transfer back to Hungary its Hungarian minority, but met with indifferent success.[325]

Yet, while the Americans were cautious not to appear to reward Hungary for being an enemy state,[326] they ended up rewarding the Czechs (and the Rumanians and Serbs) for being obstinate and refusing to act statesmanlike and to follow the example provided by the enlightened Tyrol solution, by returning the territories they had lost due to the Vienna Arbitals to them, without any guarantee of respecting minority rights.

---

324 "Catalonia" in GROLIER.
325 James F. Byrne SPEAKING FRANKLY (New York: Harper & Brothers, 1947) p. 149.
326 See #138 above.

Autonomy in Italy presents a unique picture in that every Region possesses considerable autonomy, but five selected regions, mostly on linguistic grounds, had been granted an extra measure of autonomy concerning culture and use of language.

> The modern Italian nation state dates from 1861, when the title King of Italy was conferred on VICTOR EMMANUEL II, king of Sardinia. Before that time, Italy consisted of many separate states. These have retained a strong sense of regional identity and are identifiable today in the nation's 20 administrative regions. Eight of the regions are located in northern (or Upper) Italy, six are in central Italy, and Southern Italy contains four. The other two are the island regions of Sardinia and Sicily. .
>
> The Italian people are not ethnically homogenous, reflecting a long history of foreign invasions and migrations. A variety of physical types is present in the population. Nevertheless, most speak Italian or dialects or languages related to Italian. These dialects vary considerably from region to region and are considered separate languages in the case of Sardinian, spoken by about 1.2 million people; and 53,000 Slavic Italians, scattered in several areas in Friuli and Venezia-Giulia. In addition, some isolated minority groups live in southern Italy, including Greek-speaking communities in parts of Apulia and Calabria; Albanian colonies in Sicily and Calabria; and Serbo-Croatian communities in parts of Molise. French is spoken in the Aosta valley.[327]

According to the 1948 Italian Constitution each of the 20 regions has an elected council, a president, and a giunta regionale that exercises executive power and is responsible to the regional council. Five of the regions: Friuli-Venezia Giulia, Sardinia, Sicily, Trentino-Alto Adige, and Valle d'Aosta, are granted "particular forms of autonomy, in accordance with special statutes adopted by Constitutional law."[328] In the northeastern district of FRIULI-VENEZIA GIULIA, Friulian, a Rhaeto-Romanic language is spoken by about 520,000 people. In TRENTINO-ALTO ADIGE Ladin, another Rhaeto-Romanic language is spoken in the mountains. The principal non-Italian minorities of about 260,000 German-Italians also live in the Alto Adige (formerly Austria's South TYROL) and speak the German dialects of Austria and Bavaria.[329] In this essay we shall focus on Trentino-Alto Adige.

---

327 "Italy," in GROLIER.
328 The Constitution of the Republic of Italy, Title V., The Regions, Provinces and "Comuni", Art. 116.
329 Cf. "Italy" in GROLIER.

Trentino-Alto Adige is bordered by Switzerland to the northwest and Austria to the north. With its capital at Trent (Italian: Trento), the region has an area of 13,613 sq. km (5,256 sq mi.) and a population of 891,421 (1990 est.). Formerly known as Venezia Tridentina, the region was annexed to Austria in 1814 as part of the Tyrol and was ceded to Italy in 1919. Most of the inhabitants of the northern province, with its capital at BOLZANO, speak German, whereas a majority of those in the southern province of Trento speak Italian.[330]

Trentino-Alto Adige is governed by a Special Constitution. The current constitution, dated August 31, 1972, is based on the provisions contained in Constitutional Law of 26th February 1948 and subsequent amendments. It begins by pronouncing that

> Trentino-Alto Adige, comprising the territory of the provinces of Trento and Bolzano, constitutes an autonomous region, with legal status within the political unity of the Italian Republic, one and indivisible...[331]

> The equality of citizens' rights is recognized in the region regardless of the language community to which they belong and respective ethnic and cultural characteristics are safeguarded.[332]

The next several Articles list various general powers and functions of the regional government. The question of language and ethnicity comes up in several provisions, guaranteeing equal treatment.

Article 19, dealing with education in the Province of Bolzano makes detailed provision for education of pupils from nursery to secondary schools in their mother tongue, by teachers of the same mother tongue. The Article even makes a provision for proportionate representation of the teachers of the various language communities on the Provincial School Council.

The Special Constitution also provides for proportionate representation on the Regional Council,[333] and requires that Councilors take "an oath of allegiance to the Republic and swear to carry out their duties for the sole inseparable good of the State and the Region.[334] The regional council has a 5 year term, and the President and Vice-president of the Regional Council alternate for each half of the 60 month term: the first 30 months the President

---

330 "Trentino-Alto Adige" in GROLIER.
331 Trentino-Alto Adige, Special Constitution, Art. 1
332 Ibid., Art. 2.
333 Ibid., Art. 25.
334 Ibid., Art. 29.

is Italian, and the Vice-president is German, and for the second 30 months it is reversed.[335]

If a bill is considered prejudicial to the equality of rights between citizens of the different language communities and the ethnic and cultural characteristics of those communities," they may request separate voting, and ultimately may appeal to the Constitutional Court.[336] There is also provision to publish the Official Bulletin of the region in two languages, although interpretation of the text is based on the Italian version,[337] and to publish laws of the Republic, affecting the Region in German in the Official Bulletin.[338]

The Special Constitution not only requires proportional representation of language communities in local councils, [339] and guarantees representation of the Ladin language community on the Regional Council, [340] but also reserves positions for the language groups on government staff positions, including the judicial and prosecutorial offices, and requires that Italian and German speaking judges alternate as chairman of the section.[341]

"To satisfy the needs of bilingualism," the Province of Bolzano can assign integration quotas in local government,[342] and require "perfect knowledge of the Italian and German languages" for several job categories.[343] In submitting budgets, the rights of language communities must be kept in mind, and challenges to the budget can be appealed[344] just as "administrative acts of the civil service authorities considered prejudicial" by a language community.[345] Finally, four separate Articles deal with and protect the rights of the two language communities[346] and two protect the language rights during the transitional period.[347]

This section about autonomy in practice could not be closed without quoting the full statement of the President of the Autonomous Province of Trento, the Honorable Pierluigi Angeli, written in 1988.

> Forty years ago, on 26 February 1948, the Constituent Assembly of the Italian Republic passed the special Statute for the self-

---

335 Ibid., Art. 30.
336 Ibid., Art. 56
337 Ibid., Art. 57.
338 Ibid., Art. 58.
339 Ibid., Art. 61.
340 Ibid., Art. 62.
341 Ibid., Art. 89.
342 Ibid., Art. 81.
343 Ibid., Art. 94.
344 Ibid., Art. 84.
345 Ibid., Art. 92.
346 Ibid., Articles 99-102.
347 Ibid., Articles 107, 114.

government of Trentino-Alto Adige thus opening the way towards solving one of the most important problems in connection with linguistic minorities in post war Europe.

The celebration of this event is of particular historic significance and it deserves profound and responsible meditation at a time when Europe, and not only Europe, has an increasingly urgent need for ethnic minorities in an atmosphere of collaboration and reciprocal respect, in a dimension that has been progressively spreading towards Europe and in the knowledge that autonomy cannot and must not be interpreted as provincialistic isolation but, on the contrary, as an incentive for a constructive and pacific society.

In this light the Autonomous Province of Trento is promoting the "culture of autonomy ," with various measures that can provide the local community with the cultural and civil facilities required for any future development and comparison, to satisfy the spirit of the times and the challenge that progress, from all points of view, launches day after day.

Autonomy means not only the protection of one's rights but moreover a historical awareness and sense of responsibility: two aspects that cannot be divided, the former being founded on a sense of identity with the original characteristics of a community, in a continued effort to broaden its cultural outlook; the latter, on a sound administration that involves not only the institutions but the whole community so that they participate in and are directly responsible for the government of local issues.

These, then, are the reasons for submitting to the European citizens, administrators and students, this booklet which contains the basis of own (sic) social life: that part of the Italian constitution dealing with the regions and the autonomous Statute which, this year, the Italian Government has fully carried into effect.

With this publication Trentino wishes to give the readers an opportunity to became acquainted with a "European case", and the constitutional laws that rule the life of citizens, belonging to the same nationality but different linguistic groups, in the respect and defence of their culture and identity.

Since this is the only basis on which freedom and democracy grow and prosper. Only if we learn how to defend and make better use of our regional and minority cultures shall we be able to become citizens of united Europe in the near future.[348]

Thus, we have a practicing politician living in an autonomous Province singing the praises of autonomy, assuring us that "autonomy cannot and must not be interpreted as provincialistic isolation but, on the contrary, as an incentive for a constructive and pacific society."

Earlier we have heard the philosopher Ervin Laszlo that regional autonomy and preservation of traditional cultures is the key to world peace. Next, we were instructed by a military man, Retired General Boyd that what Bosnia needs is ethnic autonomy, and were told by a political scientist, Gideon Rose, that only "a clear division and stable balance of power," that all the involved parties would support, could solve the Bosnian crisis. Last but not least, we have read the arguments of the most relevant source, the ethnic groups themselves: the Federal Union of Ethnic Groups (FUEN) argued that only territorial autonomy can solve effectively the minority problem.

What more is the world waiting for? Why is the US Administration concerned with loss of prestige, when it could gain tremendous new prestige if it would finally develop a new foreign policy doctrine, as this author has already recommended in several letters to US policy makers, including Madam Secretary of State Madeleine Albright. Now that the cold war between the super powers seems to be over and we seem to be free of a world-wide conflict, the Administration and our able Madame Secretary of State could lay down the foundation of a world free of small wars also.

The first and most urgent step should be, of course, to replace the Dayton Agreement with a new agreement, granting territorial rights and security to the three ethnic groups ready to jump at each other's throat as soon as the IFOR leaves Bosnia. It might take long and arduous negotiations, but based on historic precedents, it could be done.

Separatism and Terror

We have seen several cases where autonomy is working successfully, without breaking up historic states. But the process has not always been peaceful, and not every minority problem has been solved yet. Sebestyen-Teleki

---

348 Statement of Pierluigi Angeli, introducing the updated text of the CONSTITUTION OF THE REPUBLIC OF ITALY, and the TRENTINO-ALTO ADIGE SPECIAL CONSTITUTION commemorating the fortieth anniversary of the establishment of Autonomous Provinces in Italy. The text of the translation is reproduced without an attempt to correct or improve the translation.

collects in his essay several cases when minorities responds with violence and acts of terror if their demands are not met.

One such case is the French minority in Jura canton in Switzerland.[349] This is an interesting and complicated situation. The problem started when in 1815 the Vienna Congress attached the Jura region to the Bern Canton of Switzerland, against the protests of the peoples of both Jura and the Bern Canton. As the Catholic French national identity of the Jura people started to awaken in the 1830's, they started to protest the annexation. The immigration of German peasants and the Canton's anti-clerical policy further increased the dissatisfaction and in 1917 the first Separatist Committee was formed. The discontent increased in 1947 when the Departments of the Canton were reorganized.

Although in 1950 the Jura people were recognized as a minority in the Canton's constitution, in 1952 the Jura National Assembly (Rassemblement Jurassien, RJ) was organized demanding separation from the Canton. In the same year they also formed the Union of Jura Patriots, an organization pledged to play according to the rules of democracy. This was followed by the formation of a number of separatist organizations.

In 1957 a movement was started asking for a referendum of creating a separate Jura Canton. As the result, the referendum was held in 1959, and to everybody's surprise, the proposal was defeated, indicating that the three distinct peoples of Jura District, the French Catholics, the French Protestants, and the German Catholics do not agree on the future of the Canton. It seems that separatism is the strongest among the French Catholics, and the other two groups are hesitant to submit themselves, without further protections, to the nationalistic French group. In the mean time they also organized the Front de Liberation du Jura, an underground military arm of the RJ, to conduct terror acts to advance the cause of liberation. In an 18 month period during the early 1960's they had committed at least eight acts of terror, including arson and bombing.

Although the ultimate goal of the French group is "a separate state for all the French people of Jura," with full sovereignty, the Rassemblement Jurassien voted in 1974 to support a separate, Autonom Jura Canton. The establishment of a separate canton, according to the concept of territorial autonomy took place only on January 1, 1979. This did not satisfy, however, the separatists. Acts of terror, including stealing arms from military depots, continued. The highest number of such theft was in 1981, with 656 instances, 47 bombings, and in 1979, the first year of Autonom cantonhood, with 620 instances of theft and 38 bombings. In the 1970's these robberies have netted

---

349 Sebestyen-Teleki, pp. 2-6.

392 machine guns, 513 hand grenades, 204,000 rounds of ammunition, and thousands of other weapons. So this must had been the work of a fairly large number of individuals.

Sebestyen-Teleki's conclusion is that even where the borders are spiritualized, as it is within Switzerland, the minority problem still continues. Other conclusion can also be drawn, of course. For example, if there is a small, determined group of ultranationalist-separatists, nothing would satisfy them short of total victory or total defeat. There does not seem to be such a group working, however, among the minorities in the Carpathian Basin where, in spite of the severe oppression, the minority has not resorted to terror--yet. Another possible conclusion is that in the Jura case territorial autonomy is not the proper solution. Based on the shared territory concept, all three groups should have shared authority. And finally, perhaps more emphasis should be placed on trans-border autonomy to satisfy some of the Jura people. The Jura case seems to be a textbook example of an extreme case of "territorial grievance" committed at the Vienna Congress in 1815.

Another case of violence to achieve separation, also involving a French speaking population, is the Province of Quebec, Canada.[350] The Quebec separatists are not satisfied with autonomy and bilingualism that applies not only to Quebec but even to the English speaking provinces with practically no French speaking population. Even the resulting economic hardships do not deter the separatists from forcing the separation of Quebec from Canada. This is ironic, because Canada has one of the most progressive minority policies in providing ethnic cultural development of their numerous ethnic minorities, including public subsidy for ethnic project, newspapers, book publishing, etc.

It seems that both cases, involving French speaking minorities on two continents, are based on the territorial rather than human rights argument. While the Jura case might have had a human rights aspect at one time, radical nationalists now demand secession based on a historic grievance. The Francophone Quebec, seemingly gearing up for another referendum, has neither historic grievance nor human rights complaints, only a linguistic difference from the rest of Canada. But it seems that with their violence they cause more harm than good for their causes, as Brilmayer suggested about terror acts. It seems that claims based on territorial grievance lead to violence more frequently than claims based on human rights abuses.

Therefore the case of Quebec, and to some extent, the Jura problem is much less relevant to the problem of minorities in other countries who still struggle to obtain a measure of autonomy, than the South Tyrol or Basque examples.

---

350 Ibid., pp. 6-8.

Nevertheless, Sebestyen-Teleki's conclusion that even where the borders are spiritualized, the minority problem still continues and some form of autonomy may be required to satisfy the needs of the ethnic minorities, even if some radicals and demagogues who demand complete separation are left dissatisfied.

VII.

AUTONOMY PROPOSALS IN THE CARPATHIAN BASIN.

As we have seen, territorial autonomy is not a new concept, nor is it a magic cure-for-all. It has been used in history up to our own days, quite often with great success to quell demands for separation, resulting from oppression and discrimination. We have also seen that Benes had promised a Switzerland-like federal and republican form of government for Czechoslovakia, and it would be interesting to dust off that old document and find out the details, just what did he promise? It is quite likely that had Czechoslovakia carried out those promises, there would have been no minority problems there, and the Czechs and Slovaks, along with the satisfied Germans and Hungarians would still be united, in a rich and prosperous country under a federal arrangement, instead of a separated and Slovakia, suffering from the consequences of years of oppressive minority policies of Meciar is almost an economic basket case, torn by ethnic conflict, and locked out of the European Community.

Territorial autonomy also existed in Yugoslavia and Rumania as they both were forced after World War II as part of the post-war settlements to grant territorial autonomy to their ethnic minorities, namely the Hungarians in Transylvania and Voivodina, and the Albanians in Kosovo. These autonomies were eventually revoked by the majority governments of Rumania and Yugoslavia, respectively, not because they were unsuccessful, but because they managed to prevent forced assimilation! Restoring those autonomies would be a great step in the right direction, with constitutional protection and international supervision making sure that they will not be revoked again.

The International Context and Guidelines for Negotiating Minority Autonomy

It is in this spirit that I introduce and discuss the following proposals for autonomy for Hungarians that were prepared by representatives of the Hungarian minorities in their respective regions, who also face harsh discrimination and attempts at ethnic cleansing as soon as the attention of the world is turned to another conflict in another part of the world. These proposals have been prepared by politicians not only as representatives of an oppressed minority, but often themselves suffering victims of persecution and ethnic cleansing in their thousand year old homeland. According to Karoly Kiraly, in Transylvania "in eighty years they have beaten fear into us. Now not our physical annihilation is the primary goal but the destruction of our freedom even to think."[351]

Unfortunately, this kind of intimidation seems to work even on international level. As we have seen, Ms. Taft, a member of the US delegation to the 1977 ODIHR meeting in Warsaw had taken to task the Hungarian delegation for a Hungarian politician's statement about border changes. That same year the US had severely criticized a meeting of Hungarian representatives and representatives of Hungarians in neighboring countries for mentioning the word "autonomy." These efforts on the part of the US must have had a chilling effect on the international community.

Reading the Final Resolutions of the 1999 "Hungary and Hungarians beyond the Borders"[352] conference one must wonder if the Orban government is also intimidated, or follows a course of wisdom in not stirring up controversy that could hurt on the one hand the minorities on the short run, and the slowly warming relations between the US and Hungary.

It would be tragic if even the Orban government is intimidated by the US's blind opposition to the mere mention of autonomy. This is why it took so long for the US to finally give in on the autonomy issue in Kosovo, when it seems to have been too little too late. In Kosovo, unfortunately, by the time the US recognized that on Hannum's scale the conflict has reached level when autonomy was more than justified, it actually escalated to next level, where only complete secession can satisfy the needs of the majority population of Kosovo. Only the Co-chair and the ranking minority members of the CSCE have recognized this escalation![353] The wise course for the Orban government would be to quietly support this position and urge the US administration to be more flexible and bring the matter before the United Nations.

This susceptibility of both the oppressed minority and of interested governments to domestic and international pressure and intimidation places heavier responsibility on independent NGO-s to take the lead in promoting the causes not only of human rights but of autonomy and secession, if necessary.

Because of this intimidation and uncertainty of international support some of the following proposals, written under harsh oppression, asks (and very seldom demands) a great deal less, than other ethnic groups have received from their respective governments. Barna Bodo's accusation that "western

---

351   Karoly Kiraly, at the Civic Forum at Csernahat, on May 4, 1997; quoted in TRANSYLVANIA, vol. 38 (1997), #1-2, p. 29.
352   See #261 above.
353   See #201 above

politicians, in their rhetoric, focus on the question of European stability instead of respecting basic human rights and the rules of democracy," explains the milieu in which these proposals about national autonomy had been written. According to Bodo, international documents ostensibly aimed at protecting minority rights,

> instead of strengthening the locally initiated processes of legalizing minority rights, have proved to have the contrary effects because of the standpoint manifested by international politics that have left it up to the minority groups to help themselves, which negatively effect efficient organization. To the majority they convey ample support for the accusation that the minority groups are never satisfied; they want more than what elsewhere is "enough", thereby creating tension in the country and surrounding area.

> The subject of stability that is raised, makes the established demands of minority groups relative, moreover, by claiming that their (the minorities') actions are tension-creating, they are accusing them with charges which place international responsibilities on them, which they do not have the scope or the desire, in the international political field, to give a worthy answer to.[354]

In other words, the minorities are fighting for the rights that international agreements have established and which Rumania had also ratified, not only without international support, but against accusation that they are never satisfied and they create tension that endangers stability and world peace, as if the true cause of the tension was not the denial of their rights and the oppression of their rightful aspirations. It is highly unfair to buy security for an oppressive majority at the expense of the insecurity of an oppressed minority and it would be downright immoral to preach human rights without the willingness to make some radical changes, if necessary, to implement those rights. Using international stability as an excuse not to make the necessary changes to free the oppressed minority is like refusing to operate on a patient because it might upset the fiscal balance of the hospital.

But it seems the international climate is gradually changing and the world will not only realize who really creates the tension and who endangers world peace, but also will recognize the value on preserving ethnic, linguistic and cultural plurality. This recognition and the appropriate correction, allowing

---

354 Barna Bodo, BASIC CONTRACT AND MINORITY RIGHTS (unpublished and un-dated essay). The Basic Contract to which the title refers is the bi-lateral treaty that also contain provisions about minority rights, made at the insistence of Western powers, including the United States, between Hungary and Rumania about relations between the two countries.

autonomy, and secession if necessary, shall also place future stability on a much stronger footing that sweeping problems under the rug.

In this new atmosphere it should be expected that once the minorities in Transylvania or Slovakia realize the high standards that minorities in other countries routinely enjoy, they will raise their expectations as they should, to become fully equal and enjoy the full range of human rights including the right to life, liberty, and the pursuit of happiness that, as the American Declaration of Independence states, they "are endowed with, by their Creator." No government or chauvinistic majority should take away what God gave to every human being.

It should be noted that there are some cases where the minority lives in a geographically compact and isolated territory, like the Aaland Islands, and there are cases where the minority lives in ethnically mixed regions, like in Northern Italy. Yet, their rights can be and should be adequately protected even if by different means. There are models that do not require exclusive minority regions, as we have seen in a previous chapter. Also, it may be necessary to use different forms and degrees of autonomy for different regions and groups even in the same country. Therefore the details of any arrangement will have to be negotiated, with third party or international mediation if necessary, between the governments and the representatives of the respective minorities. The bottom line is that none should be discriminated against or suffer a disadvantage, let alone persecution, in the 21st century, because of language or ethnic background. Thus, the above cases should be used only as guidelines for the negotiations in each individual case.

Another general comment is in order at this point. The documents we are going to discuss next seem to be political statements, made by politicians, disguised as proposals. This tactic can backfire. If the proposal contains too little, the minority paints itself into a corner. If it contains too much, the majority can use it as an example of exaggerated demands, as Bodo suggested above. Also, if the negotiators negotiate away some of their publicly stated positions, as it always happens in good-faith bargaining where each side has to give to gain some concession from the other side, they might be labeled "traitors" to the cause. It is impossible to negotiate in good faith in such a situation!

From a study of the American Constitutional Convention to the most recent union-management negotiations, one can conclude that success depends to a great extent on secrecy and confidentiality. The American Founding Fathers, after electing a chairman, started as their first order of business, to establish a rule of secrecy. The secrecy rule was continued even after the constitution was published and adapted. Details of the proceedings became public knowledge only a generation later when Madison's notes were published. Yet, it did not hinder the success of the new Constitution. Diplomatic or union and management negotiators also keep their positions to themselves, at least until the actual negotiations are completed, but often even beyond. Details of diplomatic negotiations often are not disclosed even after the agreement is reached. As we have seen above, the terms of the Franco-Russian Military Convention of 1894 were not published until 1918, after the war ended. "Even the French parliament, when it declared war on Germany, did not fully know the exact nature of the obligations which the French government had assumed toward Russia."[355]

In the case of minorities, they should publicly state and document the problems to be solved by autonomy, present examples how other minorities have solved their problems through autonomy, but keep the concrete demands and proposals to themselves. Instead of coming out with demands and "proposed laws" (and often different and conflicting demands by different groups and politicians claiming to represent the same ethnic minority), they should first get an agreement from the majority government that it is willing to negotiate, and select a team of negotiators that the minority trusts and is acceptable to the majority, and let the negotiating team come up with concrete proposals. There should be a complete and absolute moratorium on publishing details of autonomy demands!

Another secret of effective negotiations is to include in their initial list of proposals "throw away" items that they can keep, or give away during the negotiations, in order to gain something else. Of course, these throw-away items should also be kept strictly confidential: you do not weaken your position by giving away strategic information in advance!

Minorities might use the FUEN model document as a starting point. The advantage of this would be that it is a general list prepared by experts, which is pretty inclusive, taking care of most items minorities need for the survival of their ethnic identity yet it cannot be used to deride the proposals of the particular minority as too demanding. Depending on the local needs, adjustments will be made during the negotiation, but in general, it is an excellent model and starting point. As for negotiating techniques, once the majority has agreed, even if under pressure, to negotiate, the minorities might use the help of FUEN or other international organizations and experts to act as advisors or even as members of the negotiating team. Also, members of ethnic groups who live in Western countries, and therefore might feel freer to do some hard negotiation, might participate in negotiations for their compatriots.

---

355 Cf. #102 above.

In the meantime, of course, the minorities hoping to negotiate effective autonomy must learn the art of negotiation which is a special field of politics. Unfortunately, the following documents indicate little familiarity with this art form.

Istvan Sebestyen-Teleki of Switzerland and Laszlo Maracz of the Netherlands have prepared a list of axioms of national self-determination for minorities in the Carpathian Basin. The last axiom states that "to carry out successfully their efforts at self-determination, every nation and national group first must get rid of the psychological shackles forced on them."[356] One cannot negotiate successfully when one starts from a position of inferiority. If one wants equal treatment, one must feel equal, otherwise the opponent realizes this feeling of inferiority and will take full advantage of it!

Another basic principle in negotiations is the use of the "positive sum approach." Presently the oppressive majority attempts to benefit in a way that seems to be at the expense of the minority. This is called the "zero sum" approach, which means that for every gain of one side, the other side must make a sacrifice. Negotiations would be doomed from the beginning, if the minority also uses the zero sum approach and attempts to gain at the expense of the majority. The minority must find a way to show (as we have tried to show it in this study) that the solution would benefit both sides: convince the majority that they would also be better off if they grant autonomy to the minority. This is the positive sum approach.

Sebestyen-Teleki and Maracz also include an axiom designed to deal with the results of past efforts at changing the ethnic composition and balance of a region. In many cases, as we have seen already, governments conducted repeated and often forced movements of population to change the ethnic composition of regions. This often involved forcing minorities to move out of their original region by restricting educational and/or employment opportunities, and enticing members of the majority group to move into minority areas by offering certain rewards and privileges. This is being currently done in Transylvania by providing low interest bank loans to Rumanians who move to Transylvania, to weaken the relative position of the minority, endangering their opportunity to preserve their ethnic identity, and making regional autonomy demands seem less justified.

There is a basic legal principle, that one should not keep the benefits illegal, immoral, or fraudulent acts. Although it might not have been illegal under the law passed by the majority, it would be immoral for them to benefit from such underhanded technique at the expense of the minority. Therefore

---

356 Unpublished document, Istvan Sebestyen-Teleki and Laszlo Maracz, "Az Onrendelkezes tizenket axiomája; The Twelve Axioms of Self-Determination," 1992; p. 2

Sebestyen-Teleki and Maracz present the axiom that "according to the international legal principle, the right to decide the affiliation of a native land should be awarded only to those whose ancestors have been residents for a number of generations,"[357] which, in the case of the Carpathian basin would mean three generations, i.e. those whose ancestors, Germans, Hungarians, Romas or Rumanians, have been residents of the community at the time of the border changes after the Trianon Peace Treaties changed the sovereign of the affected regions. Similar solutions should be applied in the cases of other regions and other minorities.

Finally, it is also surprising and somewhat disheartening that none of the demands put forth by the minorities explain how they plan to secure autonomous status. Somehow they all seem to hope that once their demands are published, somebody somehow will grant it to them! Although many documents refer to the methods used, including violence, by other ethnic groups (e.g. Basques, French-Canadians in Quebec, etc.), and some want to distance themselves from those groups and emphasize the peaceful means they rely on, there is no plan outlined how to pressure the majority governments even just to sit down and discuss the minority issue, let alone to convince them to negotiate and ultimately grant autonomy to the minorities. Why should the majority agree to grant autonomy when they do not even want to recognize that there is a problem, or worse yet, if they create the problem deliberately, as part of the ethnic cleansing process, to induce "foreigners," i.e. the minority, to escape?

Hungarian Autonomy Proposals in Serbia

The "Proposal for establishing personal autonomy for the Hungarians living in the Republic of Serbia," is a document prepared by the Democratic Community of the Hungarians in Vojvodina in 1995, as the ethnic conflict in Bosnia was developing,[358] the northern part of rump Yugoslavia. It is a good example of the naiveté of these minorities who have been isolated from the West for three generations. In the Introductory part they seem to place their fate in the hands of the Serbian legislature and the international community:

---

357 Sebestyen-Teleki and Maracz, Axiom # 10, p. 2.
358 The document was prepared and adopted on March 11, 1995, in Subotica (Szabadka), a major Hungarian populated city in Vojvodina.

"...trusting the leaders of the peace process that they will not apply double standard in the solution of the open and unresolved problems of minorities on the territory of Yugoslavia, and if necessary, their mediators will help creating a democratic agreement,

presuming that the Republic of Yugoslavia ... would like to become a member of the democratic European Community...",

and conclude that they "will present (the proposal) to the House of Representatives of the Republic of Serbia for adoption." No matter how excellent the proposal is, and it is one of the better ones, it is not going to be accepted. Instead of working on detailed plans and proposals, "trusting" their oppressors to change, they should convince the world, and the majority government in their respective countries, that there is a minority problem that should be solved, and that all would be better off if it will be solved, and that granting autonomy would offer a positive sum solution.

It should be realized that the "leaders of the peace process" are politicians who are under certain pressures from their home constituencies and will do as little as possible, place as small a burden on their country and still preserve a semblance of peace. They will not go out of their way to take on additional burdens unless it can be shown that it benefits their constituents, or be convinced by international pressure that it is necessary. This also explains why international law experts are more open and bold in supporting reform: they have no constituencies and do not have to stand for election.

Therefore, this blind and unconditional trust in the "leaders of the peace process" is unjustified. Only public pressure will convince them to attempt to solve the unresolved problems of the minorities." The idea that the United States or any other western country is "policing" the world to eliminate injustice and enforce international resolutions is naive.

As for the idea that Yugoslavia is anxious to join Western Europe, one only has to remember that Serbian nationalists assassinated Ferdinand, the Austrian crown prince to prevent Serbia's joining the Austro-Hungarian Monarchy as an equal partner, and wanted an independent Greater Serbia under Russian protection. Many Serbs feel the same way: joining the EC would diminish their sovereignty, so they are opposed to it.

Finally, submitting their proposal to the nationalistic Serbian House of Representatives seems an empty gesture: there is absolutely no chance of approval, unless sufficient pressure is applied, preferable from outside, western forces, including the threat of economic and possible military sanctions. This takes us back to the first point: how to convince the world leaders that it is in their best interest to solve the minority problems in Europe?

Although the autonomy proposal for Vojvodina is interesting, because it seems to propose three kinds of autonomy, it does not present a realistic plan of action. It refers to the appropriate international documents (except the Copenhagen Document that has the one of the most comprehensive list of minority and democratic rights) that are binding Serbia to protect human and minority rights, and seem to take it for granted that once they ask for it, the Serbs will grant it.

The proposed models of autonomy include Hungarian autonomous district for blocks of Hungarian populations, municipal autonomies in municipalities where the population is mixed, and personal autonomy. The actual structure and functions will have to be clarified and negotiated with the majority, if they can convince them to sit down and negotiate an end to the mis-treatment of the minority.

Hungarian Autonomy Demands in Rumania

The first proposal for an autonomous Transylvania was made in 1918, before the Trianon peace treaties were signed, by Elemer Gyarfas,[359] proposing a fully independent Transylvania, with a fair division of representation between the three nations, the Germans, Hungarians, and Rumanians. It was supposed to be submitted to the Great Powers negotiating the peace treaty with Hungary. Events, however, soon overtook the proposal, and it was never considered. Under the plan the eventual affiliation of Transylvania should be decided by the people of Transylvania, once peace and order has been restored.

The Democratic Alliance of Hungarians in Rumania issued a PROPOSED LAW ON MINORITIES AND AUTONOMOUS COMMUNITIES IN RUMANIA in 1993. The proposal is a textbook example of how three generations of oppression that Karoly Kiraly and Bodo Barna referred to above can intimidate a minority in their own homeland. In light of the previously discussed examples of autonomy, their proposal is so weak both in substance and form, that it is surprising the Rumanians did not grant it, to turn away the spotlight from Rumania at the time of their being considered for NATO and EC membership.

This is not to blame the authors of the proposal. Their timidity is quite understandable: the Western world, led by the United States, has rigidly and self-righteously refused any consideration of autonomy, and the authors, due

---

359   The document had been preserved in Elemer Gyarfas, ERDELYI PROBLEMAK (PROBLEMS OF TRANSYLVANIA), Kolozsvár (Kluj), 1923 and has been re-printed by MAGYAR NEMZET, in 1988. Bo date is available.

to their isolation from the rest of the world, and perhaps lack of information about other autonomies, would have been satisfied with a weak law that promises a little, and would deliver almost nothing! And this was their initial position, from which they probably would be glad to retreat to even less, if the Rumanians started to bargain, and the minority would end up with some worthless paper-promises.

So, breaking with the pattern followed so far, instead of a mere presentation of the features of the proposed law and listing its relevant provisions, here I will also add some constructive, critical comments.

The whereas... part of the document is full of nice phrases that could be the foundation of true ethnic peace, but in the circumstances they sound hollow and false. The Rumanian parliament is just not ready, even after the last election, to put its seal on this statement.

Even if the Rumanian government would accept the fact that the "existence of ethnic communities is conditioned by the preservation of their own traditions and characteristics," just to pick one statement, the goal of the Rumanian majority is not the continued existence of ethnic communities but the extinction of them! So, to extinguish these communities, Rumania must make impossible the practice and survival of the ethnic traditions and language of the Hungarian minority. For evidence, see the hysterical reaction to Moldova's giving autonomy to their own ethnic minority. Nice words mean nothing in a life and death struggle, as is taking place in Rumania, and in some other countries in Central Europe between the dominant nation and the native Hungarian minority. The Rumanian parliament is anything but ready to "proclaim (at least when it comes to the Hungarian minority) the commitment to the ideas of democracy and humanism as well as the intention of mutual understanding and friendly cooperation among peoples and nations."

Under the circumstances, forget the meaningless niceties, play hard ball, and negotiate a deal that may not sound nice, but can guarantee the survival of the ethnic communities. It would be a grave mistake to expect the Rumanian parliament to ratify this preamble. If anything, such a preamble make it politically impossible for the nationalist Rumanians to even negotiate about the rest of the proposal, which is so weak that, to quote a critique of the 1963 Civil Rights Act of the US, is not worth the paper it is printed on!

It might be more useful to admit that Hungarians understand the Rumanian's desire for an ethnically pure Rumanian nation, just like Hitler wanted a pure German nation, but the times have changed, and it is time to compromise and either grant true autonomy, as the European trend is, or accept a smaller but ethnically pure Rumania. Also, instead of politicians, making a political statement or a wish list, as the document does, the proposal should have

186

been written by lawyers and constitutional scholars, to give it practical meaning and enforceability.

As for the proposal itself, first of all, it calls for a law, when they should know from experience that even constitutional provisions are violated by extreme nationalists. In every case studied, autonomy as a minority protection is enshrined into the constitution, at least be reference. Second, instead of concrete, enforceable provisions like the other autonomies are based on, this proposal includes a list of principles, like "The national identity is a fundamental human right and both individuals and communities are entitled to it."[360] How does one expect this "law" to be enforced?

Another proposed article states an otherwise fine principle: "The national minorities are entitled to be represented in public offices and in the judiciary."[361] What does it mean? Should a certain pre-determined number or proportion of judges selected from the minority community, or is it enough if a single Hungarian clerk is appointed to the court system in the entire Transylvania to represent the millions of Hungarians in Transylvania?

The phrase is used over and over, and seems to be the corner stone of the proposed law: "communities, which have personal autonomy."[362] Something might be lost in the translation, but it is never defined, so it can mean anything or nothing. Also, "(N)ational minorities, which declare themselves as autonomous communities shall have the right to personal autonomy."[363] How does a minority make this "declaration", what are the conditions, who shall accept the declaration, are the "autonomous communities" local, regional or spiritual/cultural communities? If they are local authorities, as Art. 53 seems to suggest, how does it have "personal autonomy" as the same article states? Also, how does a local community "elaborate its own statute concerning the local self-administration?" Does the proposal provide for sovereign powers to the autonomous community? This might be nit-picking, but that is what lawyers do when they interpret a law! The proposed law would provide a field day to nit-picking lawyers, and a ton of headache to judges, with little benefit to the minorities!

Also, if the ethnic groups are to have true equality, the provisions should be reciprocal. According to the proposal, in communities where Hungarians ("persons belonging to a national minority") would constitute a majority, the Rumanian minority "shall use its mother tongue as an official language."[364]

---

360 The Democratic Alliance of Hungarians in Rumania PROPOSED LAW ON NATIONAL MINORITIES AND AUTONOMOUS COMMUNITIES IN ROMANIA, Article 2.
361 Ibid., Art. 5.
362 Idem.
363 Ibid., Art. 51.
364 Ibid., Art. 6.

Yet, there is no corresponding right proposed to Hungarians where they are in a minority.

Another provision would grant to the minority "limited right to veto in questions affecting their self identity."[365] Just what does "limited veto" mean, and what are the standards for "affecting self-identity"?

Another shortcoming of the proposed law is that it sets no enforcing mechanism and provides no sanctions. For example, there is a provision that a person belonging to a national minority "may not be subject to any attempt of assimilation against their will."[366] But who shall enforce this, and what will be the penalty if one will attempt to force assimilation?

There are also nice sounding provisions about education in the mother tongue. But it does not specify, who shall teach such courses? Could a nationalist Rumanian, who happens to speak Hungarian, perhaps even broken Hungarian, teach in Hungarian or should such teachers be from the Hungarian language community, as the Special Constitution of the TRENTINO-ALTO ADIGE Autonom region requires?

Perhaps the best illustration of the servile mentality so evident from the entire document is the proposal that "(O)n special occasions, the members of parliament, who belong to a national minority or autonomous community, may use their mother tongue. The parliament shall be notified about the intention to deliver such a speech in order to provide translation."[367] What is wrong if, in the name of equality, members of a national minority use their mother tongue routinely, and translation is provided automatically? How can one expect their national tradition and identity to survive if future generations see that Hungarian members need special occasions to speak Hungarian in their parliament? No other case of ethnic autonomy has such a humiliating and meaningless provision. Yet, in Rumania the deputies still may use only the Rumanian language.

How can one speak of autonomy and self determination if no independent regional self- government is set up that would govern the minority communities with limited jurisdiction but sovereign authority in certain domestic matters? That is the essence of national autonomy: self government. "The competence of self government" should be defined by constitutional provisions and a Regional Autonomous Government, not the "European

---

365 Ibid., Art. 8. In this Article the term used in the English translation to indicate a proportion of less than 50%, "numeric inferiority," is a poor choice of words.

366 Ibid., Art. 15.

367 Ibid., Art. 37.

Charter for Local Self Government,"[368] although it might be consulted for guidance and justification of certain provisions.

There should also be provision made for an orderly appeal process in cases when minority rights are violated. Given the history of ethnic relations in Rumania, it would not be unreasonable to include binding arbitration by an international human rights authority to settle disputes that cannot be resolved domestically.

This is not intended as a criticism of the people who prepared the Proposed Law, nor is its purpose to add oil to the fire and encourage perhaps some radical Hungarians to resort to violence. Instead, it is telling them what the international standards are, and encouraging them to reach for not only realistic and peaceful but also effective solutions that would really solve the minority problem in Rumania. If the entire proposal would be accepted by the Rumanian Parliament, it still would not solve the problem and the conflict would continue, until an adequate solution is found. But in the process the concept of autonomy would be discredited as inefficient, and it would be much more difficult to find a democratic, non-violent solution. If you shoot for autonomy, you better hit the target the first time, because the second time it will be much more difficult! At least this seems to be the above quoted message of the President of the Autonomous Province of Trento, the Honorable Pierluigi Angeli.

As for the Rumanian partner, they should also heed and take comfort in the words of President Angeli: "autonomy cannot and must not be interpreted as provincialist isolation but, on the contrary, as an incentive for a constructive and pacific society."

A more recent effort in Rumania took a different approach. Instead of proposing a concrete plan, the movement of Transylvanian Hungarian Civic Society held a forum in May 1997 with more than two hundred Hungarian intellectuals of Transylvania participating. The Forum issued a general statement, prepared by Karoly Kiraly, demanding autonomy.[369] They supported their demand with concrete examples of discrimination and quotes from various politicians, public figures, and official documents, including two documents from 1918 and 1920 when Rumanians promised autonomy, but never delivered on their promise. An important quote is taken from the 1201 Recommendation of the European Council:

---

368 Ibid., Art. 56.
369 Kiraly Karoly, "Erdelyi Onrendelkezesi Charta--Charta az onrendelkezesrol, felelem nelkul" Charter of Transylvanian Autonomy--Charta on Autonomy, without fear, in TRANSYLVANIA, vol. 38, #1-2, pp 29-32.

In those regions, where national minorities constitute a majority, those persons have the right, according to their special historical and territorial situation, and in harmony with the nationality laws of their state, to have home rule or Autonom public authorities, or special status.[370]

The problem with this statement, however, is that it refers to the laws of the state, and if the laws of the state do not permit effective autonomy, than the minorities end up with paper autonomy. As it is, the statement is a truism, and not a standard! The standard is the state law. Whatever it permits, is permitted and whatever is prohibited, is prohibited, the 1201 Recommendation notwithstanding.

It is interesting to note that according to the statement issued by the Forum, the situation in many ways was worse in 1997 than before the 1989 collapse of the Ceausescu regime.

There are also interesting recent developments concerning Hungarian autonomy requests in Transylvania. The Rumanian-Hungarian Democratic Federation (RHDF) did come out with a very weak autonomy proposal. But after last years election it became a member of the governing coalition and has received some cabinet and sub-cabinet positions, and several concrete promises from her coalition partners. Thus, in terms of Hannum's three levels of demands, the RHDF somewhat backtracked from level two to level one in exchange for these promises.

After less than a year in the coalition, the leaders of the coalition have learned that most of the promises went unkempt, and the most important, although largely symbolic demand, the restoration of the Hungarian University in Kolozsvar (Cluj), which was part of the coalition deal, was voted against even by other coalition members. Even the leaders of the RHDF had been quoted that they had been had, they were naive, etc., as some of the following quotes illustrate.

> According to Marko, "the problem is the basic approach, that is, the development of the relations between Rumanians and Hungarians, both within the country and between the two countries, the situation of the minorities, the conceptual clarification of 'nation' and 'national identity'...[371]

> Marko warns that the real problem is not the question of the Hungarian university but the road to the future that Rumania had

---

370 Ibid., p. 32.
371 August 18-24 1988 RMDSZ - HETI FIGYELO (RHDF Weekly Observer), published by the RHDF

chosen. He noted with great concern that the Rumanian elite can easily be influenced by certain elements in the media and "follows the political exigencies of the moment rather than the challenges of the future." The Federation's president reminded [us] that last year's heated debate was about the language of history and geography instruction, but in reality it wasn't only the language of these two subjects, just like today it is not the matter of the university. "The issue was, and still is, the road to be followed by Rumania, and this makes me very uneasy."[372]

This has put the Hungarian community before a cross road: continue with a useless coalition, or raise the demands one level and ask for autonomy? So one of the leaders of the Hungarian community, and an honorary president of RHDF, the Most Rev. Bishop László Tökés, called an open mass meeting for September 12, 1998 at Alsocsernaton to discuss the future of the RHDF and the Hungarians in Rumania, officially called "Sekler-land Forum for the Renewal of the RHDF."

The National Federation of American Hungarians (NFAH), the largest Hungarian organization outside the Carpathian Basin having over 100 member organizations, follows the events from the United States and wrote a letter to Bishop Tökés and also issued a statement welcoming the conference. The letter urged the participants to put all demands aside and focus on the autonomy issue and in return for an acceptable autonomy, they might want to renounce, as long as the autonomy is kept, any secessionist claims or desires, or any future request for border changes, the most feared possibility by the Rumanians. This way there would be something in it for the Rumanians too, and the conflict in terms of a zero sum approach, where one party's gain is at the expense of the other, could be turned into a cooperative, positive sum relationship, where both parties would gain: Hungarians would gain autonomy, the Rumanians would gain security of their borders. To this day, this seems to be the only viable and peaceful way to obtain autonomy, especially, if the Hungarian government would also renounce any border changes in return for autonomy..

The RHDF leadership had boycotted the meeting, and instead, issued an ultimatum to the coalition partners that if the case of the Hungarian University is not settled by September 30, they will quit the coalition. But while Marko presents a good analysis of the symptom, he is inconsistent in continuing to fight for a single demand, the Hungarian university, which at the time of this writing as of March 1999 is still not settled.

---

372 Ibid., August 26, 1998

While the issue of the university was being discussed, the Tökés conference issued a resolution in which autonomy is the only demand, and the other issues are listed as goals. This seems to bring the issue clearly to Hannum's third level. The Conference refrained from calling it a right, which would question the legitimacy of the regime as far as Hungarians are concerned. Also, at this stage the autonomy demand still seems negotiable, so there is no open conflict between the Tökés approach and the RHDF approaches.

One of the most respected Hungarian leaders in Transylvania, Karoly Kiraly, went a step further and issued a statement at the September 12 Alsocsernaton Conference in which he not only demanded autonomy, but renounced secession, thus finding the common denominator of the two sides. Although is his statement the autonomy and renunciation of secession are not linked, the proposal is a significant step in moving the issue off the dead center. The Kiraly position takes into consideration the Rumanian fear of territorial demands and wants to assure them of the territorial integrity in return for autonomy, thus bridging the intellectual and conceptual gap between the two sides.

After the Kiraly proposal addressed the territorial concerns of the Rumanians, there is no excuse for them to deny autonomy, or at least to refuse to discuss and grant the several Hungarians demands, on a case by case basis. If Rumania denies both the individual demands on a case by case basis and also fails to negotiate autonomy in good faith, the Hungarian community's demand of secession will be justified. The next step, earning from the Kosovo example, in order to create an international crisis they might be forced to resort to the only possible argument: violence. Let us hope that it will not be necessary.

So now the question seems to be: can the Hungarian community in Transylvania unite to demand autonomy? If they can, the ball will be in the Rumanian court: grant the minority demands in exchange for a pledge of renouncing secession, or risk escalating the conflict to the point when secession will be the only realistic solution. If the Hungarians cannot unite, the international community will forget them, and there is little hope left for them.

Hungarian Autonomy proposals for Slovakia

and the Sub-Carpathian region.

Some 3500 representatives of more than 600,000 Hungarian living in Slovakia, including hundreds of elected public officials, held a Congress on January 8, 1994 in the Komarom Sport Hall, with a crowd of some four hundred people standing outside the packed Hall, listening to the speeches through a P.A. system. Komarom is a major Hungarian city in Slovakia, divided by the Danube into a Slovak and a Hungarian part. The President of Slovakia was also present, along with cabinet representatives. Madame Catherine Lalumieres, secretary-general of the European Council also sent letter to the Congress.

The Congress took place in a hostile atmosphere as some Slovak nationalists incited a hostile campaign against the participants with the aim "to stain the honour of the Hungarian community in the sight of the world ... casting Hungarians as irreconcilable and chauvinists."[373]

In spite of the hostile atmosphere the Congress took a very courageous stand on a number of issues. They complained about three major problems, First, they declared that

> the legal circumstances are not satisfactory, because the self-governing rights are defined only in general terms, and in the course of realisation they have free scope of misinterpretation.... Moreover it may have an application of conscious destructive effect on self governing corporations.

> The second principal item of the assembly was the administrative and territorial reorganization of the country [that was proposed and carried out by the nationalist Slovak government, to destroy the historic administrational structure, and create new county structure to reduce the proportion of Hungarians in the new counties in regions where they had traditionally been in the majority]....

> The third principal point of the assembly was the legal status of the Hungarian people living in Slovakia.[374]

The detailed demands and resolutions all relate to these points, in reverse order. But first they make a general declaration about security and stability in Europe, and claim that settling the ethnic issue is a condition of reduced tensions and improved peace and cooperation.

Next, the representatives note that despite the decades of legal restrictions, repeated persecution and repression, including efforts for forced assimilation "Hungarians living in Slovakia have retained their ability to redefine themselves as a political entity ... and define themselves as a national

---

373 THE KOMAROM RESOLUTIONS; SUMMARY--The Highlands, p. 1.
374 Ibid., pp. 1-2.

community and are fighting resolutely for their collective rights, in addition to the individual rights to which all citizens are entitled....".[375]

In this respect, their demands include recognition of language rights based on the principle of reciprocity, proportional representation in state offices, fair share of budgetary allocations, and most important, in order to protect their national identity, they request special status in regions with "considerable" Hungarian population, with constitutionally recognized and democratically elected representative bodies.

They also included a key point: they "desire to work (with) the Slovak nation, on a footing of equal rights, in building the Slovak Republic."[376] To reinforce this point, they add that "implementation of the above principles ... would serve the interest and territorial integrity of the Slovak Republic and would contribute to the creation of a democratic constitutional State."[377] In other words, if these demands are not met, next time Hungarians might demand border changes, and in the mean time, they do not consider, and rightfully so, Slovakia a democratic constitutional state.

The next point protests against the Slovak move to re-district the Hungarian region by creating gerrymandered districts so as to dilute the Hungarian concentration without relocating anybody. This is done at a time where throughout Europe the emphasis is on minority rights! They declare that "the Hungarian community cannot accept the plan and make counterproposals to protect the historic territorial integrity of the more than half million Hungarians."

The third point suggests to increase the powers of local government and transfer some powers from the State to local government that is closer to the people and makes a pluralistic system possible, where the minorities can easier retain their identity and protect their interests. They also recommend that Slovakia adhere to the European Charter of Local Self-Government, and that the increased home rule powers of local government be spelled out in the constitution.

The demands of the Slovakian Hungarians in the Komarom Resolutions are much closer to the European norms that that of the Transylvanian Hungarians, but even this leaves room for considerable improvement to be useful as a negotiating starting point.

It should be noted, that in the recent elections the chauvinistic Meciar government was defeated and a new coalition took over, and representatives

---

375 Ibid., pp. 4-5.
376 Ibid., p. 5.
377 Ibid., p. 6.

of the Hungarian community do participate in the new coalition. Hopefully, this coalition will have more successful minority policy than the previous Meciar government had, or the Rumanians still have.

The Hungarians of the Sub-Carpathian region that came under Ukrainian sovereignty after the break-up of the Soviet Union, also issued a demand on the "Establishment and Functions of the Cultural Self-Government of Minorities in 1996.[378] The statement contains some general principles the authors would like to see realized, including a detailed description of the proposed functions and the system of election of representatives to a National Minority Council that would handle the affairs of the minority.

---

378 Cf. KARPATALJAI SZEMLE (Sub-Carpathian Review) 1996 #1.

CONCLUSION:

How could it be done Without War or Violence?

There are several possibilities, assuming that the international community is ready to take some strong action. Since most countries involved have dire economic conditions, partly due to the time, energy and other resources wasted due to the minority conflict, not to mention interruption of productive activities and the actual destruction that results from war-like fighting among ethnic groups, an attractive developmental package could be offered as an incentive to resolve the minority problem and the ethnic conflict. Such a package could serve the interest of both the western nations offering the package, in making these countries better trading partners, and of the countries in question,

To make this work, strict alternatives should be provided as the stick, ranging from partial or complete ban and boycott of the countries that do not go along, to military pressure, declaring the government illegitimate, and possible intervention if the oppression of minorities endangers peace and order in the region.

There are suggestions from Hungarian nationalists that "Trianon should be re-visited." This could mean anything, depending on the group, from complete restoration of the old borders to make border changes or to enforce the minority guarantees promised at Trianon. But Trianon had created a unique situation. While "re-visiting Trianon" may solve some specific problems of the Hungarian minorities in neighboring countries, a more general solution is desirable, because the minority and the resulting refugee problem along with the threat of ethnic violence has become a global issue.

Therefore we must find a global solution, and of all the international agencies and organizations it seems at this time the United Nations is the best equipped to develop, propose and institute a global solution and to impose global sanctions if they would become necessary, since all involved countries are members of the UN. The European Community also should develop the tools necessary to protect minorities within its jurisdiction. Unfortunately, however, the most delinquent Central European nations, Rumania, Serbia and Slovakia are not and are not likely to become EC members in the near future, although according to news reports, after the elections Slovakia's chances have tremendously improved.

As for the UN action, once the major powers in the world are convinced that the time is ripe and the package is ready, one government must bring it to the United Nations Security Council and the General Assembly. With the help of international legal experts the UN must consider the entire issue of national self-determination. Piecemeal work will just delay the resolution of the problem, and confuse both the majorities and minorities as to what their rights and responsibilities will be! The UN should not repeat the mistake the previous generation had committed in freezing the status quo in Africa and the rest of the world after the collapse of colonialism.

Such UN action is urgently needed, in light of the Kosovo fighting. Even if there will be eventual agreement in Rambouillet, France, with Milosevic, the international community cannot afford the kind of frustrating negotiation that Milosevic has been conducting every time a small time dictator or a chauvinistic majority decides to kill off its minority population. The UN should be in a position to have an international court make a decision, and the UN issue an ultimatum with a deal-line to comply with the court decision, and use military force against countries that fail to comply respect the most basic rules of humanity. International outlaws cannot get any better treatment than domestic ones.

The UN resolution[379] should provide for respect of minority rights, or adequate autonomy. If the country in question fails to provide adequate autonomy, which is a domestic matter for each country, the UN should order separation from the majority country and recognize the minority territories, on the basis "of extreme or other ways inevitable necessity"[380] as sovereign countries that will decide their future themselves. It should also include a warning that if the minorities would be subjected to violence as the result of the UN decision, it would not only authorize use of force to protect the minorities from violence (as it has been done already in Bosnia), but would declare the guilty government undemocratic and deny its right to govern, as the OAS had done in the case of the Samoza government of Nicaragua.

Accordingly, the UN must establish guide lines on three level:

1. To what minimum rights are the minorities entitled to, individually and collectively.

---

379 A proposed Resolution, as a starting point for discussion purposes, shall be included in Appendix 1.
380 Cf. #123 above.

2. When is autonomy warranted, and what are some of the functions and rights that should be de-centralized, with the actual provisions to be negotiated, under international supervision and assistance, by the parties involved on a case by case basis.

3. Provisions should be made by the UN to carry out the separation of a part of a country when secession, as the consequence of the treatment of the minority, is approved according to the principles of Grotius in an internationally organized and supervised referendum by the minority.

An important aspect of these rules should be to provide appropriate sanctions for its peaceful enforcement, if possible, but not excluding force, if necessary.

The UN will also have to decide if historical territorial claims should be considered, and if yes, to what extent, how far must the claim go back, etc. But the UN should also be cautioned that in some parts of the world borders have changed so much that it might be impossible to find or decide the rightful owners, unless the rule of "first sovereign" will be instituted. In considering territorial claims care should be taken not to render the human and minority rights argument secondary. It is suggested that peace and stability would be best served if the territorial argument is accepted and used only to strengthen claims based current human rights situations.

In the Carpathian Basin the legal, moral and political justification for such a move is multi-fold and includes both territorial claims based on a historic grievance, and human rights claims:

*   The argument that Hungary was "greatly responsible" for the outbreak of World War I, the premise for the partition of Hungary and the creation of the successor states, is absurd, as the evidence above demonstrated, while the parties truly responsible, including Serbia, were rewarded, violating the principles of Grotius. If the treatment of Hungary by the victorious parties at Trianon would become general practice, the international community would turn into chaos.

*   These multi-ethnic countries with unresolved minority issues are a threat to the peace of the region and of the world. The breaking up of Yugoslavia and Bosnia gave us a sample of the fierce genocide that can occur if the passion of nationalism is allowed to run free in a country, and if no provision is made for the orderly and peaceful resolution of the minority issue before violence erupts. An international aspect of these conflicts are the flood of refugees, and ironically, Hungary is the first target country of the masses of refugees. Nobody wants, or even expects at this time, internal revolution in Serbia, Rumania or Slovakia, but if the string is tightened too much, nobody knows what desperate people

might do. And if any violence would occur, the responsibility and guilt would be shared between the chauvinistic majority and the negligent international community.

- A New World Order must be based on respect of ethnic and cultural differences, and cultural fault lines should be recognized and respected in drawing and/or re-drawing state boundaries when possible, or, when border changes are impractical, at least by creating autonomous regions, so one culture cannot threaten or absorb another;

- The territories were ceded to these countries by the Treaties of Trianon with the condition that they will respect minority rights, as President Wilson has emphasized, and all parties had agreed. So creating autonomous regions would be little more than belated enforcement of the Treaties signed by the countries involved, or their lawful predecessors (except in the case of Ukraine, which did not even exist at that time). Further, the so called "successor states" failed to carry out their freely agreed obligations regarding the treatment of the minorities. This should be sufficient reason even to cancel those contracts.

- The partitioning of Hungary by the Treaty of Trianon, at the height of the hysteria during and following the war, violated the Wilsonian 14 points, and the partition of Hungary, at least in its actual form, was unjust and unlawful, so it is incumbent on the international community, especially the countries that have signed and guaranteed the upholding of the provisions of the treaties, to restore as justice and order much as possible as preconditions of regional and perhaps world peace, since major superpowers on opposing sides of the fault line could also find themselves on opposing sides in a political conflict.

- Given the conditions and the restrictions on the Hungarian delegation in Versailles and the threat to the Hungarian government and the entire country, the Treaty was signed under duress, and therefore as a contract it is morally null and void, and the procedures applied at Trianon have never become precedents. Therefore, even if conditions cannot be returned to as it was before the injustice was committed, some remedy should be found. Therefore it is incumbent upon the International Community to restore justice without any further suffering to those innocent peoples who were thrust into minority role under violently oppressive regimes.

It is not easy to correct a major mistake and injustice that had occurred almost eighty years ago. But the unresolved minority issue is stalling both political democracy and economic development both in those successor states and in Hungary. On the other hand, solving this thorny issue could be not only a precedent for solving thorny minority issues in other parts of the world, but could be a giant step in the direction of world peace and economic progress, toward a New World Order, as Ervin Laszlo suggested.

Once the minority issue is solved, without unnecessary border changes and in principle by a new universal law and effective UN action not only the Carpathian Basin and Europe but the entire world will be a more just and more peaceful place.

But policies do not just come out of nowhere. They have to be developed and carefully promoted. Since there is only one such international agency in the world that can accomplish this, the United Nations, all peace loving citizens, many of them one time refugees, who live in the West and have oppressed compatriots under foreign domination and hope to improve their lot, should unite in Non Governmental Organizations (NGO's) and through sympathetic governments pressure the United Nations for effective action. They also must inform, educate and convince the governments of the countries in which they live and of which they are often voting citizens, to take the necessary steps to preserve regional and world peace by introducing and supporting appropriate forms of self-determination before terrorism erupts and while it can be done without the introduction of peacekeeping forces under the United Nations flag.

Finally, political émigrés of all nations whose members suffer in minority status and have the most at stake, should cooperate with each other and with national and international peace organizations. They must initiate and coordinate this activity, or nobody will do it, and the world will remain a more dangerous, violent, and unjust place at the commencement of the next millennia.

APPENDICES

APPENDIX I.

PROPOSED UN RESOLUTION ON
NATIONAL SELF-DETERMINATION

Based on the classic definition of self-determination by Grotius, the 1921 League of Nations Resolution on the Aaland Islands, various subsidiary sources of international law, expert opinion and "opinio juris," of which several were mentioned and discussed in this book, the following RESOLUTION ON MINORITY SELF-DETERMINATION is recommended for consideration by the United Nations.

1. "In case of extreme or otherwise inevitable necessity a part may by itself transfer to other hands the sovereignty over itself without the consent of all the people." (Grotius, THE LAW OF WAR AND PEACE, 3, XX, 5.)

2. "Extreme necessity" shall consist of

> a. Refusal by the government to grant and protect against forced assimilation or against invasion of the minority's rights to maintain its cultural, religious or linguistic identity, and to practice the same freely, under similar conditions as the majority does, or if necessary, under positive protection.

> b. Refusal by the government to consider, grant, and comply with appropriate forms of autonomy, including personal, shared, cross-border, or territorial autonomies, to protect the above listed and other rights that civilized communities through traditions and/or various bi- and multilateral treaties and other instruments recognize.
> c. Creation of an international disturbance by producing border incidents, inducing a flow of refugees into other countries, disrupting international trade, travel, and satisfaction of international contracts.

3. The World Court/International Court of Justice shall have jurisdiction to hear complaints under this provision, and decide, without regard to the sovereign status of the offending party

> A. if the situation is indeed an "extreme necessity" under the above standard, and

B. If it is, what remedy should be ordered. The court can
    a. suspend the offending government and institute a temporary care-taker government until new elections are held,
    b. order one or more forms of autonomy, or
    c. in extreme cases, order a referendum on secession in the affected area.

4. At least two UN member organizations, one of which is not an interested party in the dispute, or appropriate organs of CSCE, ODIHR, EC., or other multi-lateral organizations, and a special committee established by the UN Secretariat to monitor compliance with this Resolution, shall have standing in the court. NGO's are urged to work with one or more of the above parties to document and bring minority rights violations to their attention.

5. The offending nations shall have no more than one year to comply with the Court's order. Any act of harassment, violence or escalation of anti-minority activity during the period from when the charges are brought to the full compliance will be dealt with, and the individuals, including government officials, shall be severely punished.

6. The United Nations Security Council shall have the power to enforce the court's decision by all peaceful means if possible, and using appropriate force if necessary.

Additional suggestion:

Until the United Nations passes this or similar and effective Resolution, it is suggested that based on the factors listed in the Introduction to this proposal, especially subsidiary sources and opinio juris, Parties that have standing in the Court, attempt to get the Court to accept minority rights violation cases on the above outlined basis. In International Law cases are often initiated without existing prior positive law.

APPENDIX II

DOCUMENT OF THE COPENHAGEN MEETING OF THE CONFERENCE ON THE HUMAN DIMENSION OF THE CSCE

The representatives of the participating States of the Conference on Security and Cooperation in Europe (CSCE), Austria, Belgium, Bulgaria, Canada, Cyprus, Czechoslovakia, Denmark, Finland, France, the German Democratic Republic, the Federal Republic of Germany, Greece, the Holy See, Hungary, Iceland, Ireland, Italy, Liechtenstein, Luxembourg, Malta, Monaco, the Netherlands, Norway, Poland, Portugal, Romania, San Marino, Spain, Sweden, Switzerland, Turkey, the Union of Soviet Socialist Republics, the United Kingdom, the United States of America and Yugoslavia, met in Copenhagen from 5 to 29 June 1990, in accordance with the provisions relating to the Conference on the Human Dimension of the CSCE contained in the Concluding Document of the Vienna Follow-up Meeting of the CSCE.

The representative of Albania attended the Copenhagen Meeting as observer.

The first Meeting of the Conference was held in Paris from 30 May to 23 June 1989.
The Copenhagen Meeting was opened and closed by the Minister for Foreign Affairs of Denmark.

At the Copenhagen Meeting the participating States held a review of the implementation of their commitments in the field of the human dimension. They considered that the degree of compliance with the commitments contained in the relevant provisions of the CSCE documents had shown a fundamental improvement since the Paris Meeting. They also expressed the view, however, that further steps are required for the full realization of their commitments relating to the human dimension.

In order to strengthen respect for, and enjoyment of, human rights and fundamental freedoms, to develop human contacts and to resolve issues of a related humanitarian character, the participating States agree on the following:

(30)　　　　The participating States recognize that the questions relating to national minorities can only be satisfactorily resolved in a democratic political framework based on the rule of law, with a functioning independent judiciary. This framework guarantees full respect for human rights and fundamental freedoms, equal rights and status for all citizens, the free expression of all their legitimate interests and aspirations, political pluralism, social tolerance and the implementation of legal rules that place effective restraints on the abuse of governmental power.

They also recognize the important role of non-governmental organizations, including political parties, trade unions, human rights organizations and religious groups, in the promotion of tolerance, cultural diversity and the resolution of questions relating to national minorities.

They further reaffirm that respect for the rights of persons belonging to national minorities as part of universally recognized human rights is an essential factor for peace, justice, stability and democracy in the participating States.

(31)　　　　Persons belonging to national minorities have the right to exercise fully and effectively their human rights and fundamental freedoms without any discrimination and in full equality before the law.

The participating States will adopt, where necessary, special measures for the purpose of ensuring to persons belonging to national minorities full equality with the other citizens in the exercise and enjoyment of human rights and fundamental freedoms.

(32)　　　　To belong to a national minority is a matter of a person's individual choice and no disadvantage may arise from the exercise of such choice.

Persons belonging to national minorities have the right freely to express, preserve and develop their ethnic, cultural, linguistic or religious identity and to maintain and develop their culture in all its aspects, free of any attempts at assimilation against their will. In particular, they have the right

(32.1) - to use freely their mother tongue in private as well as in public;

(32.2) - to establish and maintain their own educational, cultural and religious institutions, organizations or associations, which can seekvoluntary financial or other contributions as well as public assistance, in conformity with national legislation;

(32.3) - to profess and practise their religion, including the acquisition, possession and use of religious materials, and to conduct religious educational activities in their mother tongue;

(32.4) - to establish and maintain unimpeded contacts among themselves within their country as well as contacts across frontiers with citizens of other States with whom they share a common ethnic or national origin, cultural heritage or religious beliefs;

(32.5) - to disseminate, have access to and exchange information in their mother tongue;

(32.6) - to establish and maintain organizations or associations within their country and to participated in international non-governmental organizations. Persons belonging to national minorities can exercise and enjoy their rights individually as well as in community with other members of their group. No disadvantage may arise for a person belonging to a national minority on account of the exercise or non-exercise of any such rights.

(33) The participating States will protect the ethnic, cultural, linguistic and religious identity of national minorities on their territory and create conditions for the promotion to that effect after due consultations, including contacts with organizations or associations of such minorities, in accordance with the decision-making procedures of each State.

Any such measures will be in conformity with the principles of equality and non-discrimination with respect to the other citizens of the participating State concerned.

(34) The participating States will endeavour to ensure that persons belonging to national minorities, notwithstanding the need to learn the official language or languages of the State concerned, have adequate opportunities for instruction of their

mother tongue, as well as, wherever possible and necessary, for its use before public authorities, in conformity with applicable national legislation.

In the context of the teaching of history and culture in educational establishments, they will also take into account of the history and culture of national minorities.

(35)   The participating States will respect the right of persons belonging to national minorities to effective participation in public affairs, including participation in the affairs relating to the protection and promotion of the identity of such minorities.

The participating States note the efforts undertaken to protect and create conditions for the promotion of the ethnic, cultural, linguistic and religious identity of certain national minorities by establishing, as one of the possible means to achieve these aims, appropriate local or autonomous administrations corresponding to the specific historical and territorial circumstances of such minorities and in accordance with the policies of the State concerned.

(36)   The participating States recognize the particular importance of increasing constructive co-operation among themselves on questions relating to national minorities. such co-operation seeks to promote mutual understanding and confidence, friendly and good-neighbourly relations, international peace, security and justice.

Every participating State will promote a climate of mutual respect, understanding, co-operation and solidarity among all persons living on its territory, without distinction as to ethnic or national origin or religion, and will encourage the solution of problems through dialogue based on the principles of the rule of law.

(37)   None of these commitments may be interpreted as implying any right to engage in any activity or perform any action in contravention of the purposes and principles of the Charter of the United Nations, other obligations under international law or the provisions of the Final Act, including the principle of territorial integrity of the States.

(38)   The participating States, in their efforts to protect and promote the rights of persons belonging to national minorities, will fully respect their undertakings under existing human rights conventions and other relevant conventions, if they have not yet done so, including those providing for a right of complaint by individuals.

(39)   The participating States will co-operate closely in the competent international organizations to which they belong, including the United Nations and, as appropriate, the Council of Europe, bearing in mind their on-going work with respect to questions relating to national minorities.

They will consider convening a meeting of experts for a thorough discussion of the issue of national minorities.

(40)   The participating States clearly and unequivocally condemn totalitarianism, racial and ethnic hatred, anti-semitism, xenophobia and discrimination against anyone as well as persecution on religious and ideological grounds. In this context, they also recognize the particular problems of Roma (gypsies).

They declare their firm intention to intensify the efforts to combat these phenomena in all their forms and therefore will

(40.1) - take effective measures, including the adoption, in conformity with their constitutional systems and their international obligations, of such lawas may be necessary, to provide protection against any acts that constitute incitement of violence against persons or groups based on national, racial, ethnic or religious discrimination, hostility or hatred, including anti-semitism;

(40.2) - commit themselves to take appropriate and proportionate measures to protect persons or groups who may be subject to threats or acts of discrimination, hostility or violence as a result of their racial, ethnic, cultural, linguistic or religious identity, and to protect their property;

(40.3) - take effective measures, in conformity with their constitutional systems, at the national, regional and local levels to promote understanding and tolerance, particularly in the fields of education, culture and information;

(40.4) - endeavour to ensure that the objectives of education include special attention to the problem of racial prejudice and hatred and to the development of respect for different civilizations and cultures;

(40.5) - recognize the right of the individual to effective remedies and endeavour to recognize, in conformity with national legislation, the right of interested persons and groups to initiate and support complaints against acts of discrimination, including racist and xenophobic acts;

(40.6) - consider adhering, if they have not yet done so, to the international instruments which address the problem of discrimination and ensure full compliance with the obligations therein, including those relating to the submission of periodic reports;

(40.7) - consider, also, accepting those international mechanisms which allow States and individuals to bring communications relating to discrimination before international bodies.
V

(41)   The participating States reaffirm their commitment to the human dimension of the CSCE and emphasize its importance as an integral part of a balanced approach to security and co-operation in Europe. They agree that the Conference on the Human Dimension of the CSCE and the human dimension mechanism described in the section on the human dimension of the CSCE of the Vienna Concluding Document have demonstrated their value as methods of furthering their dialogue and co-operation and assisting in the resolution of relevant specific questions. They express their conviction that these should be continued and developed as part of an expanding CSCE process.

(42)   The participating States recognize the need to enhance further the effectiveness of the procedures described in paragraphs 1 to 4 of the section on

the human dimension of the CSCE of the Vienna Concluding Document and with this aim decide

(42.1)   - to provide in as short a time as possible, but no later than four weeks, a written response to requests for information and to representations made to them in writing by other participating States under paragraph 1;

(42.2)   - that the bilateral meetings, as contained in paragraph 2, will take place as soon as possible, as a rule within three weeks of the date of the request;

(42.3)   - to refrain, in the course of a bilateral meeting held under paragraph 2, from raising situations and cases not connected with the subject of the meeting, unless both sides have agreed to do so.

(43)   The participating States examined practical proposals for new measures aimed at improving the implementation of the commitments relating to the human dimension of the CSCE. In this regard, they considered proposals related to the sending of observers to examine situations and specific cases, the appointment of rapporteurs to investigate and suggest appropriate solutions, the setting up of a Committee on the Human Dimension of the CSCE, greater involvement of persons, organizations and institutions in the human dimension mechanism and further bilateral and multilateral efforts to promote the resolution of relevant issues.

* * *

(44)   The representatives of the participating States express their profound gratitude to the people and Government of Denmark for the excellent organization of the Copenhagen Meeting and the warm hospitality extended to the delegations which participated in the Meeting.

(45)   In accordance with the provisions relating to the Conference on the Human Dimension of the CSCE contained in the Concluding Document of the Vienna Follow-up Meeting of the CSCE, the third Meeting of the Conference will take place in Moscow from 10 September to 4 October 1991.

Copenhagen, 29 June 199

CSCE HIGH COMMISSIONER ON
NATIONAL MINORITIES

(I)   The participating States decide to establish a High Commissioner on
National Minorities

Mandate

(2)   The High Commissioner will act under the aegis of the CSO and will
thus be an instrument of conflict prevention at the earliest possible stage

(3)   The High Commissioner will provide "early warning" and, as
appropriate, "early action" at the earliest possible stage in regard to tensions
involving national minority issues which have not yet developed beyond an
early warning stage. but. in the judgement of the High Commissioner, have
the potential to develop into a conflict within the CSCE area, affecting peace,
stability or relations between participating States, requiring the attention of
and action by the Council or the CSO.

(4)   Within the mandate, based on CSCE principles and commitments, the
High Commissioner will work in confidence and will act independently of all
parties   directly involved in the tensions.

(5a)   The High Commissioner will consider national minority issues
occurring in the State of which the High Commissioner is a national or a
resident, or involving a national minority to which the High Commissioner
belongs. only if all parties directly involved agree, including the State
concerned.

(5b) The High Commissioner will not consider national minority issues in
situations involving organized acts of terrorism.

(5c)   Nor will the High Commissioner consider violations of CSCE
commitments with regard to an individual person belonging to a national
minority

(6)   In considering a situation, the High Commissioner will take fully into
account the availability of democratic means and international instruments to
respond to it, and their utilization by the parties involved.

212

(7)   When a particular national minority issue has been brought to the attention of the CSO, the involvement of the High Commissioner will require a request and a speciflc mandate from the CSO.

Profile, appointment, support

(8)   The High Commissioner will be an eminent international personality with long-standing relevant experience from whom an impartial performance of the function may be expected

(9) The High Commissioner will be appointed by The Council by consensus upon the recommendation of the CSO for a period of three years which may be extended for one further term of three years only.

(10)   The High Commissioner will draw upon the facilities of the ODIHR in Warsaw and in particular upon the information relevant to all aspects of national minority questions available at the ODIHR.

Early warning

(11) The High Commissioner will:

(11a)   collect and receive information regarding national minority issues from sources described below (see Supplement paragraphs (23)-(25));

(11b) assess at the earliest possible stage the role of the parties directly concerned.
the nature of the tensions and recen~ developments therein and. where possible.
the potential consequences for peace and stability within the CSCE area:

(11c) to this end. be able to pay a visit in accordance with paragraph (17) and Supplement paragraphs (~7)-(30) to any participating State and communicale in person. subject to the provisions of paragraph (25). with parties directly concerned to obtain first-hand information about the situation of national minorities.

(12)   The High Commissioner may during a visit to a participating State while obtaining first-hand information from all parties directly involved, discuss the questions with the parties, and where appropriate promote dialogue, confidence and co-operation between them.

Provision of early warning

(13) If, on the basis of exchanges of communications and contacts with relevant parties. the High Commissioner concludes that there is a prima facie risk of potential conflict (as set out in paragraph (3) he/she may issue an early warning which all be communicated promptly by the Chairman-in-Office to the CSO.

(14) The Chairman-in-Office will include this early warning in the agenda for the next meeting of the CSO. If a State believes that such an early warning merits prompt consultation, it may initiate the procedure set out in Annex 2 of the Summary of Conclusions of the Berlin Meeting of the Council ("Emergency Mechanism").

(15) The High Commissioner will explain to the CSO the reasons for issuing the early warning.

Early action

(16) The High Commissioner may recommend that he/she be authorized to enter into further contact and closer consultations with the parties concerned with a view to possible solutions, according to a mandate to be decided by the CSO. The CSO may decide accordingly.

Accountability

(17) The High Commissioner will consult the Chairman-in-Office prior to a departure for a participating State to address a tension involving national minorities. The Chairman-in-Office will consult, in confidence, the participating State(s) concerned and may consult more widely.

(18) After a visit to a participating State, the High Commissioner will provide strictly confidential reports to the Chairman-in-Office on the findings and progress of the High Commissioner's involvement in a particular question.

(19) After termination of the involvement of the High Commissioner in a particular issue. the High Commissioner will report to the Chairman-in-Office on the findings. results and conclusions. Within a period of one month, the Chairman-in-Office will consult, in confidence, on the findings, results and

conclusions the participating State(s) concerned and may consult more widely.

Thereafter the report, together with possible comments, will be transmitted to the CSO.

(20) Should the High Commissioner conclude that the situation is escalating into a conflict, or if the High Commissioner deems that the scope for action by the High Commissioner is exhausted, the High Commissioner shall, through the Chairman-in-Office, so inform the CSO.

(21) Should the CSO become involved in a particular issue, the High Commissioner will provide information and, on request, advice to the CSO, or to any other institution or organization which the CSO may invite, in accordance with the provisions of Chapter III of this document, to take action with regard to the tensions or conflict.

(22) The High Commissioner, if so requested by the CSO and with due regard to the requirement of confidentiality in his/her mandate, will provide information about his/her activities at CSCE implementation meetings on Human Dimension issues.

Supplement

Sources of information about national minority issue

(23) The High Commissioner may:

(23a) collect and receive information regarding the situation of national minorities and the role of parties involved therein from any source, including the media and non-governmental organizations with the exception referred to in paragraph (25);

(23b) receive specific reports from parties directly involved regarding developments concerning national minority issues. These may include reports on violations of CSCE commitments with respect to national minorities as well as other violations in the context of national minority issues.

(24) Such specific reports to the High Commissioner should meet the following requirements:

- they should be in writing, addressed to the High Commissioner as such and signed with full names and addresses;

- they should contain a factual account of the developments which are relevant to the situation of persons belonging to national minorities and the role of the parties involved therein. and which have taken place recently, in principle not more than 12 months previously. The reports should contain information which can be sufficiently substantiated.

(25) The High Commissioner will not communicate with and will not acknowledge communications from any person or organization which practises or publicly condones terrorism or violence.

Parties directly concerned

(26) Parties directly concerned in tensions who can provide specific reports to the High Commissioner and with whom the High Commissioner will seek to communicate in person during a visit to a participating State are the following:

(26a) governments of participating States, including, if appropriate, regional and local authorities in areas in which national minorities reside;

(26b) representatives of associations, non-governmental organizations, religious and other groups of national minorities directly concerned and in the area of tension, which are authorized by the persons belonging to those national minorities to represent them.

Conditions for travel by the High Commissioner

(27) Prior to an intended visit, the High Commissioner will submit to the participating State concerned specific information regarding the intended purpose of that visit. Within two weeks the State(s) concerned will consult with the High Commissioner on the objectives of the visit, which may include the promotion of dialogue, confidence and co-operation between the parties. After entry the State concerned will facilitate free travel and communication of the High Commissioner subject to the provisions of paragraph (25) above.

(28) If the State concerned does not allow the High Commissioner to enter the country and to travel and communicate freely, the High Commissioner will so inform the CSO

(29) In the course of such a visit, subject to the provision of paragraph 25 the High Commissioner may consult the parties involved, and may receive information in confidence from any individual. group or organization directly

concerned on questions the High Commissioner is addressing. The High Commissioner will respect the confidential nature of the information.

30)   The participating States will refrain from taking any action against persons, organizations or institutions on account of their contact with the High Commissioner.

High Commissioner and involvement of experts

(31)   The High Commissioner may decide to request assistance from not more than three experts with relevant expertise in specific matters on which brief, specialized investigation and advice are required.

(32)   If the High Commissioner decides to call on experts, the High Commissioner will set a clearly defined mandate and time-frame for the activities of the experts.

(33)   Experts will only visit a participating State at the same time as the High Commissioner. Their mandate will be an integral part of the mandate of the High Commissioner and the same conditions for travel will apply.

(34)   The advice and recommendations requested from the experts will be submitted in confidence to the High Commissioner, who will be responsible for the activities and for the reports of the experts and who will decide whether and in what form the advice and recommendations will be communicated to the parties concerned. They will be non-binding. if the High Commissioner decides to make the advice and recommendations available, the State(s) concerned will be given the opportunity to comment.

(35)   The experts will be selected by the High Commissioner with the assistance of the ODIHR from the resource list established at the ODIHR as laid down in the Document of the Moscow Meeting.

(36)   The experts will not include nationals or residents of the participating State concerned. or any person appointed by the State concerned, or any expert against whom the participating State has previously entered reservations. The experts will not include the participating State's own nationals or residents or any of the persons it appointed to the resource list, or more than one national or resident of any particular State.

Budget

(37)   A separate budget will be determined at the ODIHR, which will provide, as appropriate, logistical support for travel and communication. The budget will be funded by the participating States according to the established CSCE scale of distribution. Details will be worked out by the Financial Committee and approved by the CSO.

(Helsinki, July 1992)

COMMISSION ON
SECURITY AND COOPERATION IN EUROPE

237 FORD HOUSE OFFICE 8UILDING
WASHINGTON, DC 205 15

(202)225-1901

CSCE'S HIGH COMMISSIONER
ON NATIONAL MINORITIES
June 1993

The High Commissioner's Mandate

The CSCE created the post of High Commissioner on National Minorities at its July 1992 summit meeting in Helsinki, in response to the emergence of minonty-related unrest as one of the main sources of conflict in Europe. Originally proposed by the Netherlands, the proposal received wide support as an innovative approach to national minority problems unleashed by the disappearance of superpower confrontation in Europe.

The High Commissioner is envisioned as an independent, unbiased individual of high stature, who can investigate national minority-related problems confidentially, before they reach crisis proportions. These are to be problems which, in the opinion of the High Commissioner, have the potential to develop into conflicts endangering international peace and security. The High Commissioner is empowered to gather information, including through visits, and to promote dialogue.1

Before beginning a visit, and again after consideration of an issue is completed, the High Comrnissioner must consult with the CSCE's Chair-in Office. If the issue is deemed to be of grave concern, an "Early Warning" of a threat to peace and security may be issued by the High Commissioner and discussed by the CSCE's Committee of Senior Officials (CSO), CSCE's central political body including represcntatives of all 53 participating states.2

Limitations

Some of the most innovative aspects of the original proposal for a High Commissioner were substantially watered down in response to individual state's concerns.

1. The High Commissioners mandate is Section II of the Helsinki Document 1992: Challenges of Change.

2 CSCE's members include the United States and Canada and all the states of Europe and the former Soviet Union, except Macedonia, which has observer status. The "Federal Republic of Yugoslavia" (Serbia Montenegro) has been suspended since July 1992

The High Commissioner may not become imolved where armed conflict has already broken out or in areas already under consideration by the CSO, unless the permission of the CSO is given. Communication with or response to communications from organizations or individuals who practice or publicly condone terrorism is prohibited, as is involvement in situations "involving organized acts of terrorism."

The High Commissioner's mandate is constructed with emphasis on quiet diplomacy. This choice was deliberate in order to avoid pressuring governments or inflaming delicate situations, but it also deprives the High Commissioner of certain tools. Not only could this prestigious position exert considerable moral authority and pressure on governments and groups, but its potential for public diplomacy could be a boon for the little-known and less understood CSCE. Additionally, quiet diplomacy also justifies the strictly limited reporting to participating States comissioned by the mandates. The High Commissioner is only required to report to the CSCE's Chair-in-Office and through the Chair to the participating States; even a report to CSCE's bi-annual Human Dimension Implementation Meeting must be requested by the CSO.

Activities to Date

Former Dutch Foreign Minister Max van der Stoel was appointed the first High Commissioner in December 1992; his office began to function in January 1993, with premises donated by the Dutch government and a staff of three diplomats seconded from the Dutch, Polish and Swedish foreign ministries.

Van der Stoel chose for his first mission Estonia, Latvia and Lithuania, three small countries whose emancipation from Russian occupation left large Russian minorities with uncertain legal status. Estonia had previous}y requested and received a mission under the CSCE's Human Dimension Mechanism to consider whether its citizenship law met international standards; short}y after van der Stoel's visit, the CSCE placed a long-term mission in Estonia to help stimulate dialogue between the Estonian and Russian-speaking communities. Both in statements to press, government, and public in the three countries, and in a subsequent report presented to the

CSO, van der Stoel chose to avoid direct criticism of any of the governments. His recommendations included pragmatic steps such as increasing availability of language instruction and the establishment of Ombudsmen or National Commissioners and other institutions to further dialogue and consideration of concrete problems.

Subsequently, van der Stoel turned to the prickly question of ethnic Hungarians in the newly-independent Slovak Republic, whose concerns had been a topic of much discussion in non-governmental circles. In his reporting to the CSO (subsequently made a publicly available CSCE document, as were the Baltic reports), van der Stoel avoided any judgements

on the situation of Hungarians in Slovakia.3 Instead, he developed a dual-sided approach which considered Slovaks in Hungary as well as Hungarians in Slovakia—to the surprise of experts, who have not considered Slovaks in Hungary as a problem of major proportions.

Acknowledging that the question needed further surveillance, van der Stoel proposed to the CSO a program of visits to Slovakia and Hungary by experts ~affiliated with his office - not to exceed four to each over two years. After some discussion, the plan was adapted by the CSO and will require reporting from the High Commission after each visit, with a final report at the end of the two-year period.

The CSO at its April 2~28, 1993 meeting also tasked the High Commissioner to study the problems of Roma (Gypsies) and their relevance to his mandate, in response to concern for the situation of Roma voiced in the report of the rapporteur mission to the newly admitted Czech and Slovak Republics. The High Commission visited Romania in June 1993, at the invitation of the Romanian government, and is working with Macedonia and Albania as well.

Early Assessment

While six months is evidently too short a period of time to pass judgment on the success of the High Commissioner's efforts toward early warning, conflict prevention, and problem solving it is not too soon to note certain trends. Most significant are the results of the limitations imposed by the mandate. These include the High Commissioner's half constrained relations with participating States; the restrictions on his activity, limiting his ability to address many pressing minority issues; and the difficulty in coordinating his work with other initiatives.

First, the High Commissioner's independence effectively separates him from CSCE deliberations, activities, and structures, permitting a situation in which he traveled to Estonia precisely between a CSCE rapporteur mission and the establishment of a CSCE long duration mission to that country. One wonders whether some of the resources could not have been re-focused elsewhere, or at least better coordinated, particularly as the High Commissioner's mandate precludes activity in areas where the CSO is already engaged. Follow-up might be better coordinated with the participating States as well, increasing the role of the High Commissioner, and the profile of his issues, within CSCE's structures.

The limitations on High Commissioner activity are subject to some interpretation.

---

3 The relevant decisions are available in the Journal of the 21st CSO, April 26-28, 1993. This and other CSCE documents referred to, including the High Commissioner reports, are available through the CSCE Secretariat in Prague, Czech Republic

---

The interpretations which van der Stoel has chosen to make so far lead, in the view of the Commnission, to some unfortunate anomalies. For example, it is regrettable that the High Commissioner's office has remained entirely silent to date on the problems of Turkish Kurds, thus seeming to brands all Kurds with the terrorist label which prohibits High Commissioner activity, and displaying indifference to one of Europe's major human rights tragedies. Given the troubling handling of this serious human rights issues by the CSCE community to date, it seems to the Commission that the High Commissioner has abdicated what could be a leading role. Likewise, attention to the problems of Roma has thus far been limited to a study of their "relevance to the mandate of the High Commissioner," and that only after a decision by the CSO mandating him to do so. Arguments have been made that Roma issues do not "have the potential to develop into a conflict within the CSCE area affecting peace, stability or relations between participating States, requiring the attention of and action by the Council or CSO(4) While wars over Roma may well be unlikely, ignoring the problems of a group as badly mistreated and forgotten as the Roma casts favorable light neither on the High Commissioner nor on the participating States who have let it be known that Roma are not a fit topic for the High Cornmissioner's work.

A further consequence of the High Commissioner's limited mandate is the difficulty in connecting treatment of national minority issues with other economic or social problems that may increase or even underlie national minority tensions. For example, van der Stoel's initiatives cannot address the delays in Russian troop withdrawal that have done so much to poison ethnic relations in the Baltics; nor can they address general human rights shortcomings affecting all citizens of a given state. Thus far, van der Stoel's interpretation of his mandate has led him to function at a considerable mental as well as physical distance from CSCE's other activities. More efforts to be involved in CSCE activities relating to early warning and conflict prevention would improve CSCE's ability to address security comprehensively and to polish its image as a protector of human rights.

On a positive note, fears that the High Commissioner's separate role would further marginalize human rights issues within the CSCE have not materialized. Participating States' desire to scrutinize his work has ensured discussion of his activities in the CSO and the human dimension seminars of the CSCE Office for Democratic Institutions and Human Rights (ODIHR). His presentations at both types of meeting have been well-received (he delivered the keynote address at ODIHR's May 1993 Seminar on Case Studies on National Minorities Issues: Positive Results).

In his first report to the CSO, in April 1993, van der Stoel presented his proposals for follow-up in Estonia and Slovakia/Hungary that were mentioned above. Although they may be viewed as modest or disappointingly so, they were carefully prepared to be acceptable to the states concerned and were accepted without controversy. In the field of

----

4 Section II, paragraph 3 of the 1992 Helsinki DocumenL

----

national minorities, this may in itself be regarded as something of an achievement. His success in visiting states and crafting reports which treat issues seriously without meeting vocal objections also casts a positive light on van der Stoel himself and the respect shown his post.

This being said, some might have hoped that the office of the High Commissioner would take a more aggressive approach. Van der Stoel has clearly chosen, however, to maximize his role as a governmental insider, slightly distanced from CSCE governments but acting on their behalf rather than as a voice in the wilderness. An early positive result is the acceptance he has won; more concretely, at least one country, Canada, has responded positively to his appeal for language teachers for Estonia.

As long as the High Commissioner remains such an "insider," it is particularly to be hoped that he can cooperate more broadly with CSCE structures to maximize the impact of CSCE's limited resources and to inject valuable human rights perspectives into as broad a spectrum of CSCE concerns as possible. The Commission looks forward to further developments, including the chance at the 1994 Budapest Review Conference to review and revise the High Commissioner's mandate in ways that would allow him to address more completely and openly the problems of minorities in CSCE countries.

For More Information

The mandate of the High Commissioner is printed in the Helsinki Document 1992; the decisions to name van der Stoel to the post and set up his office are appended to the decisions of the 18th CSO, December 11-13, 1992, and the Stockholm Meeting of the CSCE Council of Ministers, December 14-14, 1992. Analyses of the mandate and of his role include:

Conflict Management Group/Harvard Negotiation Project, Early Warning and Preventive Action in the CSCE: Defining the Role of the High Commissioner on National Minonties, Cambridge, MA: Conflict Management Group, 1993.

Staff of the Commission on Security and Cooperation in Europe, "The High Commissioner on National Minorities," in Beyond Process: The CSCE's Institutional Development, 1990-92, Washington, D.C.: The Commission on Security and Cooperation in Europe, 1992, pp. 27-28.

Hannie Zaal, "The CSCE High Commissioner on National Minorities," in the Helsinki Monitor, Utrecht: Netherlands Helsinki Committee, 1992, no. 4, pp. 33-37.

To contact the office of the High Commissioneer:

CSCE High Commissioner on National Minorities
P.O. Box 20062
2500 EB The Hague
The Netherlands

Telephone: (31 70) 362 25 88

APPENDIX III

PLEASE NOTE: UNDERLINED PAGE NUMBERS CORRESPOND TO THE ORIGINAL FUEN EDITION.

PROTECTION OF ETHNIC GROUPS IN EUROPE

Updated **FUEN**-draft Convention:

I. Fundamental Rights Of Persons belon ging to Ethnic Groups in Europe

Draft for an Additional Protocol to the ECHR

II. Autonomy Rights of Ethnic Groups in Europe

Discussion Document for a Special Convention

1994

FUEN-team of experts

PREFACE

With the new European order begun in 1990, a definitive settlement of the issue of ethnic groups within the framework of human rights and on a basis of democratic rule of law has proved to be an indispensable necessity.

The efforts which have started at international level reflect two different strategic concepts:
- the strategy of preventing conflicts, e.g. by establishing standards, as laid down in the efforts of the international communities of states UN, CSCE, Council of Europe and EU as well as the federal union of ethnic groups FUEN;
- the strategy of damage limitation and peace-making as developed by the same communities of states by means of international peace conferences as in the case of Yugoslavia and Bosnia-Herzegovina.
Some results of these efforts have already had legal effects both on international and on national levels by being incorporated in bilateral treaties since 1991 or made a condition for the international recognition of new states in Central and Eastern Europe. However, a standardized European law on ethnic groups has not yet resulted.

The draft Convention on the Fundamental Rights of Ethnic Groups in Europe presented, as a common point of view by the FUEN in May 1992, has met with general approval. It has sometimes been described as maximalistic, since its claim to a comprehensive solution has been mistakenly confused with a maximalist one.

With the decision of the Council of Europe Summit in Vienna on 9 October 1993 to commission the draft of two conventions, i.e. a framework convention and an additional protocol to the ECHR to deal with rights in the cultural field, the way has now been cleared for the development of a standardized European minority law.

A framework convention may be useful. It will probably not contain more than general principles and so it will hardly become legally effective immediately.

Nevertheless it is in the interest of ethnic groups to welcome such a framework convention of the Council of Europe provided that it contains the fundamental principles elaborated in the draft-Convention of the FUEN (Declaration of Cottbus of 28 May 1992) and that reasons of state are not advocated as a pretext to consider the process of legislation as finished, thus preventing the adoption of further instruments of international law with immediate effect.

The decision of Vienna was a compromise. There were good reasons to expect a decision in favour of a special convention in the place of a framework convention. But it must not be overlooked that now the way has become politically free for the development 'of an Additional Protocol to the ECHR even if limited to the cultural field. There is thus some progress, although considerable resistance will have to be overcome before this instrument has been passed and ratified.

An Additional Protocol to the ECHR would be an instrument with two unquestionable advantages: firstly, it incorporates the protection of ethnic groups into the European system of the protection of human rights, and secondly, the rights contained in it become enforceable at the Council of Europe direct. Therefore an Additional Protocol on the protection of ethnic groups was and still is the paramount aim of the FUEN.

However, such an Additional Protocol, owing to the instructions given by the Council of Europe Summit in Vienna, cannot contain any rights of groups whereas a comprehensive European-standardized protection of ethnic groups must complement the rights of individuals with the rights of groups.

Page II

If not only a superficial and partial protection of ethnic groups but a comprehensive one is to be the aim - and only that kind of protection is able to avert the dangers for peace and stability in Europe deriving from the unsolved questions concerning ethnic groups - a further instrument in the form of a special Convention is needed in order to settle all the questions sufficiently which are not solvable by means of the Additional Protocol and the framework convention, such as in particular those of the rights of groups and autonomy.

As a constructive contribution to the dialogue between the interests of States and the interests of ethnic groups the FUEN is submitting an updated version of its draft- Convention (Declaration of Cottbus 1992) on a comprehensive protection of ethnic groups in Europe, which consists of two complementing parts, namely,

1. a draft for an Additional Protocol to the ECHR on the fundamental rights of persons belonging to ethnic groups in Europe;

2. a discussion document for a Special Convention on the rights of autonomy of ethnic groups in Europe.

On account of developments since 1992 it was necessary to revise the draft-Convention of the Declaration of Cottbus in its technical and legal aspects and to supplement and improve its contents. The division into two parts was necessary for reasons of procedure.

Bozen/Bolzano, 28 April 1994

Page III

I. FUNDAMENTAL RIGHTS 0F PERSONS BELONGING TO ETHNIC GROUPS IN EUROPE

Draft for an Additional Protocol to the ECHR

227

Page IV

II. AUTONOMY RIGHTS OF
ETHNIC GROUPS IN EUROPE

Discussion Document for a Special Convention

228

Page 1

I. Fundamental Rights of Persons belonging to Ethnic Groups in Europe

Draft for an Additional Protocol to the ECHR
(Updated FUEN-draft Convention of May 1992)

ACCOMPANYING REPORT

The Council of Europe summit in Vienna decided on 9 October 1993 to instruct the Committee of Ministers to begin work on drafting a protocol complementing the European Convention on Human Rights in the cultural field by provisions guaranteeing individual rights, in particular for persons belonging to national minorties".

229

To implement this resolution the Committee of Ministers established a Committee of Experts (CAHMIN) to submit a draft for such a Protocol by the end of the year 1994. The Committe of Experts, on the other hand, decided at its first meeting on the 25-28 January 1994 to begin work on the draft requested in the second half of the year 1994 so that the first half year was left to the drafting of a framework convention.

By that way, in comparison with spring 1992 when the FUEN submitted its draft Convention on the Fundamental Rights of Ethnic Groups in Europe, for this reason new and changed initial conditions had arisen.

It was, therefore, necessary to revise the contents of the FUEN draft-Convention in view of the specific characteristics of an Additional Protocol to the ECHR as defined by the mandate of the Council of Europe summit of Vienna because the FUEN-draft had been designed in such a way as to offer the possibility of an Additional Protocol as well as a special Convention.

The well-known requirements of a direct reference to human rights and to immediate enforceability was joined, after the resolution of Vienna, by the requirement to limit the contents of the Additional Protocol to individual rights in the cultural field.

In addition, it was necessary to consider in the revision the relevant results of nearly two years of discussion on an international level.

The Council of Europe Summit of Vienna limited the Additional Protocol to individual rights. With the help of the principle of the exercise of individual rights "by single individuals or in community with others" essential contents of the FUEN draft-Convention proposed as group rights, could be integrated into the updated version without loss of substance.

The limitation of the contents to the cultural field - according to the mandate of the Council of Europe summit of Vienna - is not to be seen as restrictive. Culture cannot be understood as being limited to language and education, but it necessarily comprises also the spiritual substrata of a people or ethnic group and the totality of the institutions common to the members of a society. A dispute about this is superflous in view of the fact that also protection of the language and education also assumes the existence of the persons entitled to these rights and thus necessarily implies a right of identity, existence and protection from threat as well as a right of non-discrimination, equal treatment and equal opportunities. Moreover, the rule of non-discrimination with reference to language and education demands the right of special organizations in the cultural field (educational institutions) and in addition in the political sphere (political parties) in order to be able to represent and protect cultural interests through democratic-legitimate means. From this follows the right of free and unimpeded contacts, of the free use of mass-media for information in the language of the ethnic groups, of proportionately equal access to public offices and to public service as well as of co-determination in the settlement of affairs of their own. Finally even the right of autonomy results from it because the principle of majority, i.e.

the law of the higher number, as ultima ratio for the formation of power, in the end excludes those entitled to it because their number ex definitione, is too small to be able to enter, without protection through appropriate forms of autonomy, into a numerical competition with the members of the cultural majority of their State.

<u>Page 2</u>

As the rights of groups and also the more far-reaching settlement of the rights of autonomy of ethnic groups would go beyond the frame given to the Additional Protocol to the ECHR, this matter is left to the second part of the updated FUEN proposal, i.e. to the draft of a special Convention on the rights of autonomy of the ethnic groups in Europe.

Bozen/Bolzano, 28 April 1994

PREAMBLE

Reaffirming that one of the basic aims of the United Nations, as proclaimed in its Charter, is to promote and encourage respect for human rights and for fundamental freedoms for all, without distinction as to race, sex, language or religion,

Reaffirming faith in the fundamental human rights, in the dignity and worth of the human person, in the equal rights of men and women and of nations large and small, and in the fundamental and inalienable human right of self-determination, as expressed in art. 1 para. 1 of the Human Rights Covenants: All peoples have the right of self-determination. By virtue of that right they freely determine their political status and freely pursue their economic, social and cultural development",

Desiring to promote the realization of the principles contained in the Charter of the United Nations, the Universal Declaration of Human Rights, the Convention on the Prevention and Punishment of the Crime of Genocide, the International Convention on the Elimination of All Forms of Racial Discrimination, the International Covenants on Human Rights, the Declaration on the Elimination of All Forms of Intolerance and of Discrimination Based on Religion or Belief, the Convention on the Rights of the Child, and the Resolution and Convention of Persons belonging to national or ethnic, religious and linguistic minorities as well as other relevant international instruments that have been adopted at the universal or regional level and those concluded between individual States Members of the United Nations,

Inspired by the provisions of Article 27 of the International Covenant on Civil and Political Rights concerning the rights of persons belonging to ethnic, religious or linguistic minorities,

Considering that the promotion and protection of the rights of persons belonging to national or ethnic, religious and linguistic minorities contribute to the political and social stability of States in which they live,

Emphasizing that the constant promotion and realization of the rights of persons belonging to national or ethnic, religious and linguistic minorities, as an integral part of the development of society as a whole and within a democratic framework based on the rule of law, would contribute to the strengthening of friendship and cooperation among peoples and States,

Taking also into account the important work which is carried out by intergovernmental and non-governmental organizations in protecting minorities and in promoting and protecting the rights of persons belonging to national or ethnic, religious and linguistic minorities,

Recognizing the need to ensure even more effective implementation of international instruments with regard to the rights of persons belonging to national or ethnic, religious and linguistic minorities,

Considering that, by virtue of migrations within Europe, there are persons described as new minorities who however do not possess the characteristics of national or ethnic, religious and linguistic minorities and can therefore not be considered as such, and

Emphasizing that issues concerning national or ethnic, religious and linguistic minorities, as well as compliance with international obligations and commitments concerning the rights of persons belonging to them, are matters of legitimate international concern and consequently do not constitute exclusively an internal affair of the respective State,

Page 3

Considering that the Council of Europe Summit decided in Vienna in 1993 to begin work on drafting a protocol complementing the European Convention of Human Rights in the cultural field by provisions guaranteeing individual rights, in particular for persons belonging to national minorities,

Considering that, without prejudice to the right to the homeland and its consequences, the problems of the restoration of rights and interests of peoples displaced in consequence of the Second World War require special provisions in the form of a body of remedial measures which also takes into account the interests of the population already resident as well as in particular general Human Rights, and

Recognizing that essential issues regarding the protection of ethnic groups, such as the regulation of the protection of groups and of autonomy, issues which go beyond the frame offered here, shall be regulated in a separate Convention,

the States Parties express their determination to adapt their policies in respect of these minorities and ethnic groups to the fundamental rights set out below,

and agree to the following additional Protocol to the ECHR:

<u>Page 4</u>

L GENERAL PROVISIONS
Protection of ethnic groups within the framework of Human Rights

ART.1:

1. The international protection of the rights of persons belonging to ethnic groups is a fundamental part of the international protection of Human Rights. These rights shall be exercised by individuals single or in community with others.

2. It is an essential factor for peace, justice, stability and democracy and as such falls within the scope of international co-operation.

3 As a matter of legitimate international concern it does not constitute exclusively an internal affair of the respective state.

4. It shall be exercised in good faith among the States in a spirit of understanding, tolerance and good neighbourliness; it does not permit any action directed against the fundamental principles of international law.

Definition

ART.2:

1. For the purposes of this Protocol the term "ethnic group" shall mean a community
   a) compactly or dispersedly settled on the temtory of a State Party.
   b) which is smiller in number than the rest of the population of a State Party.
   c) whose members are citizens of that State,
   d) which have ethnic, linguistic or cultural features different from those of the rest of the population,

e) whose members are guided by the will to safeguard these features.

2. The term "ethnic group" shall apply neither to migrant workers and their families lawfully resident in the State Parties, nor to other immigrants, groups of refugees or persons seeking asylum; their rights have been established or shall be established independently of the rights of ethnic groups.

3. The persons belonging to an ethnic group falling within the terms of this definition, shall be entitled to be recognized as an ethnic group.

Fundamental principles

ART. 3:

1. To belong to an ethnic group shall be a matter of individual choice and no disadvantage may arise from the exercise of such choice. The State Parties undertake to create the legal, political, cultural and social conditions for such free choice.

2. Persons belonging to an ethnic group may exercise the rights set forth in this Protocol individually or in community with others.

II. GENERAL FUNDAMENTAL RIGHTS

Right of identity (existence) and protection from threat

ART. 4:

1. Persons belonging **to** ethnic groups shall have the right to the respect, evolution and development of their identity, i.e. they shall have the right freely to express, preserve and develop their ethnic, cultural and linguistic identity, and to maintain and develop their culture in all its aspects, free of any attempts at assimilation.

2. Persons belonging to ethnic groups shall have the right to their homeland as an inseparable part of their ethnic identity and development. in particular the right to protection of their traditional settlement areas and conditions of life as well to their promotion. Measures aimed at a modification of such settlement areas and/or conditions of life need the consensus of those concerned.

3. Persons belonging to an ethnic group shall also have the right to free economic development.

4. Persons belonging to ethnic groups shall have the right to be

protected against any activity hiable to threaten their identity. The pursuit or encouragement of any policies by the State Parties aimed at the assimilation of persons belonging to ethnic groups shall be prohibited.

5. Deliberate changes to their disadvantage to the demographic composition of the areas in which persons belonging to ethnic groups are settled, including modifications of administrative subdivisions. shall be prohibited.

6. Genocide and expulsion directed against ethnic groups in whole or in part or against persons belonging to ethnic groups as such shall be prevented and punished as crimes against humanity. Persons belonging to ethnic groups who have been turned into refugees, expellees or displaced persons in consequence of such actions - and the forced relocation within the national borders shall be considered also as expulsion - shall be guaranteed the safe and dignified return to their homeland and to their homes.

Right of non-discrimination, equality of treatment and equal opportunities

ART.5:

1. Persons belonging to ethnic groups have the right to exercise fully and effectively their human rights and fundamental freedoms without any discrimination and in full equality before the law.

2. Beyond the formal equality of treatment, persons belonging to ethnic groups shall be guaranteed material equality before the law in the sense of real equal opportunities.

3. These equal opportunities shall be guaranteed through special protective measures; these measures shall be considered to be in conformity with the principles of equality and non-discrimination with respect to the other citizens and shall not be considered as acts of discrimination.

4. Such special protective measures for the establishment and maintenance of equal opportunities shall be adopted by the State Parties with regard to the rights of in particular:

a) language;
b) education;
c) separate associations and organizations;
d) unimpeded contacts and freedom of movement;
e) freedom of information (to receive and impart);
f) proportional access to the public service;
g) political representation;
h) appropriate forms of autonomy.

5. The failure to take such protective measures shall be considered and treated as an inadmissible act of discrimination.

6. Benefits, especially in the cultural sphere, granted by a State Party to

persons belonging to ethnic groups connational to its but settled in another States to improve their equal opportunities, shall not be considered as an illegitimate interference in the internal affairs of this State.

III. SPECIAL FUNDAMENTAL RIGHTS (AS COMPENSATORY RIGHTS)

Right of language

ART.6:

1. Persons belonging to ethnic groups shall have the right to use their mother tongue (ethnic group language) in private and in public, both orally and in writing.

2. Persons belonging to ethnic groups shall have this right also in contacts with the public administration, the judicial authorities and with all public institutions or institutions intended for public purposes regardless of their legal status; they shall be entitled to receive communications from these institutions in - or also in - their mother tongue (ethnic group language).

3. The exercise of this right shall be guaranteed in all administrative units of their settlement areas preferably directly, at least through translation.

4. Persons belonging to ethnic groups shall have in particular the right

a) when arrested, to be informed promptly in their mother tongue (ethnic group language) of the reasons for their arrest and of any charge against them;

b) when charged with a criminal offence, to be informed in their mother tongue (ethnic group language) promptly and in detailed manner of the nature and cause of the accusation against them and to defend themself in this language, if necessary with the free assistance of an interpreter.

5. In the settlement areas of persons belonging to ethnic groups they shall have the right to the use and equal status of their language in legislation, administration and judiciary, in particular within public collegial bodies and in communications such as official publications, general information, officiai signs as well as all acts directed to the public sphere or intended for the public use.

6. Persons belonging to ethnic groups shall have the right to use their own sur- and given-names in their mother tongue (ethnic group language) and to have them officially recognized. This right shall also include the re-establishnient of personal names in the form of their own language free of charge.

7. In the settlement areas of persons belonging to ethnic groups they shall have the right to local names, signs, inscriptions and other similar public information in the mother tongue (ethnic group language). This does not deprive the authorities of their right to display the above-mentioned information in the official language or languages of the State; however, any arbitrary modification of traditional denominations in the mother tongue (ethnic group language) which hitherto have been used exclusively in original form in an ethnic group language shall be inadmissible.

Right of education

ART. 7:

1. Persons belonging to ethnic groups shall have the right to learn their mother tongue (ethnic group language) and to be instructed in it within the whole system of instruction and education including, besides the compulsory schooling, e.g. also the kindergartens, pre-school education, secondary school education, technical and vocational education, vocational continuing education, university and adult education.
2. This right shall be guaranteed through an appropriate number of state schools and other educational establishments, located in accordance with the geographical distribution of the persons belonging to an ethnic group.
3. Whenever outside the settlement areas of persons belonging to ethnic groups the minimum number of pupils required to build a class is not achieved in schools reasonably near, the pupils in question shall be in any case entitled to learn their mother tongue (ethnic group language).
4. For sectors outside the existing compulsory school system such as kindergartens, pre-school education, secondary school education, technical and vocational education, vocational continuing education, university and adult education, appropriate institutions guaranteeing the instruction in the mother tongue (ethnic group language) shall be established and diplomas issued abroad for courses completed in the mother tongue (ethnic group language) or in a next relative language shall be recognized.

If such institutions should not be demanded by a sufficient number of persons belonging to ethnic groups, the diplomas issued abroad for courses completed in their language or in a next relative language shall be recognized.

Page 7

5. Persons belonging to ethnic groups shall have the right to set up and manage their own schools, educational and training establishments within the framework of the legal education system.

237

6. To enjoy the right of education, persons belonging to ethnic groups shall at least be entitled at all levels and for all types of education, to a share in public grants proportion to their share in the total population; this shall apply also for education abroad in the mother tongue (ethnic group language) or in the nearest related language.

7. Schooling of and in the mother tongue (ethnic group language) shall be in principle provided by teachers for whom the respective language is also their mother tongue. For educational systems based on joint teaching for persons belonging to ethnic groups and those of the majority population, special rules shall be provided taking into account in an appropriate manner the interests of persons belonging to ethnic groups.

8. In the case of minority schools the persons belonging to ethnic groups, within the framework of the general principles of national school legislation, shall have the right to

a) co-determination in the establishment of curricula, the appointment of teachers and the   supervision of schools;

b) adapt school subjects to their particular needs;

c) instruction also of their own history and culture.

9. State Parties shall be responsible for the financing of the educational system of persons belonging to ethnic groups. The State Parties shall guarantee that pupils belonging to ethnic groups who so wish to attend private schools, may do so. Such private schools shall be promoted or financed by the State Party at least to the same extent as private schools in general are promoted or financed by that State.

10. The State Parties shall guarantee that persons belonging to ethnic groups shall be taught the national language within the compulsory schooling system.

11. In areas in which ethnic groups are settled, persons belonging to the majority population shall be guaranteed to be taught the language of the ethnic group as well as their history and culture.

Right of separate organizations

ART.8:

1. Persons belonging to ethnic groups shall have the right to establish and maintain their own organizations or associations, including political parties.

2.State Parties shall promote or finance the organizations and associations of persons belonging to ethnic groups, including their political parties, in such a way that they are enable them to complete fully their functions, but in any case to the same extent as the State Parties promote and finance such organizations and associations in general.

ART.9:

1. Persons belonging to ethnic groups shall have the right to establish unimpeded contacts among themselves as well as across frontiers with citizens of other States with whom they share a common ethnic or national origin or a common cultural heritage, with a view to promoting and reinforcing their common features.

2. This right shall also include the right to unimpeded contacts with the governmental or public organs of other States, in particular with those of co-national States.

3. The right of unimpeded contacts shall also comprise the right to freedom of movement, notably everyone's right to leave freely his or her country and to return to it.

4. The right of unimpeded contacts shall also include the right traniLontier co-operation and to the promotion thereof, in particular in the fields of culture, education instruction, youth exchange, information, environmental protection, economy and trade.

Page 8

5. Transfrontier co-operation may be realized

a) through joint commissions and territorial communities or authorities and

b) through non-governmental organizations and working arrangements such as workshops and committees.

Right of information

ART. 10:

1. Persons belonging to ethnic groups shall have the right to disseminate and exchange information through print and audio-visual media in their mother tongue (ethnic group language); they shall have likewise the right to have access to such information within and across national frontiers.

2. In particular, they shall have the right to equal access to the State's or to other public mass media, as well as the right to their own means of communication and adequate public subsidies for this purpose.

3. The right of information shall include the freedom to receive television and radio programmes broadcast from foreign countries in which the same mother tongue is spoken.

Right of proportional access to the public service

ART. 11:

1. In their settlement areas persons belonging to ethnic groups shall be entitled 'to be taken into account in the access to and in the promotion in the public service in conformity with their share in the total population.

2. Public service shall mean the public administration, the judiciary as well as other public institutions or institutions intended for public purposes, regardless of their legal status.

3. Whenever the numerical share of the persons belonging to ethnic groups in the total population is a subject of controversy, transitory regulations shall be laid down by mutual agreement between the parties.

4. In the settlement areas of persons belonging to ethnic groups, institutional multilingualism shall be compulsory in all public institutions or institutions intended for public purposes.

5. To avoid social hardships the implementation of the rights mentioned in par. 1-4 shall be realized through appropriate and mutual transitory agreements.

Right of political representation

ART.12:

1. Persons belonging to ethnic groups shall have the right to take part in the conduct of public affairs in full equality, in particular also in decisions affecting the regions where they live or in matters affecting them.

2. They may exercise and enjoy their rights and interests directly or through freely chosen representatives.

3. When exercising their civil and political rights through their own political parties, these parties shall not be subject to unreasonable restrictions in electoral laws such as seat and percentage clauses.

4. Whenever the number of persons belonging to an ethnic group should be too small to win a seat of their own in legislative bodies, the persons belonging to this ethnic group shall have the right to achieve at least one seat.

5. The subdivision of administrative units and political constituencies shall be made in such a manner that the rights of persons belonging to ethnic groups set forth in this Protocol are neither denied nor materially curtailed. For this purpose it shall be a matter of principle to establish ethnic group constituencies.

6. With regard to the personal composition of public organs of decision or consultation, persons belonging to ethnic groups shall have the right to have a share in conformity with their share of the total population. Whenever the number is too small for a full seat, it shall be rounded up.

Right of autonomy

ART. 13:

1. Without prejudice to the territorial integrity of the State Parties and in correspondence with their respective share in the whole population, persons belonging to ethnic groups shall have the right of territorial or at least cultural autonomy as well as to local self-administration (local autonomy) for the protection
- of their civil and political rights and
- of the fundamental rights and freedoms due to them as to all other persons against being outvoted by decisions by the national majority not authorized according to this Protocol.

2. Persons belonging to ethnic groups forming the majority of the population in the areas where they are settled, shall have the right, within a demarcated territory, of a special status, denominated territorial autonomy, with autonomous legislative and administrative powers to conduct their own affairs. This status may also be exercised in the form of a confederation.

3. Persons belonging to ethnic groups not forming the majority of the population in the areas where they are settled, shall have the right to cultural autonomy, in the form of association with public law status that they consider appropriate, to safeguard all spheres significant to maintain and develop their identity.

4. Persons belonging to ethnic groups not forming the majority of the population in the areas where they are settled as well as persons belonging to ethnic groups who are settled away from these in isolated settlements, shall have the right of local self-administration (local autonomy) in administrative units within which they form a local majority, i.e. individual districts, municipalities or in administrative units subordinated to these.

IV. GUARANTEE OF THE RIGHTS AND LEGAL PROTECTION

Right of remedy and duties of persons belonging to ethnic groups

ART. 14:

1. If a violation of the rights set forth in this Protocol is alleged, the persons belonging to an ethnic group individually or in community shall have the right in an effective remedy before a national authority and,

after having exhausted national procedures, before the European Commission of Human Rights.

2. While enjoying the rights set forth in this Protocol, the persons belonging to an ethnic group shall respect the national legal system of the State Party based on democratic rule of law as well as the rights of other citizens.

Right of co-determination

ART. 15:

1. Persons belonging to ethnic groups shall have the right to participate in the national implementation of the rights and fundamental freedoms set forth in this Protocol, with a view to mutual agreement. The State Parties shall create adequate conditions for that.

2. Moreover they shall have the right to participate in the conduct of all affairs concerning them directly or indirectly, through the creation of a special common organ of representation within the Council of Europe.

Page 10

Right of Ombudsman

ART. 16:

1. Persons belonging to ethnic groups shall have the right to appointment of an Ombudsman for the protection of their civil and minority rights; for this purpose one Ombudsman or more Ombudsmen on different political or administrative levels may be provided.

2. An ethnic-group Ombudsman shall himself be member of the ethnic group concerned.

Sphere of validity

ART. 17:

1. This Protocol shall not prejudice the provisions of domestic law or any international agreement which provide greater protection for ethnic groups or persons belonging to ethnic groups.

2. The exercise of the rights and fundamental freedoms set forth in this Protocol shall fully apply to the persons belonging to the majority in the whole of the State Party who constitute a minority in the areas where they live.

3. The exercise of these rights shall not be made subject to any

other restrictions but such as are prescribed by law and necessary in a democratic society in the interests of national security or public safety, for the preservation of public order, for the prevention of crime, for the protection of health or morals or for the protection of the rights and freedoms of others.

V. CONTROL MACHINERY

individual and State complaints

ART. 18:

1. Provided that States which have acceded to this Additional Protocol have by declaration recognized the competence of the European Commission of Human Rights (hereinafter referred to as Commission) to receive complaints for alleged violations of the rights set forth in this Protocol, any individual or group of individuals entitled by statute in represent the rights of such groups may file a claim with the Commission for an alleged violation, by a State Party, of the rights set forth in this Additional Protocol.

2. The Commission may receive complaints from any State Party which considers that another Party violates the rights set forth in this Protocol.

3. In respect of individual and State complaints, the Commission and European Court of Human Rights (hereinafter referred to as Court) shall apply the relevant rules of procedure.

4. If States Parties to this Protocol are not at the same time Parties to the ECHR, they shall appoint an additional member to the Commission and Court if individual or State complaints are entered against such States not being Parties to the ECHR. These additional members shall have a seat and a vote in the Commission and Court only in such cases. They shall be nationals of the State Party concerned and must fulfil the same personal requirements and will receive the same compensation as the other members of the Commission and Court.

Page 11

5. The Court shall be competent only if the State concerned has by declaration recognized the competence of the Court.

State reports

ART. 19:

243

1. The States Parties to this Protocol shall submit to the Commission, through the Secretary General of the Council of Europe, reports on the legislative, judicial and administrative implementation of the rights set forth in this Protocol as well as on any difficulties in law and in fact, within one year after the entry into force of this Protocol for the State concerned and thereafter at two yearly intervals. The Secretary General of the Council of Europe is entitled to demand a report from a State Party prematurely if circumstances become known indicating that a State has difficulty in giving effect to its undertakings under this Protocol. Groups entitled by statute to represent the interests of ethnic groups shall have the right to point out to the Secretary General such circumstances and to initiate that such reports be obtained. The States Parties are invited to consult with the NGOs and the ethnic groups' organizations on the content of the State's report.

2. In order to assist the State Parties in fulfilling their reporting obligations, the Commission shall elaborate general guidelines as to the form, contents and dates of reports. The guidelines are to help ensure that the reports are presented in a uniform manner so that the Commission and the States Parties can obtain a complete picture of the implementation of the Protocol and the progress nude therein.

3. The Commission shall examine such reports immediately in the presence of the representatives of the State concerned and may make recommendations to the representatives of the State concerned and to the Secretary General of the Council of Europe, in order to ensure respect of the rights set forth in this Protocol. The States Parties shall publish the report submitted to the Commission and the Commission's opinion on the report, as well as any resulting recommendations.

4. Whenever such reports are submitted by States Parties to this Protocol which are non-members of the European Convention for the Protection of Human Rights and Fundamental Freedoms, the Commission shall be composed as provided for in Article 18. par.4 of this Protocol.

C. Peaceful settlement of disputes

ART.20:

1. The States Parties to this Protocol shall submit to the Secretary General, within three months from entry into force of this Protocol, a list of names of personalities known for their competence and high moral standing in the field of minority and group protection. Should difficulties of any nature whatsoever arise under the jurisdiction of a State Party in executing this Protocol, the Secretary General has the right to appoint three persons from this list (Minority Rights Council) who shall carry out the tasks

provided for by the mechanism of settlement of La Valetta, in the version adopted at the Moscow Meeting of October 1991.

2. Three States Parties to this Protocol may demand that the State under whose jurisdiction difficulties have arisen fulfilling the obligations under this Protocol use the mechanism of settlement contained in this article.

A State Party to this Protocol which is not willing to accept the recommendation made by the Minority Rights Council has the right to demand an advisory opinion from the European Court of Human Rights on the necessity of the recommendations. Such advisory opinion shall be binding. The second Additional Protocol to the European Convention for the Protection of Human Rights and Fundamental Freedoms shall apply mutatis mutandis to any such advisory opinion.

<u>Page 12</u>

3. For a State Party availing itself of this mechanism of settlement, the possibility of entering a State complaint against a State in accordance with Article 18, par.2 shall be excluded.

4. The members of the Minority Rights Council shall serve in their individual capacity. They shall be independent and shall not be bound by instructions. In the exercise of their office, they shall enjoy the same privileges and immunities as the members of the Commission and Court. The members of the Minority Rights Council shall receive, for each working day, a compensation equal to that received by the members of the Commission and Court. The States Parties to this Protocol shall cover the costs of establishing and operating the Minority Rights Council; the General Secretariat of the Council of Europe will assist the Minority Rights Council. It has its seat at the seat of the Council of Europe in Strasbourg and shall be entitled, according to the requirements of its work, to transfer its seat elsewhere within the jurisdiction of the States Parties.

VI. FINAL PROVISIONS

ART.21:

1. This Protocol shall be open to the signature of the Parties to the European Convention for the Protection of Human Rights and Fundamental Freedoms. They may express their consent to be bound by signature.

2. The signed documents shall be deposited with the Secretary General of the Council of Europe.

3. Each State Party shall notify at the time of signature the ethnic groups resident in its territory in accordance with art.2 to which the

provisions of this Protocol shall apply. Each State Party may, at any time, supplement this notification. Whenever ethnic groups having the right in accordance with this Protocol to be recognized as such, should not be notified, persons belonging to such an ethnic group shall have the right to file an application for ascertainment through the Council of Europe.

4. This Protocol shall enter into force on the first day of the month following the date on which ten State Parties signed this Protocol. In respect of any State Party which subsequently expresses its consent to be bound by it, the Protocol shall enter into force on the first day of the month following the date of the deposit of the signature.

5. Pending the entry into force of this Protocol the State Parties agree to apply the Protocol provisionally from the date of signature, so far as it is possible to do so under the respective constitutional systems.

ART. 22:

1. The Committee of Ministers may invite to accede to this Protocol any State non-member of the Council of Europe but signatory to the Helsinki Documents of 1 August 1975. Such States shall be entitled to appoint ad hoc members to the Commission of Human Rights and to the European Court of Human Rights for a period of six years. Such members shall have a seat and a vote in the Commission and Court only with regard to decisions concerning the application of this Protocol.

ART.23:

1. For the purposes of this Protocol, the English and French texts are equally authentic. Also a language other than the official language of the Council of Europe may be agreed upon as a negotiating language. If necessary, a translation/interpretation shall be provided for.

Page 13

II. Autonomy Rights of Ethnic Groups in Europe

Discussion Document for a Special Convention

(Updated FUEN-draft Convention of May 1992)

ACCOMPANYING REPORT

Since 1991 nineteen new states have risen owing to the collapse or disintegration of the three multinational states: the Soviet Union, Yugoslavia and Czechoslovakia. To these a series of secessions has to be added which, however, have not (yet) received international recognition, such as the Republic of Serbian Kraina, the Serbian Republic of Bosnia-Herzegovina and the Croatian State Bosna-Herceg, the independent Republic of Tchetchenia or the union of the autonomous Republic of Abchasia with Russia.

The number of the national minorities in Europe (peoples without a state of their own and parts of peoples which are divided by frontiers) is at present estimated at about 200 with about 100 million members.

Although only a smaller number of them can potentially be regarded as subjects of the right of self- determination, the situation may change if the existence of a national minority is not guaranteed but through secession. The unacceptable discrimination of a national minority because of certain group characteristics (e.g. the prohibition of speaking its own language, of handing down its own history, expulsion even if only of parts, deliberate settlement of members of the majority population or intentional modification of the administrative subdivisions in order to put the national minority into minority on its own settlement area, arbitrary imprisonment etc.) can threaten its existence. Therefore, a threat to the existence which otherwise cannot be averted and an unacceptable discrimination can actuate the secession of a national minority, even if it cannot legitimate it according to the preveiling international law or the practice of the states.

The terms national minority" and people" only partially exclude each other, partly they overlap: a group which, in relation to the total population of the state, is in the minority, can on the one hand be a "national minority" for the purposes of the right of protection of minorities, but at the same time it can also be a "people" for the purposes of the right of self-determination, that is in the case in which it forms the exclusive or at least the significant majority population on a coherent territory of a suitable size to create a state and the settlement area is a traditional one of this people. On this condition the group is a subject of the right of self- determination althought it is also a minority for the purposes of the right of protection of minorities.

In the strained relationship between the fundamental principle of sovereignty and territorial integrity of the State under international law and the fundamental principle of the right to existence of the national minorities, neither of these principles may be interpreted in such a way that no validity is left to the other one. What substance can self-determination have if the independence of the state of residence and its territorial integrity may not be touched?

247

If an explicit right of secession is not given or - whatever the reasons may be - is not desired or not desirable, a national minority has the right to a minimum of internal autonomy and to an optimum of autonomy, i.e. as much autonomy as possible without endangering the national unity; the minimum of autonomy is in any case that extent which is necessary for the preservation of the existence and the identity of national minorities. In particular cultural rights are a part of this minimum, e.g. the right to use one's own language in public, the right to use this language also in front of administrative bodies and in courts, and the right of school education in ones own language.

Attempts at secession - even if they are against the prevailing international law doctrine and practice of the States - are possible and probable if a threat to the existence which otherwise cannot be averted and unacceptable discrimination are given. An autonomy granted in time is the best precautionary measure against attempts at secession. Is it granted too late, i.e. at a moment when a powerful movement of secession has developed, it is possible that when it is granted it is no more felt as credible, and then it is no longer suitable to stop the striving for secession.

<u>Page 14</u>

Whether the right of secession exists for national minorities or not, does not play too great a role for the political development. An autonomy granted in time is the best prevention against secession!

Therefore, in view of the political development in Europe, it seems to be highly advisable to create a European-wide unified autonomy right.

Bozen/Bolzano, 28 April 1994

PREAMBLE

The States Parties to this Convention

reaffirm that one of the basic aims of the United Nations, as proclaimed in its Charter, is to promote and encourage respect for the human rights and for fundamental freedoms for all, without distinction as to race, sex, language or religion;

reaffirm the fundamental human rights, the dignity and worth of the human person, the equal rights of men and women and of nations large and small, and the fundamental and inalienable human rights of self- determination, as expressed in art. 1, para. 1 of the Human Rights Covenants: " All peoples have the right of self-determination. By virtue of that right they freely pursue their economic, social and cultural development;"

take note that, according to the Declaration of the United Nations on the principles of International Law concerning Friendly Relations among States and Peoples of 24/10/1970 GA res.2626 (XXV), each state, as a matter of principle, has the right to safeguard its existence within the existing territorial boundaries and that in principle any attempt at dismembering or impairing, totally or in part, the political unity or territorial integrity is incompatible with the aims and principles of the Charter of the United Nations;

point out that, in the conflict between the right of self-determination and territorial integrity of the States, the State Parties declare in the CSCE-Final Act of Helsinki and in the CSCE-Charter of Paris for a New Europe that they will respect the right of self-determination of the peoples by always acting in accord with the aims and principles of the Charter of the United Nations and the relevant rules of the international law, including those which refer to the territorial integrity of the states;

are conscious that, as stated in the above-mentioned Declaration, the States run their affairs in compliance with the principle of equal rights and self-determination of peoples and thus possess a Government representing the whole people belonging to the territory without distinction as to race, creed and colour;

are fully aware that the right of self-determination of the peoples also comprises a freely chosen autonomy by which peoples can determine on their own their political, economic, social and cultural matters within the given state borders;

are conscious that autonomy, according to the specific case, has developed different features, but that its effectiveness in any case requires an autonomous attitude,

-- and agree to the following Convention:

Page 15

I. GENERAL PROVISIONS

Autonomy with safeguarding the territorial integrity

ART. 1:

1. Autonomy shall mean an instrument of protection of ethnic groups which, without prejudice of the territorial integrity of the State Parties, shall guarantee the highest possible degree of internal self-determination and at the same time a corresponding minimum of dependence on the national minority.

2. As an instrument of protection of ethnic groups, the autonomy is aimed at the protection of persons belonging to an ethnic group against being outvoted by majority decisions not authorized in this Convention, and to safeguard

a) their civil and political rights as well as

b) the fundamental rights and freedoms being due to them as to all other persons, without prejudice of the territorial integrity of the State Parties.

Definition of ethnic group

ART. 2:

1. For the purposes of this Convention the term "ethnic group" shall mean a community

a) compactly or dispersedly settled on the territory of a State Party,

b) smaller in number then the rest of the population of a State Party,

c) whose members are citizens of that State,

d) which have ethnic, linguistic or cultural features different from those of the rest of the population,

e) whose members are guided by the will to safeguard these features.

2. The term "ethnic group" shall apply neither to migrant workers and their families lawfully residing in the State Parties, nor to other immigrants, groups of refugees or persons seeking asylum; their rights have been established or shall be established independently of the rights of ethnic groups.

3. Each ethnic group falling within the terms of this defintion, shall be entitled to be recognized as an ethnic group.

4. In guaranteeing the rights of autonomy, the particular conditions given for ethnic groups forming

a) the majority of the population,

b) a substantial part but not the majority of the population,

c) neither the majority nor a substantial part of the population in the areas where they are settled, shall be respected.

Moreover shall be taken into account those persons who belong to compactly settled ethnic groups but are settled away from them in isolated settlements.

Fundamental principles

ART. 3:

1. The rights set forth in this Convention of
a) safeguarding and preserving,
b) promoting and developing
the ethnic groups as entities, shall be exercised by persons belonging to these ethnic groups in community with other members of their group.
2. Belonging to an ethnic group shall be a matter of individual choice and no disadvantage may arise from the exercise of such a choice. The State Parties undertake to create the legal, political, cultural and social conditions for such free choice.

<u>Page 16</u>

II. RIGHTS OF AUTONOMY .

Right of territorial autonomy

ART. 4:

1. Ethnic groups forming the majority of the population in the areas where they are settled, shall have the right of a special status within a demarcated territory, denominated territorial autonomy, with an autonomous legislation, government, administration and judiciary to safeguard their own affairs.
2. "Their own affairs" shall be taken to mean all matters which are situated in the exclusive or preponderant interest of the community settled in the territory and which are suitable to be conducted by the community itself within the local borders with its own means, including the free use of the natural wealth and resources of the territory concerned.
3. Safeguarding its own affairs shall take place through its own bodies for
a) legislation,
b) executive power, with corresponding administrative structure, and
c) judiciary
which are responsible and reflect the composition of the population.

Autonomous sphere of the territorial autonomy

ART.5:

1. The territorial autonomy shall comprise all the powers which the ethnic groups consider necessary for conducting their own affairs and which shall be designated in the national legislation as falling within the competence of the autonomous sphere.

2. The following competences fall within the autonomous sphere, i.e.:

a) the right to have and display the ethnic group's national emblems;

b) the right of co-determination in the regulation of eventual second citizenship;

c) education, including higher (i.e. universities), which respects the values and needs of that ethnic group;

d) cultural institutions and programmes;

e) radio and television;

f) licensing of professions and trades;

g) natural resources use, e.g. agriculture, forestry, hunting and fishing, mining;

h) health care, social services and insurance;

i) provincial communications, e.g. local roads, airports;

j) energy production;

k) control of commercial and savings banks and other financial institutions;

l) police;

m) taxation for provincial purposes.

Rights of protection of other citizens

ART.6:

The exercise of the rights set forth in this Convention shall not prejudice the enjoyment of universally recognized human rights and fundamental freedoms by persons belonging to those parts of the population which form a numerical minority within the territorial autonomy.

Page 17

Right of cultural autonomy

ART. 7:

1. Ethnic groups not forming the majority of population in the areas where they are settled as well as ethnic groups which - for any reasons whatsoever - consider the establishment of a territorial autonomy as not expedient, shall have the right to a cultural autonomy in the form of

association with public law status that they consider appropriate.

2. The association provided with cultural autonomy shall be an association of individuals comprising the persons belonging to the ethnic group concerned.

3. The autonomous spheres shall be administrated by bodies elected freely according to democratic principles.

Autonomous sphere of cultural autonomy

ART. 8:

1. The cultural autonomy shall apply to all such matters the ethnic groups consider necessary for the preservation, safeguarding and development of their identity; they shall be designated in national legislation as falling within the competence of the autonomous sphere.

2. In any case, spheres essential for the preservation and development of the ethnic group's identity shall fall within the autonomous sphere, i.e.

a) culture,
b) educational system,
c) information, including through radio and television,
d) use of the ethnic group's national emblems,
e) co-determination in the regulation of eventual second citizenship and
f) any other matters which, according to the ethnic groups, are necessary for preserving and exercising the protective rights to which they are entitled.

3. The cultural autonomy also comprises the right to establish and maintain institutions, in particular in the fields of

a) instruction,
b) the print and electronic medias,
c) care of traditions,
d) the education system,
e) the safeguarding of economic activities.

Right of local self-admninistration (local autonomy)

ART.9:

1. Ethnic groups not forming the majority of the population in the areas where they are settled, as well as persons belonging to ethnic groups who are settled away from those in isolated settlements, shall have the right of a local self-administration, denominated local autonomy, within

administrative units where they form the local majority of population, e.g. in individual districts or municipalities or administrative units subordinated to those.

2. Beyond the competences transferred to such administrative units by national law, safeguarding the affairs of an ethnic group shall fall within the competence of the local autonomous administration (local autonomy).

3. Matters falling within the sphere of local self-administration (local autonomy) which constitute an exclusive or preponderant interest of the local community incorporated into the territory, shall be managed by this community in free self-determination within its local borders.

Page 18

Autonomous sphere of local self-administration (local autonomy)

ART. 10:

1. The following competences shall in particular fall within the sphere of local self-administration (local autonomy), such as:
a) arrangement of the institutional bilinguism within the local self-administration;
b) use of names and symbols specific to the ethnic group;
c) regulation of local customs and festivities;
d) protection of local monuments and memorials;
e) local security, traffic, health and building supervising police.

2. The local self-administration (local autonomy) shall also comprise the right within the framework of its disponibility of means, to establish and maintain institutions, in particular in the field of
a) local instruction,
b) local print and electronic media,
c) care of traditions,
d) educational system,
e) safeguarding of economic activities.

3. Morever, the ethnic groups shall co-operate in correspondence with their share of population in all other administrative affairs.

Administrative subdivision

ART. 11:

1. Ethnic groups shall have the right to be taken into account and

254

to uncurtailed safeguarding of their rights in the subdivision of the national territory into political, administrative and judicial districts as well as constituencies.

2. Therefore the respective administrative subdivision shall be agreed with the ethnic group directly concerned .

Provision with financial means and financial adjustment

ART. 12:

1. The autonomous bodies of the territorial and cultural autonomies shall be provided with adequate financial means to enable them to effectively exercise their competences.

2. For the financial adjustment between the respective State Party and a territorial autonomy the latter shall be entitled to a fixed share in all pertinent State expenses in the relation of the medium value of its share in the whole population and the whole territory of that State.

3. A territorial autonomy shall be entitled in any case to a suitable share (about nine tenths) in all taxes and contributions levied within its territory. The share being due to it remains within the territory where it enjoys tax sovereignty and only the amount being due to the State shall be assigned to it.

4. Whenever the share in the revenues from taxes and deliveries being due to a territorial autonomy should fall short of its fix share in all the relevant State's depenses, the State shall pay the difference to the autonomous corporation.

Page 19

Legitimacy control

ART. 13:

The legitimacy of the legal instruments adopted by such autonomous bodies shall be subject only to supervision by independent supreme courts.

IV. PROVISIONS ON LEGAL PROTECTION

Internal implementation by the States and co-determination

ART. 14:

255

1. The States Parties shall respect and enforce the rights of the ethnic groups as set forth in this Convention, by

a) granting them an adequate position in their fundamental legal system,
b) passing all legal provisions required for this purpose.

2. Ethnic groups shall have the right to co-operate in the national implementation of the rights as set forth in this Convention through commissions which are composed by representatives of the State Party and the ethnic groups on an equal footing; the commissions decide by mutual agreement and their decisions shall be binding.
3. All pertinent legal provisions of the State made effective without a previous favourable opinion given by the equally represented commissions can be contested by the ethnic groups in front of competent courts.
4. Ethnic groups shall have the right to participate, through autonomous entities in their respective State Party, in the preparation of decisions of international organizations on matters in which they take a specific interest.
5. Enjoying the rights set forth in this Convention, the persons belonging to ethnic groups shall respect the national legislation and the rights of others, in particular those of the members of the majority population and of other ethnic groups.

IV. CONTROL MACHINERY

(In principle there are two possibilities:

- the construction of a special machinery, or
- to append these provisions to the ECHR-system.

This question is still open, also because within the framework of the Council of Europe the 11th Additional Protocol to the ECHR regarding the standardization of the European Court of Human Rights is being worked on.)

V. FINAL PROVISIONS

(The Control Machinery is a prerequisite for the Final Provisions. The latter will be defined after the Control Machinery has been determined.

**The Railroad Lines and the Trianon
Boundaries in Hungary.**

These railroad lines were strategically useless for the
Successor States, because they were within the range of the
Hungarian artillery. They were only good for making tens of
thousands of Hungarian families miserable and fomenting
hatred of the Trianon Powers

Post Scriptum.

Central Europe and the Balkans is in a mess. The treaties ending the First World War was bad enough, but the deal cut in Yalta and Potsdam was even worst.

To right the wrongs of Versailles and Trianon could have been done easily before 1933. After all, it was only the questions of Danzig, the Corridor, Czechoslovakia and the Hungarian problems to be solved in an equitable way. But after the inevitable rise of Hitler, things had changed for the worst. But most of the carnage and the Holocaust occurred after Casablanca, where the doctrine of unconditional surrender was declared.

After Potsdam, Poland was moved westward some one hundred miles, the Soviet Union was let into the Carpathian Basin, East-Prussia given to the Soviets, along with the Baltic States, and some more real estate ceded to the Soviets and Czechoslovakia. After the hostilities ended, millions were displaced, murdered and taken to the Gulag or the Romanian Danube-Delta and the Danube Canal camps to perish.

Millions of minorities were thrown at the mercy of the majority nations. The pious declarations of the human rights were just that. With no authority, and means of retribution to punish the oppressors, all "nation states" were hell bent to destroy, chase out or assimilate the minorities.

But we are living in a modern world, with instant and global communications. What went unreported and unheard before is now plastered on the monitors and newspapers all over the world, almost instantly. The minorities are increasingly vocal, demanding border corrections and/or independence. The peoples of Northern-Ireland, Corsica, Bosnia-Herzegovina, Kosovo resorted to arms to achieve their rights.

Other minorities are still waiting, but their patience is running out. At this moment they would be satisfied with territorial and personal autonomy. Tomorrow - when their patience runs out - they would want to rejoin their respective mother countries. If it takes force, so be it.

The publisher

ROLL OF HONOR
Our dedicated supporters:

Mrs. Etu Alapi
Mr. Jozsef Ambrus
Dr. Ferenc Androczi
Mr. F.F. Androczy
Mr. Jeno Arros
Mr. Otto Avvakumovits
Mr Bela Aykler
Mr. Alexander Babos
Mrs. Magdalene Bajan
Mrs. Terezia Bajnoczi
Mr. George M. Ballun
Dr. John Balogh
Mr. John Balogh
Mr. John Balogh
Ms. Cornelia O. Balogh
Mr. Elemer Balogh
Mr. Istvan S. Balogh
Mr. Nicholas Barabas
Mr. T. M. Baranski
Mrs. Katalin Baranski
Mr. Tibor Baranski
Mr. Joseph Baranyai
Mr. Julius Bartha
Mr. Oscar Bartha
Mr. Lajos Bartha
Mr. Zoltan Batyka
Mr. Andrew Beelik
Mr. Stephen W. Beke
Mr. Janos Beller
Mr.Miklos Bende
Mr. Adam Beniczky
Dr. Gyula Benko
Mrs. Marta Berta
Mr. Thomas E. Berty
Bessenyei Gyorgy cscs
Mr. Francis Bessenyey
Mrs. Eva Bessenyey
Mr. George Bethlendy
Ft. Zoltan Bihari, S.J.

Mr. Frank Horvath
Mr. John J. Horvath
Mr. Istvan Horvath
Dr. Janos Hoyos
Mr. Istvan Huff
H. Social C., Hamilton
Mr. Balazs Hunyadi
Mr. Bertalan Hunyadi
Dr. Istvan Hunyadi
Ms. Margit Iklody
Hamiltoni Irodalmi Kor
Mrs. Marta Istvanov
Mr. Laszlo Ivanyi
Mr. George Jalics
Mr. Laszlo Jambor
Rev. B. Jaschko S.J.
Mr. J. Jaszberenyi
Frau Eva Jekelfalussy
Dr. Elisabeth Jeney
Dr. Laszlo Jeney
Dr. Piroska Jeney
Mr. Nandor Jenofi
Dr. Kinga E. Jokay-Agg
Ms. Edith E. Jokay
Mr. & Mrs. Arpad Joo
Dr. Emilio Jordan
Mr. Lajos Kadar
Ms. Margit Kaffka
Rev. Arpad De Kallos
Rev. Szabolcs Kalman
Mr. Ernest Kalnoky
Mr. Emil Kanitsch
Mrs. Gabriella Kardos
Mr. Geza Kardos
Ms.I. Kasza-Szentirmay
Mr. Vince Somogyi
Mr. Laszlo Kazal
Mr. Alex Kedves
Mr. George Kekessy

Mrs. Jolan Oszlanyi
Dr. Zoltan Ovary
Mr. Antal Pak
Mr. Michael Pal
Mr. Sandor PAL
Mr. Gyula Palinay
Mrs. Dalma Pallagi
Mr. Ferenc Palvagasi
Dr. Laszlo S. Pandy
Mr. Gabor Z. Pap
Mr. Sandor Papp
Mrs. Marta Papp
Mr. Joseph Pataky
Ms. Csilla M. Patrin
Mrs. Magdalena Pattantyus
Mr. Rudolph Pechy
Mr. Ferenc Pendl
Dr. Marta Pereszlenyi
Mr. Sigmond Piller-Tahy
Mr. Steven Pimperl
Mr. Istvan Pinter
Mr. Joseph Poecze
Dr. Ervin Poka
Prof. Andras Prekopa
Mr. Istan Prileszky
Mr. Stephen Pungor
Rakoczy Fundation
Mr. Bela Ranky
Mrs. E. Rath-Mandy
Hun. Reforned Church
Ms. Katherine Rekai
Ms. Gizella Rona
Mrs. Maria S. Roy
Dr. Thomas F. Ruzics
Mr. Les Safran
Mrs. Margit Salamon
Mr. Leslie Samu
Mr. Rudolf Sandl
Mr. J. Saxon-Beregszaszi

Mr. Eugene Biro
Mr. Zoltan Biro
Dr. Tibor Blank
Mr. Andras Bobula
Mrs. Magdalena Boesze
Mr. Istvan Bognar
Mrs. Irene Bokrossy
Dr. Laszlo J. Bollyky
Mr. Steven Borbas
Mr. Denes Boronkay
Mr. Karoly Borossa
Dr. Gabor Both
Mr. László Botos
Mr. Barnabas Bozoki
Mr. Aladár Burgyán
Mr. & Mrs. Frank Butty
Dr. Edward Chaszar
The Corvin History S.
Mr. Janos Csaba
Dr. Imre Csapo
Mr. Thomas Csathy
Cs.B.K. Los Angeles
Mrs. Margaret Csendes
Mr. Gabriel de Csepel
Mrs. Zoltan Csere
Cserkesz Baratok Kore
Mrs. Eszter J. Csiga
Mrs. Esther Csiga
Mr. Ernest Csok
Mr. Eugene Csoka
Rev. Karoly Csokay S.J.
Mr. Laszlo Csordas
Mr. Bela Csordas
Mr. Barna Csuros
Mr. Ferenc Daday
Mr. Lajos Desy-Nagy
Dr. Levente L. Diosady
Dr. T. Doby
Mr. Emery G. Dora Jr.
Mr. Stephen Dragossy
Mr. Gyorgy Draskoy
Mr.&Mrs. Janos Ebner
Mr. Ignac Eder

Mr. Leslie Keller
Mr. Ernest F. Kemenes
Mr. Jozsef Keresz
Mrs. Ilona Keresztes
Mr. Zoltan Keresztes
Mr. Laszlo Kerkay
Mr. Martin Kertesz
Mr. J. Kerti
Mr. Ferenc Kis
Mr. Joseph Kish
Dr. Erno Kiss M.D.
Mr. Antal Kiss
Mr. Sandor Kiss
Mr. Bela Koczor
Mr. Tamas Kokai-Kun
Mrs. M. Koller
Mrs. M. Koller
Mr. George Kolonits
Mr. Bela Kontes
Dr. Laszlo Kontur
Mr. Edmond de Koos
Mr. & Mrs. Istan Kosa
Mrs. Emma Kosto
Mr. George De Kova
Ms. Eva Kovacs
Mrs. Iren Kovacs
Mrs. Katherine Kovats
Mrs. Ilona Kozmon
Mr. Steve Kucsma
Mr. Steve Kun-Szabo
Dr. Geza C. Kuun
Mme. Elizabeth Kvarik
H. Scout Ass'n W. Reg.
Mrs. Emilia Laczhazy
Dr. Frederick Ladanyi
Dr. Abel Lajtha
Mr. Erno Lakatos
Mr. Stephen Lakatos
Mr. Zoltan Lamperth
Mrs. Cecilia Lamperth
Mrs. Maria Langi
Mr. Tibor Lantos
Mrs. Edit K. Lauer

Mr. Gyula Say
Mr. Ferenc Beodray
The Graber Family
Dr. Peter Forgach
Ms. M. Schattenstein
Mr. Miklos Schloder
Mr. Walter Schrenck-Szill
Ms. Ilona Schroeder
Mr. Emil Schuller
A. H. Friends of Scouting
Mr. Erik Selmeczy
Mrs. Anna Seregelyes
Mr. Marton Seregelyes
Istvan v. Serenyi
Mr. Ferenc Sidlo
Mr. Lajos Simo
Mr. Barnabas Simon
Prof. Andrew L. Simon
Mrs. Elisabeth Sipos
Mr. Otto Skolak
Mr. Jozsef Solymos
Mrs. Maria A. Somogyi
Mr. Zoltan Somogyi
Mr. Frank Somoskoi
Mr. Stephen Sothy
Mrs. Albina Suba
Mr. Victor R. Sumeghy
Svedorszagi M. O. Sz.
Mr. Zoltan Szabados
Mr. Bela Szabo
Mr. Zoltan Szakal
Mr. Steven V. Szalay
Nt. Laszlo Szamoskozi
Mr. Eugene J. Szamosvary
Dr. Bela Szandtner
Mr. Istvan Szappanos
Mr. Andrew Z. Szappanos
Szechenyi Society, Inc.
Mr. George S. Szekely
Mrs. Maria Szekeres
Mr. Zsolt Szekeres
Mr. Erno Szelepcsenyi
Mrs. Helen Szendi

Mrs. Ilona A. Elek
Mr. Ferenc Engli
Mrs. Julia Erdelyi
Mr. Frank Erdelyi
Mr. Tihamer S. Erdos
Mrs. Katalin Értavy M.D.
Mr. Mathew Eszes
Mrs. E.Dezsery-Fabian
Mr. Rudolf Faulhaber
Mr. Frank A. Fazakas
Mr. Gyula Fazekas
Mrs. Gabrielle Feher
Mr.&Mrs. Leslie Feher
Mr. & Mrs. Gyula Feher
Mr. Tibor Fekete
Mr. Istvan Felszeghy
Mr. Alex Ferenczy
Mr. Albert Fodor
Mr. Nicholas Fodor
Mrs. Rozalia Forgo
Mrs. Ilona G. Frater
Mr Peter G. Fratrits
Mr. George Fuhrmann
Mr. Louis Fulop
Mr. Elmer Gabri
Mr. Nandor Gacs
Mr. Frank Gal
Mr. Thomas A. Gal M.D.
Mr. Michael Gocsei
Mr. Leslie Gombos
Mr. Kalman Gorgey
Mr. Anthony Greger
Ms. Julianna Gulden
Mr. Stephen Gulyas P.E.
Prof. Laszlo J. Gutay
Mr. Imre Gutay
Mr. & Mrs. J. Guttridge
Ms. SaroltaGyekenyesi
Mr. Zsigmond Gyenge
Dr. Louis Gyorgypal
Mr. Louis Gyori
Mr. Leslie Gyorok
Dr. Ferenc Gyulai

Mrs. Susan Legeza
Mr. Imre Lendvai
dr. Alfonz Lengyel
Mr. Michael F. Lents
Mr. Gyorgy Lesko
Mr. Laszlo Lesko
Mr. Laszlo Levius
Mr. Laszlo Levius
Mr. Laszlo Lonyay
Mrs. S. Lopert
Mr. Laszlo Lovas
Mr. Karl Lovasz
Mr. Tamas Ludescher
Mr. Steven Macskasi
Dr. George Maday
Dr. Sandor Magyar
Dr. Kriszta Magyarody
Mr. S.J. Magyarody
Mrs. Rose Magyarody
Mr. Thomas Magyarody
Mrs. Maharajak Katalin
Mr. Leslie L. Majthenyi
H-C C. Soc.,Manitoba
Mr. John Marosan
Mr. Laszlo L. Marton
Mr. John Mate
Mr. Nick Mates
Mrs. Agnes P. Maticza
Ms. Gabriella Mauthner
Mr. Frank Mayer
Mrs. Erzsebet Melics
Mrs. Margit Mentler
Mr. Lorand H. Meray
Dr. Fiore Mester
Mr. Nicholas Mezey
Mr. Joseph S. Miko
Rev. Kalman Miskolczy
Mr. Janos L.F. Molnar
Dr. J.V. Molnar
Mr. David Molnár
Mr. Janos Molnar
Dr. J.P. Molnar
Dr. J.P. Molnar

Mrs. Eva Szendrey
Ms. I. Kasza-Szentirmay
Dr. Andras Szentkiralyi
Mr. Paul O. Szentkiralyi
Mr. Julius Szentkuti
Mr. F. G. Szentmihályi
Dr. Marta Szep
Mr. Oliver Szerze
Mrs. Gizella Szigeti
Mr. Szojka K. Lorand
Mr. Laszlo Szoke
Szt Laszlo Tars. es Rend
Mrs.Maria Takacs Lambert
Mrs. Erzsebet Takacs
Mr. Endre B. Tamaska
Mr. Frank Tarcsay
Dr. Stephen Tarczy
Mrs. Eva Tarnóy
Mrs. Margaret Tasnadi
Dr. Stefan Taubinger
Mr. Joseph Telek
Mr. Joseph Teszar
Mr. Leslie Thiringer
M r. László Thomay
Ms. Julianna Tiger
Dr. Eva Tihanyi
Mrs. Elisabeth Tomory
Mr. Nicholas A. Tömöry
Mr. Csongor M. Torma
Mr. John Torocsik
Mr. Paul Töröcsik
Mr. Stephen Torok
Mr. Stephen Torok
Mr. John S. Torontali
Mr. Miklos Toth
Mrs. Julia Tudos
Mr. Csaba Tusko
Mr. Anthony Urmos
Mr. Marton M. Vagi
Mr. Thomas L. Vajtay
Mrs. Susan Valoczy
Mr. Joseph Vamosi
Ms. Eva Varady

262

Mrs. Gyongyi Gyulassy
Hun. Scouts, W. Reg.
Mr. E.J. Hajto
Dr. Bela Halasz
Mr. Otto Hamos
Mr. Leslie Hanula
Mr. Steve Hari
Rev. Dr. A.Harsanyi
Mr. Andrew Hasulo
Mr. Frederick v. Hefty
Msgr. Dr. K. Henkey
Mr. Attila Hethelyi
Mr. Tibor Hidas
Andras Hites
Gyorgy Hites
Dr. Laszlo Hites
H. Club of Kingston
Ms. Adel Hollo
Mr. Andrew Holloy

Mr. Stephen Mozes
Mr. Sandor Murguly
Ms. Ilonka Nagy
Mrs. Anna Nagy
Mrs. Maria Nagy
Mr. Louis I Nagy
Mr. Akos L. Nagy
Mrs. Maria Nagy
Mr. Edward J. Nagy
Dr. Julius G. Nagy
Mr. Louis P. Nagy
Ms. Ilona Nanasi
Mr. E. A. Nemes
Mrs. Julika Nemeth
Mrs. Magda Nemethy
Mrs. Judith Nemethy
Mrs. Helene I. Nemeti
Mr. Frank A. Novak
Drs. Laszlo Osvath

Mr. Bela Varga
Mrs. Yolanda Varga-Davis
Dr. Julius A. Vargha
Mrs. Lujza Varosy
Mrs. Margaret Szabo
Mr. Leslie Vegvari
Mrs. Agnes Viragh
Ms. Katalin Voros
Mrs. Eniko Wargha-Oss
Westside H. Ref. Church
Mr. Peter Zathureczky
Mr. W.G. Zeman
Dr. Steven Zsako
Mr. Gabor M. Zsolnay
Mr. Andrew D. Zsoter
Dr. Victor P. Zsufka
Mrs. Margaret Zydron
Hungarian United Fund
The Illyes Fundation